366 DAYS OF
One Year Devotional by Jocelyn A. Soriano

I will betroth you to me forever. Yes, I will betroth you to me in righteousness, in justice, in loving kindness, and in **compassion.**
– Hosea 2, WEBBE

The deepest wounds of the soul are healed only by compassion... People do not merely need to be clothed, they need to be embraced with love. A love that enters into their own fears and frailty, a love that suffers with them and stays with them through their darkest hour.

Love has a certain element of tenderness, which alone pierces through the heart and binds us more intimately than any force in the universe ever can.

It isn't violence that can break through our hearts. It isn't force that binds us and keeps us together. Only tenderness has the power to accomplish what the fullness of love desires to do. Tenderness that approaches us little by little, and handles our feelings with the deepest affection and delight. Tenderness that is willing to wait for the right time until we are ready and we are no longer afraid.

O, the great tenderness of God that seeks and that patiently waits for His beloved. The kind of love which alone can touch us in our frailty and in our brokenness, mending our wounds, healing our deepest pains.

God's love is quiet, yet it is strong. And its strength moves in its tenderness that never fails.

You were healed by his wounds.
- 1 Peter 2, WEBBE

3

Hi, I'm Jocelyn! I wrote this book so I may always remember how God has comforted me through the years. It isn't easy to face your troubles alone, so if you just need someone to talk to and/or pray for you as a friend would, you can write to me at **itakeoffthemask@yahoo.com** or visit my website www.itakeoffthemask.com

This life is full of beautiful things, though it is also full of suffering and pain. Many times, no matter how strong we are, we hurt. We cry from the depths of our soul and our spirit groans as we lift our prayers to heaven.

In such times, the last thing we need is for someone to come by and say that we have no reason at all to be sorrowful. The last thing we need is for someone to neglect our pain as though it didn't matter, as though none of the things we went through were real.

Pain is real. We bleed sometimes. Though we all want relief from the pain, we also want deeper **consolation.**

There at the **cross**, we see all pain and darkness conquered in such a way that it is defeated forever. Not by disregarding it. Not by denying it. But by giving value even to our tears. By loving everything about us, including our very worst hurts.

How do you wipe away pain? You don't. **You put in tenderness, compassion and joy.** You cling to hope and then you offer everything to God. And you wait, with faith you see all things anew – light shines out from darkness, happiness grows through every pain, and all things become indeed so very beautiful in His time.

Jocelyn A. Soriano

Table of Contents

JANUARY

January 1 :
Can You Stay With Me?

The best of friendships aren't necessarily those with the most laughs or the most excitement. The best of friends are those who can stay with us even in our most boring days, even in days when we could hardly remember how it was to laugh.

"...couldn't you watch with me for one hour? - Matthew 26, WEBBE

Stay

Won't you stay with me in this silence,
there isn't much to say;
Still I want you by my side,
as I watch the tides.

Let's look at the sea
as the waves crash by the shore;
Let's breathe the salty air
until I can sense peace again.

For there is a storm within me
that's raging fiercely right now,
and there is nothing I can do about it
though I've really tried.

All that remains is to wait 'til it's over,
until I can be myself again.
But until then,
can I ask you to stay?

16

January 2 :
Never Give Up

Sometimes, all we need is just one person who believes in us and who will never give up on us. Someone who sees beyond our weaknesses, beyond our faults. Who knows that though we walk in darkness, we can still find our way into the light.

He also spoke a parable to them that they must always pray, and not give up, saying, "There was a judge in a certain city who didn't fear God, and didn't respect man. A widow was in that city, and she often came to him, saying, 'Defend me from my adversary!' He wouldn't for a while, but afterward he said to himself, 'Though I neither fear God, nor respect man, yet because this widow bothers me, I will defend her, or else she will wear me out by her continual coming.' "

The Lord said, "Listen to what the unrighteous judge says. Won't God avenge his chosen ones who are crying out to him day and night, and yet he exercises patience with them? - -Luke 18:1-7, WEBBE

I pray that you may find someone who will never give up on you. Someone who sees you truly and who believes in the very best you could become.

Whatever happens, remember that you have God. And when you have Him, you have Someone who will never give up on you.

17

Never Giving Up

You are the kind
I know
who will never give up
on me.

The kind who will
believe in me
long after
I could no longer
believe in myself.

The kind who sees
my shadows
yet who never fails also
to see my light.

A light that can remain
hidden for so long
Hidden even from
my own eyes.

I can hate myself so much
that I can't even look
at my very own
reflection.

Yet I don't even need to see it
Because I see better
as I look
in your eyes.

I see someone
who will always
be there
through and through.

Whose silence
is far better
than any word

other people can utter.

Whose gaze alone
can give me hope
can help me hold on
for one more day.

Because you never give up
on me
You never did
and never will.

Though I let go
you will get me back
Though I forget
you will remember.

Though I stop
even to hope
You will hold on
for the both of us.

January 3 :
Glimpses of Love

Sometimes all that we have are moments - glimpses of heaven, sweet scents of love. They are foretastes of eternity. And though they last but for a moment, the strength they give us lasts, and the warmth they leave us lingers.

The voice of my beloved!
Behold, he comes,
leaping on the mountains,
skipping on the hills.
My beloved is like a roe or a young deer.
Behold, he stands behind our wall!
He looks in at the windows.
He glances through the lattice.
-Song of Solomon 2:8-9, WEBBE

All I Have Are Glimpses

All I have are glimpses,
a glance,
a touch,
a memory of your voice.

Glimpses that
take my breath away,
that draw me from
the monotony of each day.

Glimpses that
give me life,
that give me a new heart
and a new soul.

For when those glimpses come,
I feel a lifetime has also gone by,
a lifetime with you,
well spent in a moment of love.

And I let each memory

sink as deeply as it could,
so I may remember
and never forget.

How each glimpse of you
has changed me,
has found me,
has saved me.

And all I could ever do now,
is wait for you,
content with glimpses of your love,
until you come and make me live again.

January 4 :
Grace For Today

To find grace, we need not look so very far ahead. We need only look at the present moment. God gives us grace right now, in the very moment we need it most.

Peace I leave with you. My peace I give to you; not as the world gives, I give to you. Don't let your heart be troubled, neither let it be fearful. - John 14, WEBBE

May God bless you. May God lead you every step of the way, giving you strength for each moment, providing you with courage for each trial.

For this is all that we really need. Not to look so far away but to be right where we are, clinging to His hand and trusting in His heart.

He is there with you now. He gives you everything you need for this very moment as He carries you upon His arms.

I Love You Now

I see you,
I feel you now,
Here beside me,
Here where I also stand.

Let not the past
Trouble you
Let no heartache
Take you away
From my arms.

Is it not enough
That I hold your hand
Is it not enough
That I have come?

Think not of
your worries
For each day
that has not yet come.

No future can spoil
This moment
None of your tomorrows
Can steal this hour
That's yours and mine.

Cast away your burdens
Let still each anxious thought,
For I am here with you
I give you all of me
And I love you Now.

January 5 :
    A Time To Hide

I hope you remember that you always have a place to hide, away from the noise of the world, away from all that dares to wound your heart. You can always hide within the merciful heart of God.

He who dwells in the secret place of the Most High
will rest in the shadow of the Almighty.
I will say of the LORD, "He is my refuge and my fortress;
my God, in whom I trust."

-Psalm 91, WEBBE

When we experience difficult times, we often hear people say that things are going to be alright, and maybe they will, just not at the moment, not yet. And though we want to show the world we still have some sliver of hope, some strength remaining, we just want some time away. For there is a time to rest, isn't it? It isn't always daylight, and the season doesn't always fall into spring.

When It's Night

When life just feels so dreary,
and the world, so dark and sad,
And the load you bear is so heavy,
and you're just bruised and broken bad.

Take heart and rest awhile,
and if your heart is broken, you can cry.
No one ever said we must always smile,
no one ever said there'd be no night.

For there are times of joy and times of trouble,
there are days when you just feel so tired.
You have tried and tried and tried,
you did all you could with all your might!

Take heart and give yourself some time,
give yourself some space to hide.
No one ever said we must always toil,
no one ever said we must always shine.

January 6 :
    I See Your Beauty

When God looks at you, could He ever fail to see the beauty He Himself has made?

Behold, you are beautiful, my love.
Behold, you are beautiful.
Your eyes are like doves.
-Song of Solomon 1, WEBBE

23

Beautiful You

You must learn
To love yourself
If you can't love you for you
I hope that you
Can love you for me

If you say you love me
If you really feel you do,
Then give me you
Give me all of you
The worst and
The best of you.

See how I see you
Believe how
I treasure you
And how I want you
From the very core
Of who you are.

I am not asking you to change
Or to give up anything
If it would destroy you,
Beautiful you.

If you must change,
If you must give anything,
Do it because you want
To spread your wings
And soar,
Because it would help
Make you
Even more beautiful
Than before.

Then I couldn't be happier
I couldn't be more joyous in love,
For my happiness is
To see you happy

And my life
Is to live
Knowing you have become
The very best
Of who you are!

January 7 :
How Do You Move On?

To move on doesn't mean the pain is already gone. It means being able to go on one step at a time, bearing the pain, clinging to what little hope you've got, and all the while, letting the grace of God carry you through.

He heals the broken in heart,
and binds up their wounds.
He counts the number of the stars.
He calls them all by their names.
 - Psalm 147, WEBBE

How do you move on? You move on slowly, awkwardly, unwillingly. You move on not with your whole heart, but with all the broken pieces of you.

You try to be brave. You listen to what other people say. But no matter how courageous you are, and no matter what words of wisdom you've learned, none could ever take away the pain from your heart.

So you live each day not knowing how you're going to live through the next. Sometimes all you have are hours of survival. Sometimes mere moments of hope.

Gradually, you heal. Not entirely, but in part. Each broken piece being mended. Each painful memory being healed.

Eventually you make it through more and more days. But though you're able to stand again, it doesn't mean that you stand without tears in your eyes.

You really don't know how you even got to where you are. It's as though you have just let the waves carry your helpless soul.

But you are grateful for each grace. And you pray. And you continue to hope. Ever so awkwardly, you move on.

January 8 :
Someday We'd Understand

When I judge others harshly, I must ask this question, "Am I doing all these because I have also been so harsh with myself?"

Yes, I don't judge my own self. For I know nothing against myself. Yet I am not justified by this, but he who judges me is the Lord. Therefore judge nothing before the time, until the Lord comes, who will both bring to light the hidden things of darkness, and reveal the counsels of the hearts. Then each man will get his praise from God.
- 1 Corinthians 4, WEBBE

Someday

Someday,
We'll understand each other, you and I,
When we finally discover the reason why
Why we seemed so different from the outside

Someday,
We will see,
That there's a lot of similarity
Between you and me

We will know
That we have both tried our very best
But we were both wounded
We were lost and tired and weak

All the while
We were both just trying to find
The thing that's missing
In our lives

We were both just trying to walk
Just trying to talk
Just trying to pray
When we couldn't find our way

Someday,
We will finally come to see
We both just wanted to be loved
You and I.

January 9 :
The Birth of Joy

Only in heaven shall we know that deep space for joy carved out for us by our deepest griefs.

For our light affliction, which is for the moment, works for us more and more exceedingly an eternal weight of glory... - 2 Corinthians 4, WEBBE

It is never God's intention to cause hurt or sorrow. Yet if He ever allows any pain, it is only so that He could make way for greater joy!

We can never fully understand it here. Not when we're suffocated by darkness. Not when our hearts are broken by sorrow.

But someday we will know. We will see how each of our tears have become priceless pearls, how our most terrible afflictions have given birth to our highest bliss.

MY HEART'S DEEPEST WOUND

I guess you will always be
my heart's deepest wound.
The kind that aches terribly.
The kind that time could never heal.

I glimpse a memory of you
and I feel it!
I feel both the joy and the pain
of loving you.

27

Yes, loving you.

For I have never really forgotten.

How could the heart forget?

Had I not loved you,
I'd have moved on already.
Had I not loved you,
You wouldn't have been able
to cause me pain.

But I did.
I loved you then, and I love you now.
You will always be
the deepest wound in me.
That's how strongly
you are etched
upon my heart.

January 10 :
    The Love We Give

The love we give in this life is the only thing that can truly belong to us for eternity.

Jesus said to him, "...go, sell what you have, and give to the poor, and you will have treasure in heaven; and come, follow me." - Matthew 19:21, WEBBE

There are times when we start to ask ourselves, "What is the worth of my life? What do I possess now to prove that something has happened and that my life has not been in vain?"

We then look towards our achievements or our status in life, and we start to compare it with what other people have. More often than not however, this kind of thinking just makes us feel worse. It makes us feel that if we don't have a lot to show, we have not lived well. We feel empty as though nothing good has ever happened in our lives.

28

But if we start to see things through the lens of eternity, we may start to wonder deeper. What are the things that really matter anyway?

Then a little voice within us seems to say, "only love".

In the end, the only thing we'd ever regret is not having loved enough. The only thing we lose is the love we held back.

Hold My Hand

Hold my hand in friendship,
while I am still alive.
Come take my hand and walk with me,
along the road of life.
For I don't want your whispers,
when my ears can no longer hear,
Nor your embrace,
when I can no longer feel.
Let me know you need me,
while I can still extend my hand;
Lest I let the Savior take me,
to a far and blessed land...

January 11 :
When You Get Tired

For the many times that we wanted to quit, let us remember, maybe all we really needed to do was to rest.

In peace I will both lay myself down and sleep,
for you, the LORD alone, make me live in safety.
-Psalm 4, WEBBE

When you get tired from your trials, my friend, I pray you may find a way to rest, I pray you do not give up.

Don't think so far ahead. Don't fret!

Be where you are, stay where you need to be. Think only of your troubles today.

For there is a way with things that we cannot control. And there is a way with things that make them turn out well in the end. Though we may not know how. Though we may not know when.

So when you get tired from your trials, my friend, I pray you may find time to rest, I pray that you don't just quit.

God has a way to make things better in the end. And for now all you need is to rest and to trust Him, my friend.

When You're Too Tired To Hope

There are times in your life
when all that you could do is rest.

You cannot love,
you cannot dream,
you don't know where to start,
and you don't know where to go.

You want to change your life,
but you're too weak to move,
you're too tired to think,
too hurt to heal,
too numb to make amends,
too lost to even hope,
too tired to even pray.

Rest then O heart,
and rest then O soul,
for the journey has been too much for you,
and the world has left you wounded
and alone.

Sleep then for a while,
let go of all your woes.
Lie down in trust,
and let your tears flow down
as they should.

Somebody's watching,

Somebody's catching your every tear.
Fear not, for in the quiet of the night
you're in the arms of Him
who loves you most.

Think not of your worries,
think not of your wounds,
for they shall be healed.
In time shall you find comfort,
and you shall find peace.

O blessed peace,
claim your portion and your strength.
May your soul know what stillness means,
and may the very marrow of your bones
find ease.

Time has come to stop your restless wonderings,
and for all the useless work to cease.
Let God work while you are sleeping,
and in the morning
may you find all things new and sweet.

January 12 :
  When Dreams Fade

Don't give up now.   For all you know, your dreams are just about to come true!

Let's not be weary in doing good, for we will reap in due season, if we don't give up. - Galatians 6, WEBBE

Try

When dreams die,
as they sometimes do,
when the plans you've made
and when the things you've built
just seem to fade,
do not leave,
it is not the end.

31

When hopes disappear,
as they sometimes do,
when everything you've prayed for
and every seed you've sown,
just seem to wither away,
do not quit,
you can try again.

For those dreams that died,
they'd give way to bigger dreams,
as the things that have fallen,
will make greater things arise.
You may cry for a while,
but you will mend.
When the night is over,
a bright new morn will shine!

January 13 :
Broken People

The good thing about being broken is the opportunity to start over again, to become even better than before!

I am weary with my groaning.
Every night I flood my bed.
I drench my couch with my tears.
My eye wastes away because of grief.
It grows old because of all my adversaries.
Depart from me, all you workers of iniquity,
for the LORD has heard the voice of my weeping.
The LORD has heard my supplication.
The LORD accepts my prayer.
-Psalm 6, WEBBE

I like stories of broken people and how they rose again. They remind me that no matter how damaged you may have been, your life can still have purpose, some meaning you did not see before. They give me hope. They allow me to see that it is indeed possible to be healed, to be whole again, to be even far better than you were before.

32

The truly inspiring stories are not those with people who never fail. The most inspiring ones are about those who got really lost but somehow found their way again, those who got really sad but somehow found a way to try smiling again. These are the ones that tell us it is not yet too late for us, and no matter where we are right now, we can start over and build our dreams again.

January 14 :
Sacrifice

There are things God allows us to have not that we may retain possession of them, but that we may have something to offer as a sacrifice of love.

The king said to Araunah, "No; but I will most certainly buy it from you for a price. I will not offer burnt offerings to the LORD my God which cost me nothing." - 2 Samuel 24, WEBBE

Why do we have to lose the most important things? The most important people? Why do we have to suffer such a terrible heartbreak? Such a terrible terrible loss?

We love, we give it our all. We hope, we put everything we've got in it. And in one moment, everything is lost! Everything becomes meaningless.

Was there ever a meaning to everything we've gone through? Was there ever a worth to the love we gave, to the love we have received?

If everything's supposed to end this way, what's the meaning in all that?

But you tell me to trust in You, O, Lord. You tell me to have faith. You tell me to hope still amidst all hopelessness. And you tell me to go on loving even though my heart would eventually break from the pain of it all.

And even though the pain still lingers. Even though I still couldn't understand a thing. I will let You hold me and lead me. I will trust the Heart that has been wounded too, out of love.

Lead me each step of the way for I fall. I'm blind though I walk with the Light.

I will trust that though I walk now through the valley of the shadow of death, you will never leave me alone.

January 15 :
Where Is God?

We often fail to find Jesus not because He's not there, but because we don't know where to look.

Then the King will tell those on his right hand, 'Come, blessed of my Father, inherit the Kingdom prepared for you from the foundation of the world; for I was hungry, and you gave me food to eat. I was thirsty, and you gave me drink. I was a stranger, and you took me in. I was naked, and you clothed me. I was sick, and you visited me. I was in prison, and you came to me.'- Matthew 25:34-36, WEBBE

There are times when we wonder where God could we found. Could we really love Him even if we do not see Him? Where could we possibly find Him?

We can look for Jesus in money and we won't find Him there. We can look for Jesus in success and we won't find Him there. We can look for Jesus in pleasure and we won't find Him there.

But try to fix your gaze elsewhere. Look for Him among the humble and among the poor. Look for Him among those who are children at heart. Look for Him among those who are sick and helpless. Look for Him among those who are yearning to be loved.

Suddenly, you are not alone anymore. You are not trapped within yourself anymore. You realize that you can give something. Your life matters. Jesus waits for you, and you can finally touch His face.

January 16 :
Night Shall Pass

Sometimes, success is not being able to smile, it is merely possessing the hope that you can smile again.

He will wipe away every tear from their eyes. Death will be no more; neither will there be mourning, nor crying, nor pain, any more. The first things have passed away. - Revelation 21, WEBBE

Sometimes, the darkness that covers the present moment is so heavy and painful, that even though we know God still watches over us, even though we believe that in the end, all things would work together for good, we can't help but feel unbearable sorrow. Why must things happen this way? Why this indescribable grief?

And though we know that there will be an end to the night, even though we believe the sun will surely rise again, we can't help but weep. For though such dark hours will certainly pass, it seems to pass so slowly. And while it lasts, eternity itself seemed to have arrived at our very door. A night of eternal sorrow. A winter that refuses to surrender into spring.

What can we do but wait 'til the night is over? What can we hold on to but prayer? And even though our prayers seem empty and dry, we trust still that the One who hears them lives! He is ever the same. He has sustained us in all our past woes, and He will carry us through though we may not know when, though we may not understand how, and though the only grace we feel is the strength to hold on for one moment more.

IT'S JUST A MATTER OF TIME

When grief looms over like a cloud,
and your heart gets broken,
and your spirit's down,
it all seems like happiness
is but a distant dream,
and it loses its meaning
where it cannot be seen.

And we are lost where it's dark,
without a song in our hearts,
and we couldn't believe
it would all pass away.
If we could only hold on to a rhyme,
which could make us remember the light,
then morning might not be so far away,
IT'S JUST A MATTER OF TIME.

If we could imagine once more,
what joys are instore
with the rising of another day;
if we could only hear again
that gentle voice in the wind
reminding us that dawn is already near –
won't we break out into songs
and cheer each other on
and say IT'S JUST A MATTER OF TIME?
Won't we be able to bear
the darkness we are in,
knowing it couldn't help but end
and IT'S JUST A MATTER OF WHEN!

And though the dawn is yet to come,
and the night is yet to end,
though our pain still lingers,
and our wounds are yet to heal,
we rejoice with our hopes,
as though they've already come,
certain that our prayers were heard
and IT'S JUST A MATTER OF TIME!

January 17 :
When I Look At You

When God looks at you, shall He not see His beloved child?

The LORD is near to those who have a broken heart,
and saves those who have a crushed spirit.
-Psalm 34, WEBBE

Think not that when I look at you, I look only at your faults. That all I see are the rough edges and the shadows surrounding you. Think not that as I gaze upon you, I have come only to measure you, to find only what is lacking in you.

No, this is not how I look at you. For though I see all this darkness, all this brokenness and pain, all these things could never turn me away.

On the other hand, I have come to share your sufferings, to taste your tears, even to dwell upon your wounds. And there, where all is bitterness, I live, and I love.

I take your every weakness upon me, I claim all of them as mine. For you are mine. You are my beloved. And if you are willing, you can rest your broken heart upon Mine.

And I shall look at you as I look upon my own wounded heart. Pierced and crushed, yet overflowing with compassion. Knowing both sorrow and joy. Beating as one with love!

I LOVE YOU MY CHILD

I love you, my child
There is nothing that you can do
that can separate me away from you

You are here always,
within my strong and loving embrace
You are protected
You are loved.

37

I delight in you,
and see my own eyes upon your eyes
I take away your fears
I take away your tears
from now on you are safe
and you are where you've always longed to be.

Let the people who judged you
see how I cherish you now,
Let those who condemn you
see how close you are to me.

You are never outside of my love,
never an outcast
never a failure
never so far away

You need not do anything
to please me,
for I am already pleased
that you trust me
to guide you in everything
you wanted to do

You are beautiful
you are whole
you are healed
you are my beloved
you can rest upon my strong shoulders,
and trust that you won't ever slip away,
For it is I
who is holding on firmly to you.

January 18 :
    Give Me Eyes to See

Give me eyes to see beyond the mask of things: to see beyond weakness so I can find strength, to see beyond the disfigured, so I can find beauty and to see beyond the darkness so I can find the light!

38

The lamp of the body is the eye. Therefore when your eye is good, your whole body is also full of light; but when it is evil, your body also is full of darkness. Therefore see whether the light that is in you isn't darkness. If therefore your whole body is full of light, having no part dark, it will be wholly full of light, as when the lamp with its bright shining gives you light. - Luke 11, WEBBE

Give me eyes to see the true. Beyond the temporary, let me see the eternal. Beyond the darkness, let me see the light.

Give me eyes to see what's within. Beyond what's frail, let me see what's strong. Beyond the disfigured, let me see what's lovely and pure.

Give me eyes to see what's precious. Beyond the sacrifice, let me see the love. Beyond the tears, let me see a joy that lasts.

Give me eyes to see for I have long been blind. I have stumbled and I have lost my way for I have followed paths not leading to life.

Let my eyes be opened so I may see. And beyond all the gloom and drudgery and misery, may I find hope to guide me, courage to strengthen me and compassion to heal me from this day forth and always.

TO LOOK USING GOD'S OWN EYES

I pray I could learn
to look at people,
the way God sees each one of us –

to be able to forego the little mistakes,
maybe even the big ones

to be able to see weaknesses
turned into strength

to know something's hurting
and yet know that the hurt
would be healed in time

to look beyond judgment
to see with an understanding heart
to see what's beautiful
to appreciate what's good

to not measure anybody's destiny
with their present plight

but to see real hope for everyone
the way God sees us

To know that orphans
have their Father

To know that those imprisoned
have One who will set them free

To see how the poor
will one day bask in God's abundance

To see the brokenhearted
in days when God Himself
will cradle them upon His lap
To be able to see with God's own eyes
is to see with gladness,
with hope,
and with a love so strong
it could never ever fail!

January 19 :
    A Greater Joy!

We can be happy and sad at the same time. But as Christians, our joy should always be greater than our grief.

Blessed be the God and Father of our Lord Jesus Christ, who according to his great mercy caused us to be born again to a living hope through the resurrection of Jesus Christ from the dead, to an incorruptible and undefiled inheritance that doesn't fade away, reserved in Heaven for you... Wherein you greatly rejoice, though now for a little while, if need be, you have been grieved in various trials... - 1 Peter 1:3-4,6, WEBBE

We can find a lot of reasons to be sorrowful. As we see the plight of our suffering neighbors and as we witness evil and sin committed each day, it is but natural to grieve and to feel pain. Even our Lord suffered on the cross, the darkest and most terrible suffering!

Yet even then, He did not lose hope. Even then, His joy was not lost. For it is a joy that comes from faith, a joy that comes from love.

May no one take away the joy we have in our risen Savior, in the God who gave everything to save us.

Our joy is greater! It is far greater than any sadness or brokenness we may have in this life.

For we may have pain, but we shall be healed. We may hunger, but we shall be filled with heaven's bread. Darkness is no match for God's light. Death is nothing compared to eternal life!

Let no wound therefore bring you more sorrow than it should. Offer every tear to Him who knows your pain, to Him who has been pierced and cruficifed. It is in His wounds that we discover the greatness of His love.

A Time For Joy

This may not be a time for dances,
but this is a time for prayer.
This may not be a time for clapping,
but this is a time for songs.

This may not be a time for merriment,
but this is a time for awakening.
This may not be a time for running,
but this is a time for rest.

This may not be a time for kisses,
but this is a time for hugs.
This may not be a time for laughter,
but this is a time for smiles.

This may not be a time for parties,
this may not be a time for noise,
But this is a time for healing,
and this is a time for joy!

January 20 :
On Gentleness

Let us learn to be more gentle with ourselves. Quite often, our harshness towards others is merely a reflection of our own harshness towards ourselves.

But we were gentle amongst you, like a nursing mother cherishes her own children. - 1 Thessalonians 2:7, WEBBE

God is kind and gentle. He is kind with you. He is gentle with you. How could you not be kind and gentle also with yourself?

While it is true that we must never let sin reign over us, neither should we let discouragement and harshness fill our souls. Harshness is not compatible with love. It is never compatible with compassion.

We need to love ourselves right so we'd know how to love others. It is this love within us that will spread to those around us.

If we can only understand ourselves more and have more patience for our shortcomings, maybe we can also be more patient with others. Maybe then, we can truly love others the way Jesus Himself loves us.

January 21 :
Touching His Wounds

To love is to bear the wounds of our beloved. It is to hurt where they hurt, to weep where they weep, and to make ourselves vulnerable so we can strengthen those who faint.

...Christ also suffered for us... He himself bore our sins in his body on the tree, that we, having died to sins, might live to righteousness. You were healed by his wounds.- 1 Peter 2, WEBBE

The deepest wounds of the soul are healed only by compassion. By compassion, we do not merely love from a distance or have pity by looking down upon others. Compassion compels us to share in the very pains experienced by our brother or sister in need. We touch their wounds, and their wounds become our own. We listen with our hearts, we enter into the darkness where they are, and we walk together to find the way back home.

People do not merely need to be clothed, they need to be embraced with love. A love that enters into their own fears and frailty, a love that suffers with them and stays with them through their darkest hour.

May There Be Bridges Between Us

May there be bridges between us
Bridges of understanding between you and me,
Bridges of hope,
Bridges of honesty,
Bridges that link us,
heart to heart,
and mind to mind.

May there be bridges between us,
Bridges that break down walls
and the coldness of words misunderstood,
May those bridges stand strong
May they reach out far and wide,
And may no one burn them
that they might fall.

May there be bridges between us
May it unite us evermore,
Bridges that bring us closer
heart to heart
and mind to mind,
Bridges between friends,
Bridges between brothers,

43

that we may know we're not alone,
and that we could always – always find our way back home!

January 22 :
Found By God

And after much seeking we finally discover, all that we really needed was to be found.

But while he was still far off, his father saw him, and was moved with compassion, and ran, and fell on his neck, and kissed him. The son said to him, 'Father, I have sinned against heaven and in your sight. I am no longer worthy to be called your son.' "But the father said to his servants, 'Bring out the best robe, and put it on him. Put a ring on his hand, and sandals on his feet. Bring the fattened calf, kill it, and let's eat, and celebrate; for this, my son, was dead, and is alive again. He was lost, and is found.' - Luke 15, WEBBE

Home. There is no place quite like it, and some of us are blessed to have it or at least to have it in our memory. To others however, it is a place that is yet to be found. And behind all our strivings, all our efforts and wanderings is a secret hope of one day being able to get there.

For where is that place where we might finally be at peace with those who love us? Where is that place where we can finally feel that we belong?

We seek it all our lives but what we do not know is that it has been waiting for us all along. We were the ones who have gone astray as we sought other things that pale in comparison to its warmth. We chased other dwellings wherein we might rest but we have found no rest.

God is our home, our true home. In Him our hearts can rest and find its dwelling. In Him we know we are loved. We are not lost anymore, we are found.

44

January 23 :
Quiet Days

It is not only the days of battle that count. Many times, it is how we make use of the days that we can rest.

...a time to tear,
and a time to sew;
a time to keep silence,
and a time to speak;
a time to love,
and a time to hate;
a time for war,
and a time for peace.
-Ecclesiastes 3, WEBBE

Some days are neither happy nor sad. In those days, our eyes are not filled with tears nor our hearts filled with too much happiness. We are not fighting a battle. We are not facing a storm.

In those days, it seems all we could do is wait and let time pass us by. We do our chores, we show up, we carry on even though we feel whatever it is that we do won't make a big difference at all.

But even in a song, we must remember that beyond the low and the high notes, there are spaces of silence in between. Spaces to take a deep breath until we can raise our voice again, until it is time to sing.

Many times, what truly makes a difference in our lives are the many spaces in between, spaces of waiting and of being faithful to the work at hand. Days such as these when we silently go about our lives, holding on to memories of joy, to hopes of dreams yet to come, and to the love that gives us strength to carry on.

This Is The Great Pause In Between

This is the great pause in between work and play
the great silence between a song, and another song

This is Selah, this is s p a c e

This is the point at which the earth neither slumbers nor wakes up

This is the great pause in between crying and laughing
between getting sick and getting well again

This is the time of waiting
without expecting for something soon to come

This is the space between heartbeats
between a heartbreak and a new-found love

This moment is silence
but this is not worth nothing

Everything is stored in this very moment
where everything else proceeds,
and where every great dream is born.

January 24 :
Precious Now

Amidst all our worries and all our regrets, let us never lose sight of the precious moment we are being given right now just where we are.

For everything there is a season, and a time for every purpose under heaven:...
a time to weep, and a time to laugh; a time to mourn, and a time to dance... Ecclesiastes 3:1, 4, WEBBE

Many times, in our anxious attempt to predict or control the future, we lose sight of the valuable things that are there for us in the present moment. Even if all we have at present are trials and heart wrenching difficulties, even these have treasures that they can share with us.

Instead of losing much time worrying about a future we can never control, let us make the most of each moment that is being given us.

Embrace each joyful hour, taste the sweetness of each passing day, treasure even the tears that fall, even the anguish of a heart that is broken and bruised.

You will never pass this way again. Live each moment fully that you may keep what's truly precious for all eternity.

I'm Taking It All In

I'm taking it all in now
savoring each precious moment
that I have with you.
I'm breathing the air you breathe,
I'm touching your skin,
I'm looking at your face,
trying to memorize your smile.

I'm taking it all in now
for I shall never pass this way again,
I'm hearing your voice,
I'm hearing your laughter,
I'm seeing you,
I'm smelling you,
I'm walking side by side with you,
down the streets we've always loved to walk.

I'm taking it all in now
and I can't waste a precious moment.
Each second counts, each minute is a gift,
no moment shall pass by, without me seizing it!
Living it! Taking it!
Filling it with all the love
I could possibly give away!

I'm taking it all in now,
I'm filling my soul with things that last,
etched upon my heart forever,
embedded always in my mind,
in my soul, in my very spirit!
I take what God has given,
eternal treasures that won't ever slip away.

I'm taking it all in now,
I'm drinking it, receiving it,
basking in it with arms opened wide!
I'm here
You are here
This time is sacred,
and I'm taking it all in right now.

January 25 :
Receive His Love

From Him who is Infinite Love and Infinite Mercy, only one thing is asked, that we receive Him with all our hearts.

We love him, because he first loved us. - 1 John 4, WEBBE

Before you give, receive from Him who has every good thing to offer you. Before you love, allow yourself to be loved.

It is only by being loved first that our love can be grateful, humble and pure. For we do not love anymore in order to be loved. We do not love in order to boast of our righteousness. And we do not love merely because we have an obligation to do so.

We love because we have been loved. We give because we have been given much. We make others happy because we are filled with joy!

There Is No Greater Love

You've got to allow God to LOVE You
From the very core of you;
Not the form that everybody sees,
Not the mask that you want
Everybody else to see.
You've got to allow God to enter
The innermost chambers
Of who you are;
To taste and see the real essence
Of your being,
Not the strength that gets sapped up

48

In your difficulties,
Not the outer beauty that ages
And soon fades away.
For you are not your height
Nor your stature.
You are not the color of your skin.
You are not your capabilities
Or your disabilities.
You are not the tone of your voice,
Or the power of your stride.
You are not your health,
You are not your sickness.
You are not your wealth,
Or the greatness of your name.
You are not your good deeds,
You are not your sins.
You are not the fears
That cripple you,
Or the courage
That makes you win.
You are whom God made you to be.
You are a spark from that
Unquenchable Flame.
You are His,
You've always been and always shall be.
You are the apple of His eye,
You are His delight,
You are the vessel that catches
The great outpouring of His love.
You are His beloved,
The one He awaits and longs for,
The one He teaches,
The one He leads,
The one He watches over
As you slumber,
The one He rejoices over
As you awake.
What greater joy is there than to know
How marvelous you are
In His sight?
What greater peace than knowing
You will never be alone?

That you are pursued,
That you are most of all desired
By the One who changes not,
And fails not
With all the burning passion of His LOVE!

January 26 :
I Give You Rest

God loves us not only when we work, but also as we rest upon His arms.

It is vain for you to rise up early,
to stay up late,
eating the bread of toil,
for he gives sleep to his loved ones.
-Psalm 127, WEBBE

Sleep Now, My Child

Sleep now my child,
day has passed
and night has come,
come and rest upon my arms.

You have done much,
you gave it your all,
and now it's time
to walk your way home.

Weep not for your falls
or for things left undone,
Worry not for tomorrow
for it is yet to come.

You have done all you could,
you have done your very best,
It is enough that you trust me,
and I will do the rest.

You are my child,

whether you work or you slumber
I gaze at you and I smile
just because of what you are.

You are mine, all mine
I have borne you in love
and in love I draw you closer
even as you rest upon my arms.

January 27 :
The Miracle of Faith

Miracles are not done to produce faith. It is faith that makes miracles happen!

He didn't do many mighty works there because of their unbelief. -Matthew 13:58, WEBBE

Faith is an open hand, willing and able to receive the many blessings being poured upon it. It is an open window, able to let the sunshine in, allowing the fresh air to come. It is the door of the heart through which the love of God can freely come to dwell.

Many times, we wait for miracles to have us believe. When we do not see any, we say that there is no reason to believe anyway.

But miracles need even faith. Miracles are always there, coming down from heaven. But how do we see it without the eyes of faith?

To Believe What the Eyes Cannot See

To believe what the eyes cannot see,
To trust when you cannot see the way,
To keep on believing when there's no one else
to cheer you on,
To keep on hoping
To keep on dreaming
Even when your way seems blocked,
Even when you've waited for so long,
Just carry on, carry on.
Drop by drop

Your cup shall overflow,
Inch by inch
You'll walk the mile.
Be impatient not for the day
For it will surely come!
It will give way
To the man who knows
What he truly desires.
Clouds shall gather without your knowing,
Seeds shall grow beneath the ground,
And soon the clouds that have gathered
Shall pour as heavy rain,
With showers of blessings before your very eyes.
Soon the seed shall be a tree,
Mighty and strong,
And yielding a hundred fruits for the picking.
Trust that none can stop that rain from falling,
Or that seed from breaking free.
And you shall break free!
One day you, too, shall see
How God's own plan comes true
How He shall make a way for you
Until you reach your destiny!

January 28 :
Room For Your Mistakes

Remember that God loves you even in your worst day.

I, even I, am he who blots out your transgressions for my own sake;
and I will not remember your sins. - Isaiah 43:25, WEBBE

We can get so used to doing our very best that we can feel a bit of
suffocation sometimes when we run out of strength and we make
mistakes along the way.

We may feel then that the eyes of everyone have suddenly turned
towards us, ready to cast a blame, even ready to condemn us just
for that one error we never wanted to commit.

Have all our prudence come to nothing? Wasn't it enough to have
tried and given everything we've got?

When that time comes, remember that love, if it be true, leaves enough room for understanding and forgiveness also. Love knows how much we've tried, and love accepts us both in times when we're radiant as well as in times when we're really miserable.

Love has left a room even for your mistakes, even for your sins. Love goes with you not only when you stand, but even when you fall, especially when you fall. It does not laugh. It does not cast a look of sarcasm.

Love instead casts a look of faith and is ready to help you rise again.

January 29 :
  Forget Not To Be Human

We must not forget the things that make us human. Friends, family, love – these are the things that truly give meaning to our lives.

Woe to you, scribes and Pharisees, hypocrites! For you tithe mint, dill, and cumin, and have left undone the weightier matters of the law: justice, mercy, and faith. But you ought to have done these, and not to have left the other undone. - Matthew 23:23, WEBBE

Our humanity is a gift. We may experience moments of weakness or pain. We may get frustrated at times for all the imperfections of life. But we must never forget the valuable things that we do have in this life.

Life is not all about efficiency and productivity. It is important to meet our goals, but we must never forget the substance of all our undertakings.

What are we really trying to accomplish? Are we forgetting something along the way?

To be human is not to be like a machine who can perfectly accomplish its tasks. It is to be able to rise from our falls again and again because we have a spirit that knows how to love, because we have a higher calling that reaches out towards eternity.

January 30 :
The Same Wounds

Is there a greater way to encounter Jesus than by knowing His wounds?

But he was pierced for our transgressions. He was crushed for our iniquities. The punishment that brought our peace was on him; and by his wounds we are healed. - Isaiah 53:5, WEBBE

Not everyone may be acquainted with happiness, but each one, to some extent, has been touched by some kind of pain or suffering. We have all traveled this valley of tears, and each one has his or her wound to tend to.

We may not know each other well, but we could all relate to the hurt each one felt for the loss of a loved one, for the injustice experienced, for the rejection and judgment one has received at one time or the other.

And because of this, we each have the capacity to reach out to another. We each have the chance to be compassionate, to show mercy, to love.

They who have experienced true sorrow are the ones who can best comfort those who mourn. They who have felt the most pain are the ones who can best assist those who struggle with anguish.

All is not yet lost then. And even in this fallen world, there may yet be a light for us all. We need only to see that our neighbors are not so different from us after all. We are not alone, and we can let others feel that they too, have someone to lean on to.

January 31 :
How Much We Are Loved

Why not seek love where it can surely be found?

For your Maker is your husband; the LORD of Armies is his name. - Isaiah 54:5, WEBBE

We are loved... so much and so deeply. Our problem is that we don't know and we seek this love constantly from those who could never give it to us.

If we only knew, our lives would never be the same again. If we only understood, we'd be so happy we'd think this place called earth is already heaven itself. For how could it not be heaven?

Heaven is knowing that you are valued and cared for. That someone knows you just as you are and loves you even more because it is so.

It is knowing that you are ever present in someone else's thought. Day and night you are thought of, thought of with so much sweetness and affection.

You are beautiful in someone else's eyes. You may not know it, but it doesn't change the truth about how much you are loved.

INVISIBLE

I have always been there for you,
watching over you, loving you.
All these years I have known you,
but you knew me not.

You should have known
how beautiful you were to me,
how delighted I was to see you,
to hear your story,
to watch your every step.

You should have known
you were special,

you should have known
how you were never truly alone.

I've tried to let you know.
I've tried to find the best words
to tell you.
But for some unknown reason
you've never truly heard
what I've been really trying to say.

You were always looking faraway.
you were always yearning
for someone else's love.
O, if you only looked at me,
the one beside you
all these years.
If you only tried to let go
of the one who hurt you
and sought another heart
who will leave you not.

You could have found me.
You could have seen me.
But I had always been the invisible one.

With Love,
JESUS

FEBRUARY

February 1 :
Accepting Imperfections

Life isn't perfect. But that doesn't mean it could never be beautiful.

But as it is written,
"Things which an eye didn't see, and an ear didn't hear,
which didn't enter into the heart of man,
these God has prepared for those who love him."
- 1 Corinthians 2, WEBBE

Perfectionism has many levels. Sometimes we think we have already learned to accept life's many imperfections and our own inability to accomplish a task. But once in a while, something happens beyond our worst nightmares. We are caught by surprise and our perfect world is shattered once again.

How do you deal with imperfections? You deal with it as you deal with earthquakes that come out of nowhere. You try your best to survive it and not blame anyone for not being able to control the movement of the earth.

Deep within our own minds, we already have a story that we want to be played. We have in it expectations of how our dreams can work out if only we do this and that. We tell ourselves how evil must never triumph and how good must always shine.

But that is not often how things really work. Sometimes we need to go through a storm before we could see the sun again. And many times, we must endure longer winters than we've ever expected until we see the flowers bloom again.

Let us try not to be disheartened when things don't work out the way we wanted them to. Let us instead try to trust God, who is ultimately the one in control, the one who lovingly weaves all stories into something truly beautiful and far more wonderful than we could ever imagine on our own.

The Courage to Smile

Let me deal with life as it comes,
not as how I wanted it to be
Let me have the courage to smile
when things don't work out for me.

Let my heart be able to trust
that all can still be well,
for you are there my Lord and God
you can make things whole and fair.

No matter the storm that comes,
No matter the raging seas,
may I have the hope that never fails,
and faith that always trusts in Thee.

February 2 :
> Be Free

Not all open doors can lead us to the place where we want to be. Not all semblance of freedom can break the chains that bind our spirits down.

Out of my distress, I called on the LORD.
The LORD answered me with freedom.
-Psalm 118, WEBBE

There is something within us that rebels whenever we are prevented from doing something. The human spirit, it seems, does not want to be restrained, but yearns to be free. Free to do as we wish, free to roam as we desire.

Yet even the highest of freedoms do not free us from the consequences of our choices. When we choose one door, we reject another. When we choose to be bound in one direction, we reject the freedom to go the other way.

Which paths then shall we choose? In which shall we truly be free?

58

February 3 :
As God Desires

In heaven we shall be grateful not only for the times God said YES, but even for the times He said NO or NOT YET.

...for your Father knows what things you need, before you ask him. -Matthew 6:8, WEB

Most of our worries are based on our fear that things won't happen as we have planned. But when we come to think about it, shouldn't it be more important that things happen as God Himself has planned? We may not always know what is best for us, or what can really make us happy. But it is for certain that God knows. And it is His will that shall save us in the end.

Not As I Dreamt It

Not as I dreamt it,
Not as I thought with my mind,
but as you have conceived it, Lord,
far better than I planned.

Not as I desired it,
thinking how glad I might be,
but as you have designed it, Lord
to be far more joyful then for me!

February 4 :
Love Yourself Also

God wants us to forgive not because He thinks we don't deserve justice, but because He desires to give us peace.

Let all bitterness, wrath, anger, outcry, and slander be put away from you... be kind to one another, tender hearted, forgiving each other, just as God also in Christ forgave you. -Ephesians 4, WEB

Sometimes we find it hard to forgive because we feel that it isn't fair for us to just let go of our grudge against someone. We feel that the people who offended or hurt us deserve our hatred, not our love.

59

But O, how great a sacrifice on our part! How we suffer from lack of peace. And how our hearts are burdened by the pain of their transgressions.

Letting go of our grudge is not a sign of weakness but of strength. It is not being unkind to ourselves, but of truly loving ourselves.

It is never an easy task to let go of negative emotions. But we should do our very best and ask also for God's help so that we may be able to let go of them.

Only when we're able to free our hearts from the darkness would we be able to feel the light. And this light is the peace and happiness we have long been searching for.

LET GO

Let go of your tears,
and you will see the light.
Let go of your worries,
for tomorrow is alright.

Let go of your troubles,
or you might lose your peace.
Let go of your fears,
and you will find your dreams!

You will find your life,
is more meaningful to live.
You will find your burden,
getting lighter like your soul.

You will find happiness,
always waiting on your way.
You will find heaven,
getting nearer each day!

February 5 :
Mercy and Hope

Justice need not deprive anyone of compassion. For with true justice comes mercy, and He who is most just must also be most kind.

Jesus, standing up, saw her and said, "Woman, where are your accusers? Did no one condemn you?"
She said, "No one, Lord."
Jesus said, "Neither do I condemn you. Go your way. From now on, sin no more."
Again, therefore, Jesus spoke to them, saying, "I am the light of the world. He who follows me will not walk in the darkness, but will have the light of life."
-John 8:10-12, WEB

Much as we want to, we don't always succeed in doing the right thing. We fail, we have bad days, we do things we can't be proud of.

It is during such days that we become prone to criticism and humiliation from those around us. We feel ashamed and many times, we don't know how we ought to react. We may react with fear and disgust with ourselves, or we may react with anger, trying to hide our shame. At times, such days become memories that wound us deeply, and we carry a sense of unworthiness and despair all our lives.

God is so good however, that He offers us healing just when we need it most. In our most humiliating moment, He offers us His hand, far from the reaction of those who fear to even be associated with us.

God lifts us up at our lowest, and instead of condemning us to utter despair, He offers hope and forgiveness.

God loves us, even at our most humiliating day. He takes us in even when we can't face ourselves in the mirror.

Remember this the next time someone condemns you. Remember God's face of love and mercy. Remember the warmth of His hand, inviting you to be free from your painful past and leading you towards a future full of hope and of light.

February 6 :
Your Own Path

You have your own path, your own phase, your own destiny. You need not compare your life or your growth to another.

For I know the thoughts that I think toward you," says Yahweh, "thoughts of peace, and not of evil, to give you hope and a future. - Jeremiah 29:11, WEB

You need not measure your success by any other man's measure. Your success is to be measured by how you have lived the life given you. It is to be seen in how you have used your gifts, your opportunities, even your difficulties and struggles.

Do not deprive the world of the gift of your being. Do not block the blessings that were meant to flow through you.

Be patient with yourself, with every little step you take in growing and in becoming a better you. Follow your own path, the path God Himself has prepared for you.

February 7 :
God's Protection

Who could ever surive without the protection of God?

Haven't you made a hedge around him, and around his house, and around all that he has, on every side? You have blessed the work of his hands, and his substance is increased in the land. - Job 1:10, WEB

God is protecting us. In ways unknown and invisible, in ways mysterious and wise. We may not see it, we may not feel it; but God is keeping us from harm.

O, if we could only see the invisible walls surrounding us, defending us from evils we cannot see. If we only knew how many times we have been saved from harm, protected from crosses too hard for us to bear! Without this shield, who knows what tragedies we'd have faced already, or what enemies would have already entered into our lives?

God loves us so much that He would not allow any pain or problem to touch us if it would not lead to our greater good and glory. He watches over us and has put us under the shadow of His wings.

February 8 :
To Forgive Is To Love

To forgive is not to forget what's evil but to remember the good, and there is some good even in the worst of us.

Hatred stirs up strife, but love covers all wrongs. -Proverbs 10:12, WEBBE

It is impossible to forgive without love. We can grant pardon from punishment towards those who offended us. We can say that we have decided not to seek vengeance anymore. We can even say that we desire the good of those who hurt us. But without love, we cannot achieve true forgiveness, for forgiveness requires love.

Yet how can we love without knowing what love is? How can we give that which we have not received? That which we have not felt?

When we find it impossible to forgive, let us seek the God of Compassion. Let us seek Him who loves us and never gives up on us no matter how many times we have fallen and lost our way.

Let His words of mercy resound always in our ears. Let His tender touch melt the hardness of our hearts. Let His gaze of kindness break through our own guilt and our many burdens. And let these words be a balm that the heals the wounds of your soul: "You are loved. You are forgiven. You were lost, but now you are found."

February 9 :
    To Really See Him

For all our presumptions and best imaginings we shall find that we can never really know what it's like to see Him until we see Him with our own eyes!

Beloved, now we are children of God. It is not yet revealed what we will be; but we know that when he is revealed, we will be like him; for we will see him just as he is. - 1 John 3, WEB

We all have our preconceived ideas about God. Maybe we have read about Him somewhere. Or maybe we have heard things about Him from other people. And so we heard that He is just. And so we heard also that He is merciful.

But one day, we'll know Him for who He really is. And won't we be surprised? When we really get to know Him, I believe we'd say, "He is so much more than what they said He is!"

To See Him

To see Him as He is
Not as I thought He was
Not as I thought He would be

To really know Him
To know what it's like
to be His friend

To be able to gaze at His face
To hear His voice
To feel His touch

To walk with Him
To talk with Him
To be able to stand by His side

What greater joy
could there be?
What greater destiny?

To see Him at last is Heaven,
and Heaven is to behold Him
as He is at last!

February 10 :
Jealous Over You

God is jealous over me! It would take eternity for me to even get a good idea what that is all about.

For I am jealous over you with a godly jealousy. For I married you to one husband, that I might present you as a pure virgin to Christ. - 2 Corinthians 11, WEBBE

Is it even possible? For God to be jealous over me? His love, I can still grasp. His mercy, I can accept. Yet how can I even start to think about Him being jealous over me?

It is not the kind of jealousy that is self-serving and is borne out of pride. It is not the kind that is whimsical or vengeful.

But it is the kind that yearns the total devotion of the other. The kind that expects all because it gives all. It is the kind that is borne out of purity, simplicity and holiness. The kind that desires nothing else but my complete happiness and wholeness and that would never rest until it is certain that I am able to love true and without end, that I am able to love without letting anything to ever take me away from my true joy.

February 11 :
What Matters In The End

It is not the beginning of the journey that counts but the end of it. After all that we go through, how shall it all be at the end?

For what does it profit a man, to gain the whole world, and forfeit his life? Mark 8:36, WEBBE

At the end of our lives, many of the things we gave importance to won't matter anymore. The things that stressed us so much, the tasks that worried us, the issues that we argued so much about, how much of such things do we think would still stand vital in that moment?

It wouldn't even matter then how rich we are or how popular we've been. It won't matter how much power we possessed or how many people are there to do our bidding.

At the end of our lives, what would surely matter is whether we have lived a meaningful life, whether we have loved well. Have we done all that we could to spread laughter and understanding and compassion? Have we tried to alleviate other people's pain instead of causing it? Have we been men of peace instead of enmity and division?

For it is there at last that we will reap what we have sown. It is there where we can finally see the true fruits of our labors. At the end of it all, only truth, goodness and beauty shall prevail. If we have much of it, then we have lived rich lives indeed.

February 12 :
Days of Faith

Not everything will be to our liking, but all things will be for our good, though all that we can see for now are days so ordinary there are no miracles except those that have been concealed from our eyes.

... though now for a little while, if need be, you have been grieved in various trials, that the proof of your faith, which is more precious than gold that perishes even though it is tested by fire, may be found to result in praise, glory, and honour at the revelation of Jesus Christ— whom, not having known, you love. - 1 Peter 1:6-8, WEB

The truth on faith is that it does not and should not depend on our feelings. Because though by faith we are given grace for each moment and strength for every trial; though we are at peace and we are grateful for the incomparable blessings given us; we are still human beings bound with our frailties, trying to make our way each day through all the ups and downs of real life.

The truth is that there are days when we could hardly remember the feeling of consolation in prayer or the joy of our first revelations, when we could barely recall the sweetness of the many glimpses of heaven we once knew.

The truth is that there are days when we just feel tired and lonely and aching and we could hardly get up from bed; days when we see more darkness than stars, more rain than sunshine, more tears of sorrow than of bliss.

This is the truth. And this is the faith that conquers even when by our own strength, we're already at the point of breaking or giving up.

February 13 :
How to Fight Temptation

Whenever we are tempted, let us ask ourselves, "Is this going to be worth it in the end?"

No temptation has taken you except what is common to man. God is faithful, who will not allow you to be tempted above what you are able, but will with the temptation also make the way of escape, that you may be able to endure it. - 1 Corinthians 10:13, WEB

1. Prepare. Avoidance is still the best defense. The time of peace is the best time to prepare for war.
2. All grace comes from God. Pray to receive grace to overcome temptation.
3. Fill your mind with good thoughts. Remind yourself of the things that give the most meaning to your life.
4. As yourself: Is this something you'd be ashamed of? Then don't do something you'd be ashamed of.
5. Ask yourself: Do you somehow know it's not right? Then don't do it, period. Stop talking, bargaining or reasoning with a deceiver.
6. Ask yourself: What is it stealing from you?
7. Ask yourself: Whom are you offending or hurting?
8. Ask yourself: What kind of person is it turning you into?

9. Keep on fighting even if you fall. Do not despair. Trust in God's infinite mercy.
10. Ask for help whenever possible. Avoid isolating yourself.

February 14 :
   Love Is a Promise You Keep

We often don't know the sacrifices we'd make in order to keep our promise, but that is just what love is for. Love gives us the strength and the will to keep the promises we've made.

Set me as a seal on your heart,
as a seal on your arm;
for love is strong as death...
Its flashes are flashes of fire,
a very flame of the LORD.
Many waters can't quench love,
neither can floods drown it.
-Song of Solomon 8, WEBBE

Love is a promise. It is a promise you make when everything is good and nice and bright. It is a promise you make when you truly believe it is worth it, that though the rest of the world goes against you both, you will still fight for it because there is never anything else you'd rather look forward to.

Love is a promise. It is a promise that is tested through time and many trials. It is a promise no longer just written or declared by mouth, but testified to by sweat and blood and tears.

Because love is a promise. Love is a promise you keep even when everything seems going the wrong way, even when you could barely see the joy of it or the hope of it. You hope for hope. And you persevere even when all that you can deal with is the present moment. You protect your love in that moment, and from one moment to the next, you keep your promise to love.

To Love is Beautiful

To LOVE is the most beautiful thing we could ever do,
The most beautiful that could ever be done for us...
Yet to love in this life, we must look beyond the crooked,

68

the dirty and the unpalatable.
To be able to LOVE, one must love in places
Where comfort is rare, and where pain is deep,
One must love where the storm is fiercest,
And where the light is faint.
For it is not mere excitement that defines love,
It is not a fleeting adventure,
Nor a grand but fading song…
Love is that which is strong enough
To survive the harshest winter
And the monotony of daily life…
Love is beyond skin, beyond sickness,
beyond frailty, beyond death…
Love is the only thing that remains
after all the darkness fades away,
For Love is light beyond measure and life without end,
Love is God,
And God is the most beautiful of all!

February 15 :
   What Is Trust?

Quite often, what we need is not sufficient strength to win our battles, but enough trust in the God from whom all victories come from.

Now faith is assurance of things hoped for, proof of things not seen.
- Hebrews 11, WEB

What is trust? To trust is to believe that there is something else beyond what you can see. It is to have the heart to hope in something farther, something deeper, something that is currently veiled from plain sight.

To trust is to place one's faith in things that will happen in time. It is to have peace amidst the chaos currently surrounding you. It is to be able to hold on through the night, looking forward towards the sunrise no matter how great the darkness, no matter how strong the storm.

To trust is to never let go of miracles, such as how an acorn can grow into a towering oak, or how a caterpillar can turn into a beautiful butterfly. It is the way that things can still turn out well despite and in spite all the bad things that have already taken place.

February 16 :
Rejoice!

Life is not always fun and laughter, but neither is it always sorrow and tears. There are days of happiness, days of cheer! God gives each of us a time to remember that heaven is just within our reach.

"Go your way. Eat the fat, drink the sweet, and send portions to him for whom nothing is prepared, for today is holy to our Lord. Don't be grieved, for the joy of the LORD is your strength." - Nehemiah 8, WEBBE

There are difficult days and days of sorrow, days we must mourn, days we must fast and grieve. Yet there are also days of healing, of moving on, of trying to live again, of trying to smile again.

Sometimes we take our sorrows to heart for far too long. We punish ourselves. We let our guilt get the best of us and we think that the only thing to make it right again is to live a life of sorrow and being cast down.

Yet is this the way of love? Is love not also joy and of being whole again? Is love not also enjoying life and having a feast that will gladden not only the body but the soul?

What is keeping you from being happy again?

February 17 :
The Regrets We Have

Regrets will always be a part of being human, but we can turn them into those things that have made us better, that have given us a wiser mind and a more compassionate heart.

Purify me with hyssop, and I will be clean.
Wash me, and I will be whiter than snow.
Let me hear joy and gladness,
that the bones which you have broken may rejoice.
Hide your face from my sins,
and blot out all of my iniquities.
-Psalm 51, WEB

I guess that no matter how happy or successful we claim to be, no person is really without regret. There are choices we wish we haven't made, words we feel we shouldn't have uttered, people we shouldn't have hurt, days or even years we never should have wasted.

It makes no sense to deny we'd rather have lived better, loved more, laughed more often. To do so would sound as though we haven't grown or learned much with the life given us.

Yet what do we do with the pain within us? Or with the many questions at the back of our minds?

We bring them to our compassionate God who alone can make sense of everything, who alone can redeem every failure and every regret. We come to His most merciful heart and lay down our burdens. It is there where we can find healing and rest at last.

February 18 :
   A Merciful Heart

Our wounds are the bridges by which we receive mercy and by which we can give it in return.

Blessed are the merciful, for they shall obtain mercy. - Matthew 5, WEBBE

A merciful heart is a heart that has experienced much suffering. It is able to bless because it is able to feel the pain of those who are also hurt.

It is those who have known hunger who yearn to give bread to the poor. It is those who have known sickness that yearn to comfort

71

those in beds of affliction. It is those who have known how to be misjudged who yearn to avoid words that can break another person's heart.

Who else can guide the desperate except those who felt hopeless? Who else can understand the grieving except those who have lost those whom they loved the most?

Mercy is never looking down upon the plight of another. Rather, it is being able to see oneself in another person's eyes. The requirement for a merciful heart is not self-righteousness but suffering. The reward is not the right to boast, but the opportunity to heal one's own bleeding heart.

February 19 :
Before Christ Crucified

What is the agony of Christ for? It is to let us know that even in our darkest, loneliest and most painful hour, we are never alone.

But he was pierced for our transgressions. He was crushed for our iniquities. The punishment that brought our peace was on him; and by his wounds we are healed. - Isaiah 53, WEB

Many times, our hearts are so heavy that we can't even pray for what we need. We just feel overwhelmed. We want rest but we can't find it. We know we have many questions at the back of our minds, but we can't even start naming what these questions are.

Whenever we feel like this, may we find comfort before the crucified Christ. Sometimes, we need no words in order to pray. But we need to seek His Face and to lay down before Him our many burdens and tears.

At The Foot of the Cross

At the foot of the cross
that's where I want to be
To gaze upon my God
with boundless love for me

72

To kiss His feet pierced with nails
to worship and adore
Him who was pierced by a lance
Him who was crowned with thorns

I cannot ever understand
all the reasons why
Why He must be crucified like this
why He must suffer and die

But there at the foot of the cross
I feel His great mercy for me
Blood and water flowed from His heart
out of His great love for me

How else can I even understand
how infinite and great is His love
if not by the cross, yes, by the cross
where all is gained when all was lost

I thank you Lord for bringing me
where alone my soul can stay
It is there alone where I can find healing
it is there alone where I can be saved!

February 20 :
   Letting Go of Resentments

Let go of everything that dares to destroy your peace.

Wrath and anger, these also are abominations;
And a sinful man will possess them.
-Sirach 27, WEBBE

What makes us hold on to our resentments? Why do we hold on to so much anger that eventually consumes us and poisons our very hearts?

Maybe we think we are justified in doing so, and maybe we are. Maybe we got hurt really bad that we're afraid of being hurt again.

Yet along the way, as we keep these thorns within our hearts, they continue to hurt us even more.

Even as we pray, we can't find healing. Even as we ask for God's love, we are still left in the dark.

But let us remember that love cannot be received in halves. You either surrender to it fully and let it wash over your soul or you try to hinder its flow as you allow your resentments to block your healing.

Which will it be then? What will you choose?

Would you allow your resentments to rule over you, to rob you of happiness and to lead you farther and farther into the dark? Or will you allow love to heal you, to bring you joy and to lift you higher into the light?

February 21 :
　　A Deeper Love

Do we not love more those whom we thought we've lost?

By night on my bed, I sought him whom my soul loves. I sought him, but I didn't find him. I will get up now, and go about the city; in the streets and in the squares I will seek him whom my soul loves. I sought him, but I didn't find him. The watchmen who go about the city found me; "Have you seen him whom my soul loves?"
I had scarcely passed from them, when I found him whom my soul loves. I held him, and would not let him go... -Song of Solomon 3:1-4, WEB

What greater happiness is there than to regain something you thought you have lost forever? What deeper love than the return of a beloved you thought would never come back anymore?

We never get to value things so much as when we have almost lost them. All the while that they were just within our reach, we may have just ignored them, thinking they'll always be around.

The moment we lose them, however, we're able to see how truly valuable they are. We suddenly wish we could turn back time so we

74

can take possession of them again, so we can take care of them while we still had time.

How happy we are when we are given another chance, we are so much more happier than if we had never feared losing them at all!

February 22 :
You're Not Alone

Someone is waiting for you to be the best of who you are.

For even as we have many members in one body, and all the members don't have the same function, so we, who are many, are one body in Christ, and individually members of one another, having gifts differing according to the grace that was given to us: if prophecy, let's prophesy according to the proportion of our faith; or service, let's give ourselves to service; or he who teaches, to his teaching; or he who exhorts, to his exhorting; he who gives, let him do it with generosity; he who rules, with diligence; he who shows mercy, with cheerfulness. - Romans 12:4-8, WEB

You're not alone. Even if you're not married, even if you don't have kids, even if you think you're a loner. Still, you're not alone.

You have been born into this world from a mother and a father who gave you life. Even if you do not know who they are, you will forever be their child.

You have met people along the way, a kindergarden playmate, a classmate, a room mate, a friend, a stranger you passed by one busy morning or one lazy afternoon.

Other people you hardly knew may have prayed for you. Others pray for your help. Still others are already there, creating a link of love that goes on and on throughout the world.

You may not know it. You may not believe it. But your life is important.

Someone is waiting for you to be the best of who you are, to be strong, to be compassionate to those who are longing to be loved.

The next time you feel you are alone, think of the many people whose lives are affected by your own. Think of the way other peoples' lives have inspired you or have shed light in your darkest hour.

You can also be that person. With God's help, you can make other people know that they too, are not alone.

February 23 :
Patient Kindness

A kind love is a love that has learned how to wait.

Love is patient and is kind. -1 Corinthians 13, WEBBE

Love is patient. Being patient with others, as well as being patient with yourself.

All too often we want to achieve things in haste and in great violence. We forget that everything has its own phase, its own time.

We forget that love is not only meant to be strong, it is also meant to be gentle. And in this gentleness is kindness and patience and every sort of good fruit that blooms in its time.

Let us do what we can each day, and the entrust the rest to God. We may not always succeed, but we can keep on trying. And for as long as we really do try, one day we shall see how God has supported us and kept us safe every step of the way.

February 24 :
Choosing Heaven

I pray with all of my heart, that you will choose heaven today.

Behold, I have set before you today life and prosperity, and death and evil...
I call heaven and earth to witness against you today, that I have set before you life and death, the blessing and the curse. Therefore

choose life, that you may live, you and your descendants... - Deuteronomy 30:15, 19, WEB

We may not be aware of it, but we choose either heaven or hell all the time.

Everytime we choose to hope, everytime we choose to forgive and to let go of our resentments, we choose heaven, we choose life.

But everytime we choose to hold on to our anger, everytime we decide to seek revenge and to hate, we are choosing hell, we are choosing death.

We can choose to dwell in darkness or we can choose to seek the light. We can choose to wallow in our anguish, or we can choose to find healing for our souls.

We can choose heaven today. We can choose to free ourselves from all the things that burden our hearts. We can choose to be happy. We can choose to love.

February 25 :
   A Thirst For Love

Our thirst for love tells us that we shall never be satisfied until we find Him who alone can satisfy the human heart.

As the deer pants for the water brooks, so my soul pants after you, God. - Psalm 42, WEB

The worst feeling in the world is to have no one. It is the utmost poverty and desolation of the heart. It is a wound whose depths only those who have experienced it could ever know.

Some people don't have the slightest idea what being alone means. Some think that just because you have people around you, you are no longer lonely. They think that it is enough to be seen, to be called, to be heard.

But it isn't enough. It isn't enough to be merely seen, we must be seen for who we really are. It isn't enough to be called, our dignity must also be recognized. It isn't enough to be heard, we have a longing to be listened to out of the very depths of our soul.

For our souls were never meant to be alone. Our hearts were never meant to be ignored. Deep within us, we have a yearning to love and to be loved, to be taken care of and to take good care of someone.

Blessed are those who have found true friends and true hearts! Blessed are those who are showered each day with love.

Yet even then, there will always be a space within our hearts that will be left aching and longing for more, a space that yearns to be understood completely, to be loved infinitely, to be touched in such a way as to be lifted up from the prison of even our own selves.

Only God can touch this space, this sacred space. Only God can fill this emptiness which no one, not even the best of men can fill.

For who but God can know us more than how we know ourselves? Who but Him can enter the deepest wounds of our souls and heal it? Who but Him can stay with us forever, never to leave us even in our worst and darkest days?

February 26 :
Two Faces of Love

Love lacks nothing, will always give more than it thought it could and will always believe no matter how great the storm.

Love... bears all things, believes all things, hopes all things, and endures all things. Love never fails. - 1 Corinthians 13, WEBBE

There are two sides to love. One is the face of happiness, the face of youthful dreams and colorful summers. The face of two people in mutual attraction and admiration, proud of each other's beauty and strength. This is the face that most people know, the only face that some people are willing to receive.

But there is another face to love. The other face we hardly look upon because we do not have the strength to bear its sorrows. This

78

is the face of suffering, the face of loss, the face of winter. This is that love we bear when we see our beloved suffering, when for one reason or another, our journey with them is no longer as enjoyable as before.

This is not always to our liking, but to reject this face is to reject the fullness of love. To desire summer without suffering the cold is to have but weak feelings, not true affection. To stay only when things are enjoyable is to not have gone to the very depths of compassion, the love that endures, that fights, that triumphs through all life's troubles.

What kind of love do we really want? What kind of love do we truly possess? Say not that you love if you know only but one face and not the other. For love is both the happiness and the sorrow of it. It is both the light and the darkness of the journey getting there.

February 27 :
Who You Are

Be careful of the things that turn you into what you shouldn't be.

They made a calf in Horeb,
and worshipped a molten image.
Thus they exchanged their glory
for an image of a bull that eats grass.
-Psalms 106, WEBBE

Who we are is far more important than what we do, but quite often, it is the things that we do that turn us into the kind of people that we are.

Let us be careful then with the things we allow to fill our lives - the thoughts we think, the words we say, the habits we form, the things we worship and love. Little by little, we are changed by such things, and before we know it, we have been turned into another kind of person. May it be the kind of person we'd like to be and not the other way around.

February 28 :
Love Completely

Must our hearts be half-filled only because we only love by halves?

Two are better than one, because they have a good reward for their labour. For if they fall, the one will lift up his fellow... - Ecclesiastes 4, WEBBE

We either love a person or we don't, for love cannot be measured in halves. When you love a person, you care about him, you'd do only the things for his good and not for his harm.

When we love, we allow our beloved to enter a special chamber in our hearts, and in a way, we give something of ourselves, too, and we become a part of each other. And that is why the other person's happiness becomes also our own, another person's sorrow finds its way also into our tears.

There is no other way to love than to love completely, with our whole hearts, for only a whole heart can continue to live and beat with love.

February 29 :
Forgiven

The one that loves also forgives.

"Come now, and let us reason together," says Yahweh: "Though your sins be as scarlet, they shall be as white as snow. Though they be red like crimson, they shall be as wool. - Isaiah 1:18, WEB

No matter how good we are or how holy we tried to be, there is some part of ourselves that's burdened by past mistakes. It is that part that never quite goes away even though we try again and again to cover it or to deny that it even exists.

There is some part in ourselves that need to be forgiven, some part in our hearts that long to be freed from guilt. We need someone else to declare that our sins have indeed been blotted out, that they have been swept away. We need to hear it. We need to know that we are no longer being blamed.

Take heart, O soul. For your God is ever ready to relieve you from pain. Through a repentant heart, you obtain in Him freedom, you obtain forgiveness from all your sins. You are not blamed, you are not condemned. On the contrary, you are embraced, you are welcomed in great delight, you are loved!

MARCH

March 1 :
   What Frightens Us

Sometimes the people who seem most frightening are the people who need help the most, people who are merely longing to be loved.

The LORD himself... goes before you. He will be with you. He will not fail you nor forsake you. Don't be afraid. Don't be discouraged. - Deuteronomy 31, WEBBE

Some people, when they are afraid, they become angry too, but then all that we can see is this anger, how they explode and seem to lose all control. What we do not see is this great fear within them, a helplessness masked by the outward rage.

Underneath it all is a vulnerability that has shielded itself so it can't be touched. So no one may hear what it is really screaming about.

And that is why it takes much courage to love. While it is true that we must be cautious also, we must not be so frightened too much as to fail to see a heart that is only longing to be heard, to be loved.

March 2 :
   Being True

There is so much more than the words I'm able to say. I hope you hear me in my silence as much as you hear me when I speak.

One who loves me will be loved by my Father, and I will love him, and will reveal myself to him. - John 14, WEBBE

Honesty doesn't mean you have to reveal everything to people. There is some part in us that can be understood only by a few, some special place that can only be shared with those whom we love the most.

It doesn't mean we have to lie. But it means having the right expectations, not assuming that everyone else will be able to share your happiness or to understand the days when you cry.

We don't need the whole world's applause just to know we're living meaningful lives. Sometimes all we need is just a few people who know who we really are and who accept us and love us no matter what we're going through.

March 3 :
The Courage to Love

To love is to not be afraid. It is to be far more courageous than you ever thought you could be.

For God didn't give us a spirit of fear, but of power, love, and self-control. - 2 Timothy 1, WEBBE

Love is not a mere sentiment. It is not something that merely makes us feel all good and light inside, something that warms us on a rainy day. Love is so much more than that!

Love is the fire that propels us onwards, it is the strength that helps us bear the storm. Love is the power that changes us for the better, that inspires us to sacrifice something we hold dear for the sake of our beloved ones.

Love is that courage we have to defend our loved ones, to stay with them even if we get nothing in return. For the reward of love is love itself. And its happiness is always in the heart of the one it loves.

March 4 :
Boundless Love

God asks us to forgive without limit. Must we lose our courage when we go to Him whose Love is Boundless and whose Mercy is beyond what we can possibly understand?

If he sins against you seven times in the day, and seven times returns, saying, 'I repent,' you shall forgive him. - Luke 17, WEBBE

For The Countless Times

For the countless times I sinned
And you still took me in.
For the countless times I strayed
And you still held my hand
Willing to lead me back
Again and again.

For the countless times I faltered
And you never gave up
But continued to believe
That I can still get up.
For the countless times I've hurt you
But you never complained
And you kept on loving me
Again and again.

It is for these and for countless things more,
For things that words could never express
That I give you my praise, my heart and my soul
Hoping and praying that I could love you more.

O how I pray for the time
And how I long for the day
That I won't hurt you
And I won't fail you anymore.
But until that day
I pray you show me the way
To keep on believing
To keep on hoping
To keep on returning
Again and again
To you.

March 5 :
Of Good and Evil

Let us not fool ourselves into thinking we're accomplishing something good when we're actually doing something evil.

"The lamp of the body is the eye. If therefore your eye is sound, your whole body will be full of light. But if your eye is evil, your whole body will be full of darkness. If therefore the light that is in you is darkness, how great is the darkness!"
 - Matthew 6, WEB

"Woe to those who call evil good, and good evil;
who put darkness for light,
and light for darkness;
who put bitter for sweet,
and sweet for bitter!
Woe to those who are wise in their own eyes,
and prudent in their own sight!"
-Isaiah 5, WEBBE

Drawing The Line

You can persuade
but not manipulate
You can speak
but not kill with your words
You can sacrifice your body
but never your soul
You can give your life
but not take another's
You can seek justice
but not vengeance
You can fight monsters
but never become one of them!

There are some things we can do
and some things we cannot do
If we truly wish for light to prevail
If we truly wish for good to triumph
then we must learn to draw the line somewhere

and not be the evil
we wish so much to conquer!

March 6 :
Guard Your Heart

Always remember to fight evil with goodness, harshness with gentleness, darkness with light. Above all else, guard the purity of your heart.

Keep your heart with all diligence,
for out of it is the wellspring of life.
-Proverbs 4, WEBBE

We must learn to guard our hearts. Even if we see everyone else risking theirs, even if we feel out of place, even if it means not getting a shortcut to reaching a goal we desire, we must protect what's within us.

We cannot exchange outward success to our inner ruin. We can never find happiness if we lose the substance of who we really are.

Under all circumstances, guard your heart. For what use is everything else if we lose what's truly important in us?

How could we ever find happiness when we have ruined the heart, which alone can taste love and beauty and joy?

March 7 :
Kindness To Enemies

In the worst of situations, let us remember that we can still be human, we can still look at other people with a merciful heart.

He said to David, "You are more righteous than I; for you have done good to me, whereas I have done evil to you. You have declared today how you have dealt well with me, because when the LORD had delivered me up into your hand, you didn't kill me. For if a man finds his enemy, will he let him go away unharmed? Therefore may the LORD reward you good for that which you have done to me today." - 1 Samuel 24, WEBBE

It's never easy to be kind to those who harmed us. It's never even easy to forgive, how much more to do good to those who did evil to us?

But a chain of one evil to another evil could never result in anything but more evil. And the violence that punishes another person, no matter how we deem to be just, punishes not only that person, but the one who administers the violence itself. Like a poison, it creeps into his heart until there is nothing there but bitterness. Like a two-edged sword, it pierces through his soul and claims his own humanity.

What difference shall there be between ourselves and our enemies if we merely do what they do, or if we do even worse? What right have we to hate evil if we have allowed darkness itself to reign in our souls?

Let us pray for the strength to resist the temptation to succumb to the evil we detest. It will never be easy, but with God, it is possible. Why would He tell us to love even our enemies if it couldn't be done?

March 8 :
 Fight With Courage

It's always in the midst of fear where great courage is born.

Be strong and courageous, and do it. Don't be afraid, nor be dismayed; for the LORD God, even my God, is with you. He will not fail you, nor forsake you, until all the work for the service of the LORD's house is finished. - 1 Chronicles 28, WEBBE

It takes a lot of courage to continue to believe in the light when you're in so much darkness. It takes a lot of courage to continue doing good when everyone around you tells you nobody does that anymore.

Where do you find the strength to continue fighting for what you believe in? Where do you find the power to resist despair when you see no fruit whatsoever to everything you've worked so hard for?

Take heart for you are never alone. God whose light has led you so far will never leave you. The Lord in whose name you work for will give you the power to carry on.

Be brave and continue fighting! Fight even if you may not see how you could ever overcome your many foes. The storm itself will strengthen you. The crashing waves themselves will carry you. The wind itself that threatened to blow you away will give you wings to soar!

March 9 :
A Different Courage

It is not the wolf amongst sheep that is brave, but the sheep that dares to walk amongst wolves.

"Behold, I send you out as sheep among wolves. Therefore be wise as serpents, and harmless as doves. - Matthew 10:16, WEB

There is a different kind of courage, the kind the world does not often see or believe in. For to the world, courage has become a sort of a license to merely do what one wills. To the world, it is the violent man that is brave. It is the man that speaks loudly. It is the man that imposes and forces his own will so that others may obey in fear.

Yet what is courage? It is the willingness to stand alone if that's what it takes to express his faith. It is refusing to do something wrong even if everyone else is doing it. It is acknowledging one's mistakes. It is being able to speak softly even when others are already being rude.

March 10 :
    The Innocent Ones

Do not lose the conscience God has given you to distinguish between what is right and what is wrong.

At that time, Jesus answered, "I thank you, Father, Lord of heaven and earth, that you hid these things from the wise and understanding, and revealed them to infants. - Matthew 11:25, WEB

Have you ever had those times when something seemed to have been logically explained to you and yet somewhere within, you feel that something is just not right? Don't dispel that feeling so quickly because it may have something valuable to tell you.

For in this world, there are many things that appear to be good but are in truth evil, and many things that sound pleasing to the ear but are truly rotten to the heart.

Don't numb that little voice within you just yet. Don't dismiss it as the mere stuff of naive children. At times, children can see things clearer because things are simpler in their eyes.

March 11 :
    A Lesser Evil

Evil needs but the smallest door to get through with the greatest of sins.

"You have heard that it was said... 'You shall not murder;'and 'Whoever murders will be in danger of the judgment.' But I tell you that everyone who is angry with his brother without a cause will be in danger of the judgment. Whoever says to his brother, 'Raca!' will be in danger of the council. Whoever says, 'You fool!' will be in danger of the fire of Gehenna.
"You have heard that it was said, 'You shall not commit adultery;' but I tell you that everyone who gazes at a woman to lust after her has committed adultery with her already in his heart."
-Matthew 5, WEB

That Little Evil

That little evil you did,
You think it wasn't evil at all
You're not convinced it is evil
Just because it was small...

But that little evil you did
It crept to your heart
And you hardly felt it
Because it's just a bit.

But that little evil you did
It began to poison you
Little by little it did
That little evil you did.

Until one day that little evil
It wasn't little anymore
Because it grew so big
'Til you can't fight it anymore.

March 12 :
   Excusable Evil?

Our good intentions can never justify the evil things that we do.

God said, "Who told you that you were naked? Have you eaten from the tree that I commanded you not to eat from?"
The man said, "The woman whom you gave to be with me, she gave me fruit from the tree, and I ate it."
Yahweh God said to the woman, "What have you done?" The woman said, "The serpent deceived me, and I ate."
 - Genesis 3:11-13, WEB

We often confuse ourselves about what is good and what is evil not because we have no idea of what is right and wrong but, because we often try to make excuses for the wrong things we intend to do.

"It's for the greater good," we'd say. Or we'll reason, "there is no other way." But is this the way if the way itself is already wrong?

We'd have fallen then into the darkness even before we ever arrive at the light we say we desire.

Do not make things more complicated than they have to be. Do not call evil good or good evil. Let's not fool ourselves until we can no longer tell what it is we're doing or who we have eventually become because of the choices we've made along the way.

March 13 :
   The Face of Evil

If you ever see something attractive in evil, always remember, whatever attracted you was just a mask.

Now the serpent was more subtle than any animal of the field which Yahweh God had made. He said to the woman, "Has God really said, 'You shall not eat of any tree of the garden'?"
The woman said to the serpent, "We may eat fruit from the trees of the garden,
but not the fruit of the tree which is in the middle of the garden. God has said, 'You shall not eat of it. You shall not touch it, lest you die.'"
The serpent said to the woman, "You won't really die,
for God knows that in the day you eat it, your eyes will be opened, and you will be like God, knowing good and evil."
 - Genesis 3:1-5, WEB

It's not the face of evil. It is just a mask. So you'd think evil is beautiful and strong. So you'd think it's desirable. But it is not. It's just a mask.

And you are fooled by the mask. You thought you could achieve your heart's desires. You thought you could do good. You thought your life could be meaningful. But then it's just a mask.

The mask convinced you hatred is good, that it is power! That violence is glorious and that peace is cowardice.

The mask convinced you that war is necessary. That you can save many while damning some.

The mask convinced you that you're wise. That you are wiser than those who aren't resourceful enough, those who can't be tough enough to believe that the end will always justify the means.

But in the end you'll see, that it is just a mask.

The face of evil is behind it. The face that will terrify you! The face that will laugh at you when you realize... that you have been fooled... that everything good and beautiful about it was just a mask.

March 14 :
The Courageous Ones

You may have the most terrifying enemies, but if you have God, BE NOT AFRAID!

The LORD is my light and my salvation.
Whom shall I fear?
The LORD is the strength of my life.
Of whom shall I be afraid?
When evildoers came at me to eat up my flesh,
even my adversaries and my foes, they stumbled and fell.
Though an army should encamp against me,
my heart shall not fear.
Though war should rise against me,
even then I will be confident.
-Psalm 27, WEBBE

I salute you, courageous one. You've been broken bad. Tired and bruised and wounded. You've been terribly crushed. But you held your ground. You did not give up.

I salute you, courageous one. You've been cast away. You knew what it was to suffer loneliness. But you chose to stand alone than join in and give your faith away.

I salute you, courageous one. You've worked so hard to do good. You saw no fruit to your labors, but you were not dismayed.

92

I salute you, courageous one. You've been hurt so many times. Betrayed by those whom you've loved. But you never lost hope. You did not close your heart.

I salute you, courageous one. After working all these years, you've received no applause, you've received no reward. But you carry on. Each day you still do what is right.

I salute you, courageous one. Others thought you're weak. Others thought you're mad. But you knew your true strength and you've used it. You were mighty within and that's more than enough.

March 15 :
  The Sky Above Us

There is far more to life than the things we can see or touch. We were not born merely for this world, there is a better one above us.

Finally, brothers, whatever things are true, whatever things are honourable, whatever things are just, whatever things are pure, whatever things are lovely, whatever things are of good report: if there is any virtue and if there is any praise, think about these things. - Philippians 4, WEBBE

The world has fallen into a great pessimism. Because it cannot see beauty, it has judged that there are no colors. Because it cannot hear music, it has judged that there are no songs. Because it cannot see heaven, it has judged that there is only dust underneath our feet.

If we can fall while reaching for the ideal, what will happen if we do not even try reaching it? If we can hurt each other while trying to be good, what happens if we succumb to the beast within?

It is not good to fall into illusions, but neither is it right to give up our dreams. Dreams that inspire us to be better men, that give us strength to face our daily burdens, that help us to rise again and again no matter how hard we may fall.

93

I Dream of a Better World

I dream of a place where I can be understood,
such a place where finally,
I can be myself.
I dream of a place
where people need not be told anymore
what to do,
because they already know it,
because finally,
they're already guided by their hearts.
I dream of a place
where people can be brothers,
where people can be friends,
where people can be people
and remain to be a people of the sun.
I dream of a place
where I can paint the world
and sing to it my songs;
where I can dance
when I'm filled with joy;
and where I can cry
when I can no longer hold back
my soul.
I dream of a place,
where we all can dream,
and make those dreams come true;
where clouds are as soft
as cotton candies,
and where stars are fireflies
that roam the night;
where children
laugh
and play
and run;
where wings can fly us
'round that magic sky.
Where we don't have to worry
and where don't have to wait
for a brighter tomorrow
and a happier today.

Where we can all walk down life's road
in one direction,
walking hand in hand,
and side by side.
I dream of a place
no further than a step,
of a world
no further than a kiss.
For this world is all we need to have
if we could just
forget,
forgive,
and believe.

March 16 :
A Glimmer of Hope

God may allow us to go through the darkest of nights, but He will never abandon us without the smallest glimmer of light.

LORD, how my adversaries have increased!
Many are those who rise up against me.
Many there are who say of my soul,
"There is no help for him in God."
But you, LORD, are a shield around me,
my glory, and the one who lifts up my head.
I cry to the LORD with my voice,
and he answers me out of his holy hill.
-Psalm 3, WEBBE

In that cold night, may you see a glimmer of hope, some little light to see you through. I hope you find enough to carry you through the darkest hours before dawn. And may you keep hanging on to the very last moment of trial.

May a candle's flame warm your shaking hands. May a single star pierce through the thickest clouds for you. That you may not be lost, and that you may yet say a prayer from your heart.

We may not always be blessed with sunshine. And many are the days without mirth. Yet even then, may you find that all is not yet lost. Even in the throes of seeming defeat, there is yet a way to win.

March 17 :
The Fruits Within

We can't always see the fruits of our labor, but God sees the fruits we have within, and whatever we accomplish is nothing as much as who we have become for eternity.

But I said, "I have laboured in vain.
I have spent my strength in vain for nothing;
yet surely the justice due to me is with the LORD,
and my reward with my God."
-Isaiah 49, WEBBE

Don't ever think that the good you do is futile. It is not. It has shaped you, it has helped you become who you are. It is still moulding you to become even better than before.

Don't ever think that because you see you no fruit yet, that there will be none. Because there will be. And there are fruits now, ripening within you. There will be other fruits, and all because of what you've done.

Don't ever think that all is lost because you're alone. You are not. The Lord who sees everything sees what you do, and when you can no longer walk, He will carry you!

MAYBE NOT NOW, BUT LATER ON

Maybe not now, but later on
the words you've said will be remembered
they will come back,
full of meaning, and of truth.

They shall return
and they shall speak
as though speaking
for the very first time.

96

Maybe not now, but later on
a heart will be changed,
a grudge will be forgotten,
a hurt will be forgiven.

In that perfect time
when a light shall be cast
to help us understand
what we have failed to fathom before.

Maybe not now, but later on
we all shall walk upon one road
hand in hand
heart to heart
singing together a brand new song.

In that perfect day
when we shall each other's face
and be glad that we were friends
in that great journey we called life

In that day, we'll be looking
at the same sky
and we'll be dancing with one song
finally seeing
finally hearing
what our hearts have known
all along.

March 18 :
 Our True Image

Our true nature is not evil, but good. It is not the beast in us that must be set free, but the divine image God has made.

God said, "Let's make man in our image, after our likeness. Let them have dominion over the fish of the sea, and over the birds of the sky, and over the livestock, and over all the earth, and over every creeping thing that creeps on the earth." God created man in his own image. In God's image he created him; male and female he created them. - Genesis 1, WEBBE

Sometimes I wonder what makes people do terrible things that seem obviously evil. Why do it? For it would seem even without religious laws against such deeds, the natural conscience of man would feel repulsed in doing them.

Maybe there is really an influence of original sin in us all, and this is like a beast just waiting to be released with all its tendencies to evil. Many times, all it needs is just a license from something or someone to say that it's alright, that it can even be good to follow these instincts. And the beast is unleashed, seeking the ruin of others and eventually, the ruin of self.

On the other hand, I also believe that there lies buried beneath all these, the original image of our humanity, a humanity made in God's own image. This is our truly natural state, the core of that Divine spark within us. And this humanity is what helps us recognize the beauty of goodness, compassion and every other virtue that lifts us beyond the instincts of the beast. This is our true self, and this is what enables us to realize that it is not the beast that we want to win, it is not the beast we want to become.

And so there will be two forces throughout man's history that will always struggle with one another. The one that thinks it is the beast that must be set free. And the other that remembers its true self and its divine origin, that realizes we can never find our truest desires as long as we succumb to the instincts of the beast.

March 19 :
　　The Right Path

It's not always the easier path that can lead us to the right destination.

"Enter in by the narrow gate; for wide is the gate and broad is the way that leads to destruction, and many are those who enter in by it. How narrow is the gate, and restricted is the way that leads to life! Few are those who find it." - Matthew 7, WEBBE

Sometimes, all we want are the shortcuts in life. We want things to be done quickly even if we use means that would otherwise defeat the very principles we wanted to uphold in the first place. We convince ourselves that the end would indeed justify the means.

But what we fail to realize is that by going through the tedious yet straight path, we are gaining something else. We gain courage and strength we otherwise would not have found. We gain perseverance, a virtue that is often necessary for victory, true victory. And quite often, if we are able to pursue along this path, we find surprises too, wonderful ones we wouldn't have found or discovered had we been content to walk through the mere shortcuts in life.

In God's Perfect Time

In God's perfect time,
every pain shall be comforted,
every tear wiped away.
All our wounds shall be healed,
all our fears cast away,
in God's perfect time.

In God's perfect time,
all the good we did shall be revealed,
and what was whispered in the darkness
shall be broadcast aloud in the light.
Every sacrifice made in secret
shall be revealed,
in God's perfect time.

March 20 :
Rich in God

He is never poor who has God. He is never alone who has God. He who has God has everything!

Listen, my beloved brothers. Didn't God choose those who are poor in this world to be rich in faith, and heirs of the Kingdom which he promised to those who love him? - James 2, WEB

99

In His Eyes

Does it not feel unfair at times,
How some people seem to get
All the attention and love and care
While others work so hard
Just to be accepted
Only to be rejected
Time and time again?

The world applauds
Those who are beautiful and strong
Those who are happy
Those who already seem to have it all.
While for those who are weak
For those who seem poor in all things,
Those who thirst for love the most,
No alms are given,
No eyes are even interested to see.

Yes, the world is unfair,
And our prejudices are many.
Maybe that is why God chose to be born
Among those whose only wealth
Is hope.

God chose the humble
and the poor and the weak,
Those who are lost
and cast away,
Those who do not belong anywhere else.

Is it not enough then
That the unfairness of the world
Should be responded to
By the generosity of His love?

The world may never care,
It may not even know that you're there,
But you are never left out in God's eyes,
And never ever cast away
From His heart.

March 21 :
Hope For Tomorrow

May God give you not only grace for today, but peace for the past and hope for the future.

"For I know the thoughts that I think towards you," says the LORD, "thoughts of peace, and not of evil, to give you hope and a future." - Jeremiah 29, WEBBE

We are often told that what we can do today, we must not put off for tomorrow. And there is wisdom in doing the most important things at present because it is the only moment we really have. We must not get into the habit of delaying things and of being negligent, failing to do the things that really matter in our lives.

Yet there is also some wisdom into making sufficient room also for hope in your life. As much as we want to anyway, not all things can be done today. For all the rest, we entrust them to God. And we use them to inspire us so that we can have something to look forward to when we awake.

March 22 :
Good Things Remain

The beautiful things will always remain, we carry them with us in our hearts.

Now may the God of hope fill you with all joy and peace in believing, that you may abound in hope, in the power of the Holy Spirit. - Romans 15, WEBBE

Remember

Everyday, you have to remember
the really important things.
Otherwise, you will begin to see
only the little irritations,
the clouds, the illusions

and you begin to believe
that these are all you have.

So everyday, try to remember.
Remember who you are.
Remember what you're made of.
Remember how you've survived
so many problems and dreary days before.
Don't let anyone else
make you forget your worth.

Remember where you're headed for,
all those dreams now living
within your soul.
Remember how each step you make
takes you closer to where you
have always wanted to be.
Let no one steal your dreams away.
Remember them today.

Remember Him who loves you so.
How nobody else can fill
His place within your heart.
Remember His eyes,
how He gazes upon you with love.
And that's enough,
more than enough,
to carry you through
the saddest days.
Let no one make you forget
You are loved,
You are precious,
in someone else's eyes.

Everyday, when you start
to feel as though
your happiness is fading away,
As though your life
loses its very meaning,
Remember, Remember all the
precious things you have.
Let no soul ever take away

your faith.
Believe and Remember!
Beyond all the passing shadows,
the beautiful things remain.

March 23 :
A Greater Love

We can never really love unless we love to the full and to the very end.

"You have heard that it was said, 'An eye for an eye, and a tooth for a tooth.' But I tell you, don't resist him who is evil; but whoever strikes you on your right cheek, turn to him the other also. If anyone sues you to take away your coat, let him have your cloak also. Whoever compels you to go one mile, go with him two. - Matthew 5:38-41, WEB

Sometimes, when we love, we tend to give only what we think we ought. We strive for fairness, and we give only as much as we think we could receive along the way. We then live with the very minimum, and then we wonder why our relationships are not doing great.

God's love on the other hand is more than mere fairness. God's love is an abounding love. It is a love without limits or condition, a love that knows no end. It is a love that always seeks to do more, to give more.

If we could only learn from God's love, all our other relationships would be blessed. We'd realize that all the while, we were being content with so little when we can be blessed with an overflowing, ever growing, and abounding love.

March 24 :
His Banner Is Love

Why do we often fail to choose the kind of love that can truly make us happy in the end?

I sat down under his shadow with great delight,
his fruit was sweet to my taste.
He brought me to the banquet hall.
His banner over me is love.
-Song of Solomon 2, WEBBE

To walk with God is to grow in the awareness of His love for me. It is to grow from wanting to believe to being able to believe, from having the knowledge of His love to having the sweet experience of His presence. There is no end to knowing Him, there is no end to the joy of walking with God.

When I Feel Your Love

When I feel your love
I feel alive
And my life has depth and meaning
And all is beautiful and good
And lasting

When I feel your love
The simple life
Is a glorious life
And I don't need
Anything more
Or anyone else
To fulfill me

When I feel your love
I feel as though
I could soar
It's the only fitting thing to do
To meet you
To keep you
To fall over and over again
In a love that is so
Achingly beautiful and true.

March 25 :

God has made the Universe and all that is in it, can He ever fail to give us anything that we ask of Him today?

Therefore don't be like them, for your Father knows what things you need, before you ask him. - Matthew 6, WEBBE

The Things We Need

Sometimes we seem to be lost
We can't find what we're looking for
And even if we find it,
We still feel we've missed it,
We've missed what it was we really need.

And what is it that we need?
We need to know that
Despite our many sins
We can still be forgiven.
We need to know we are loved.
We need to find justice.
And not only justice
But mercy
Mercy that meets with Truth.
We need to know that there is
really such a thing as goodness
And beauty
And purity.
And that somehow,
There are still good things
That can last forever.

These are the things we need.
And God knows our needs
Even before we learn about them
Even before we finally found
The wisdom
And the courage
To ask.

105

March 26 :
Deeds of Love

Our aim should not be to grow us fast as we could but to grow well and to grow without breaking.

When he had finished speaking, he said to Simon, "Put out into the deep, and let down your nets for a catch." Simon answered him, "Master, we worked all night, and took nothing; but at your word I will let down the net." When they had done this, they caught a great multitude of fish, and their net was breaking. - Luke 5, WEBBE

There are times when we may feel that despite all our labors, we're barely making a difference, we're hardly seeing the fruits we wish to make.

It's never easy. Such times require great patience on our part, a certain tenacity, and a tremendous dose of hope to keep our spirits up, to keep going on.

And we go on not because we've already seen our dreams coming true, not even because we feel victory is near. We go on because just like the apostles, Jesus tells us to keep on trying, to look to Him in trust instead of looking towards our many fears.

We cast our nets to catch not what we see, but what God sees. For God sees every fruit that comes out of our labors, and every good thing that happens from each little deed that is done in love.

March 27 :
Light Of The World

It is amazing what a little light can do to dispel the darkness. Hide not the light you alone can shine.

You are the light of the world. - Matthew 5, WEBBE

106

That Little Thing You Did

That little thing you did,
that little smile,
You thought it didn't matter,
but it got through,
and thanks to you,
her day was not so blue.

That little thing you did,
that little letter,
You thought it wasn't written well,
it wasn't perfect,
But it didn't need to be perfect,
to let him know he was loved.

That little thing you did,
that little poem,
It hardly made a rhyme,
You thought no one would read it,
But somebody did and somebody thought about it,
And now his life was spared
by a poem that did not rhyme.

How many good things have not been done
just because we thought
what we do is too little?
How many beautiful things
were left unsaid
just because we thought they wouldn't rhyme?

Do not forget the little things
even the broken and imperfect ones.
God uses the little things
to accomplish His greatest work,
And it is the broken that can mend
the deepest wounds of men.

March 28 :

When Sorrow Becomes a Friend

A friend never leaves just when you needed him most.

You have turned my mourning into dancing for me.
You have removed my sackcloth, and clothed me with gladness...
-Psalm 30, WEBBE

We may find many who will gladly laugh with us, but where can we find those who can share our tears? For laughter is a quick medicine that attracts, but weeping is a burden that none may wish to carry with you. Thus it is said, that when you laugh, the world laughs with you, but when you weep, you weep alone.

Yet even weeping is a treasure, because it is in sorrow that we discover what true love is. Sorrow reveals to us the strength of our friendships. It takes away the masks that have deceived us into believing we are with someone, but in truth, we are really alone.

Let this be our consolation. That such tears take away from us only those who are not real. But they gather with us those who are faithful and true.

We weep in our pain, but we rejoice in the love we have found.

March 29 :

My Small Gift

We begin to help the world when we begin to help one needy person at a time.

"There is a boy here who has five barley loaves and two fish, but what are these amongst so many?"
Jesus took the loaves; and having given thanks, he distributed to the disciples, and the disciples to those who were sitting down; likewise also of the fish as much as they desired. When they were filled, he said to his disciples, "Gather up the broken pieces which are left over, that nothing be lost." So they gathered them up, and

filled twelve baskets with broken pieces from the five barley loaves, which were left over by those who had eaten. - John 6, WEBBE

Five Loaves and Two Fishes

Five loaves and two fishes
These are all I have
And I didn't think they'd matter much
When there are thousands to be fed.

Five loaves and two fishes
And I was ashamed to ask
If somehow they could help
To feed those hungry men

But You took them in Your hands
And you blessed them
And offered them
To heaven.

And everyone ate 'til everyone's full
And everyone believed
That you loved them
Cause you fed them.

And all these out of my small gift
The ones I thought didn't matter
With five loaves and two fishes
You satisfied the hunger of men.

March 30 :
Wait In Hope

With God, we never hope in vain.

For though the fig tree doesn't flourish, nor fruit be in the vines; the labor of the olive fails, the fields yield no food; the flocks are cut off from the fold, and there is no herd in the stalls: yet I will rejoice in Yahweh. I will be joyful in the God of my salvation! - Habakkuk 3:17-18, WEB

109

I Will Wait

I will be patient
I will wait, Dear Lord,
For I know
I don't wait in vain.

You always keep
Your promises
I have no right
To complain.

I will not be fooled
By the things I see
I will not be disheartened
By the darkness surrounding me.

But I will put my trust in You
And I will wait
I will be patient, Dear Lord
For I do not wait in vain.

Consider, please, from this day... Is the seed yet in the barn? Yes, the vine, the fig tree, the pomegranate, and the olive tree haven't produced. From today I will bless you. - Haggai 2:18-19, WEBBE

March 31 :
    A Place For Rest

God is our true home.

Jesus said to him, "The foxes have holes, and the birds of the sky have nests, but the Son of Man has no place to lay his head." - Luke 9, WEB

It's so easy for people to speak about peace and finding time for quiet and solitude when they do not live amidst noise and chaos. We all desire the relaxing sound of the waves near the shore, or the chirping of the birds in a secluded forest. But what of those who live in the midst of cities and noisy streets? Or of those who cannot afford a quiet spot of their own? Who cannot even find a place to rest after the exhaustion of the day's labor? A place to pray and ponder and heal after the countless battles one has fought?

Let us pray for God's mercy, trusting that Jesus Himself knew what it was like to have no dwelling of His own though He made all the universe and everything that's in it. He left heaven itself to abide with us, to live in this restless world right where we are.

Without a Home

There are times
when I still feel like a stranger in this world,
like nobody knows me,
and I don't know anybody who's there for me.

I want to go home,
but I can't go home yet,
and I remain where I'm lost
and cold
and forgotten.

When will I be able to see the dawn again,
when will I be free
to go where I want to go?

No more a stranger,
no more a nobody,
no more alone,
and without a home.

APRIL

April 1 :
   To Look Beyond

If you really want to know me, you must look beyond the me you think you see.

The body is sown perishable; it is raised imperishable. It is sown in dishonour; it is raised in glory. It is sown in weakness; it is raised in power. - 1 Corinthians 15, WEBBE

Past The Ragged Ends

There's a wonderful view just up these mountains
past the rough roads, and 'round the bend,
But you'll never see it, unless you climb it
and unless you make your way to the very end.

There's a beautiful soul just within him
past all the sketchy and rough edges
But you'll never see it, until you seek it
unless you look past all the ragged ends.

April 2 :
   Be Made New

We can look at the same painting twice and see very different things. Not because the painting has changed, but because we ourselves have.

"Behold, I am making all things new." - Revelations 21, WEBBE

It's a bit scary to reveal ourselves too much to other people, to share what it is that makes us laugh, what makes us cry, the things we like or not like at all. It's scary because after revealing these things, we may be judged by them, and the judgement could hurt because we have been criticized just where we are most naked and vulnerable. Furthermore, the judgement could persist even if we have already outgrown such things or made a different path.

112

People's opinion of us can be stuck even if we have already changed.

Despite that however, let us remain confident with our own path of growth. Let us not be confined to other people's idea of us, but continue to be ourselves, even if we have not remained as the kind of person they expected us to be.

April 3 :
To Love as God Loves

He who has received God's love is also the most capable of giving it.

A new commandment I give to you, that you love one another. Just as I have loved you, you also love one another. - John 13:34, WEB

I have realized that unless I know how Jesus loves me, I wouldn't know how to obey Him when He said, "Just as I have loved you, you also love one another."

My first task therefore is to know as much and as deeply as possible how much Jesus loves me. Because if I get it wrong, I won't be able to love others right.

And looking back, I know I often got it wrong.

I have often thought that Jesus loves me only when I'm good. That Jesus can only love me perfectly when I am also perfect myself.

I've been afraid of Him, of His justice, as though He has only allotted a fixed number of times for His forgiveness.

I thought Him to be always stern and serious, like He could never even smile.

Yet the truth is that His mercy is infinite. And He gave His life for me long before I ever knew Him! The truth is that He is humble and He welcomes even a little child.

He knows me even more than I could possibly know myself. He knows how weak I am, and that is why He can be gentle and so patient with me.

He knows my fears. He knows all my wounds.

He is not among those who will rejoice when I hurt, who will scold me as I trip and fall. For He is the Friend who has compassion for me, who lifts me up and carries me upon His arms.

He wants me to be happy, truly and endlessly happy. He wants to shower me with His love!

Greater love has no one than this, that someone lay down his life for his friends.

This is my commandment, that you love one another, even as I have loved you. - John 15:12-13, WEB

April 4 :
Who Is To Judge?

Who am I to judge whom I don't even know?

Don't speak against one another, brothers. He who speaks against a brother and judges his brother, speaks against the law and judges the law. But if you judge the law, you are not a doer of the law, but a judge. Only one is the lawgiver, who is able to save and to destroy. But who are you to judge another? -James 4, WEBBE

Can I Judge You?

How can I judge you
when I don't even know you?
How can I judge another
if I do not even know who I am?

All I have are clues
All I have are rumors
All I have are sketches
But sketches do not define who we are.

114

How I'd like to say things
based on what I see
based on what I believe to be true
but how little I see the truth!

I therefore withhold my judgment
and replace it with my many doubts,
I lift up my complaints to Him
who knows you as you really are.

I cast upon Him my heart's burden
and all the things I cannot see
I believe in His love and In His Justice
And He will judge between you and me.

April 5 :
What The World Needs

We need God but don't quite know it, but we will see it when we realize how badly we thirst of love.

You are the light of the world. A city located on a hill can't be hidden. Neither do you light a lamp, and put it under a measuring basket, but on a stand; and it shines to all who are in the house. Even so, let your light shine before men; that they may see your good works, and glorify your Father who is in heaven. - Matthew 5, WEBBE

The World Needs Saints

What does the world need right now?

We need more saints who are not afraid,
saints who are not afraid to speak the truth
where truth is needed,
saints who are not afraid to give
even their very lives
for the sake of compassion
for those who are lost,
saints who are not so easily disheartened
with the evil that they see,

knowing that it is God
who will have the final say
and God's will
shall always prevail.

What does the world need right now?

We need more saints who are merciful,
saints who will not so easily judge
or cast away or condemn,
saints who know suffering
and who can honor the pain of those who hurt,
saints who can understand grief,
who can understand loss,
who know how it is to be empty
and poor and forgotten,
to be without love
just when you need it most.

What does the world need right now?

We need more saints who are humble,
saints who are not always concerned
about themselves,
for they know that God is
already concerned about them;
saints who know the truth,
who know their own misery and lowliness
before the perfection and purity of God;
saints who boast not of their own righteousness,
knowing that every good thing that they may have
comes from God only, comes only from His love.

What does the world need right now?

We need more saints who are lovers,
saints who are not only concerned
with fulfilling the commandments or avoiding sin,
saints who are more like Good Samaritans,
willing to go out of their way,
so they can help those in need;
saints who have seen God's Face

and who bear His image
for all the world to see.

For this is indeed, what the world needs right now,
saints who have seen Him,
saints who let Him live within them,
ready to give as He gives,
to live as He lives,
to love as He has always loved!

April 6 :
Enduring Faith

Much of what we do with our lives depends on the things we believe with all our hearts.

For what will it profit a man, if he gains the whole world, and forfeits his life? Or what will a man give in exchange for his life?- Matthew 16:26, WEBBE

The greatest legacy we can leave our children is our faith. Faith in the God who truly cares, faith in Him who alone has the power to change the world.

We may strive to give them all the material comfort we could, all the education and opportunity to rise in their chosen careers. But if they have no faith, what would protect them from despair? What would give them true meaning and purpose in life?

All else will fade in this world. All else will fail them, even the best people, even their highest aspirations.

Only faith can guide them towards Truth so they can have wisdom to discern what is right and wrong. Only faith can stand the fierce storms of temptations that seek to devour every man's peace and wholeness.

Love your children well. Give them a legacy that will truly last.

April 7 :

When you have God, no one could ever steal your JOY!

"Go your way. Eat the fat, drink the sweet, and send portions to him for whom nothing is prepared, for today is holy to our Lord. Don't be grieved, for the joy of the LORD is your strength." – Nehemiah 8:10, WEBBE

The circumstances in life do not always bring about happiness. But this doesn't mean that we cannot find joy where we are. Ours is the greatest joy in knowing God Himself came down from heaven, suffered, died and lived again for our sake, to give us eternal happiness. And so in whatever situation we may be, we have joy, if not in actual possession of it, in our certain hope that it will be ours.

Joy

Joy is with us always,
in our hearts and in our hands,
in our triumphs and in our failures,
in our fullness and in our emptiness.

For how can we be far away from it
How can we ever be so far?
Joy can be found where God is,
And God is always where we are.

I will tell you what my joys are –

in suffering, it is Christ
in sickness, it is healing
in dying, it is the thought of new life

in defeat, it is in future triumphs
in silence, it is prayer
in confusion, it is wisdom

in calamity, it is being able to repent
in poverty, it is the charity I may give and receive

118

in sacrifice, it is the presence of love

in blessings, it is my gratitude
in uncertainty, it is hope
in happiness itself, it is the thought of far greater joys and of eternal
bliss

Joy is here
Joy is in my tomorrows
Joy always
And always, JOY!

April 8 :
The Unpopular Choice

God will always have the final say. Let us seek His opinion for His opinion is Truth and Life.

For am I now seeking the favor of men, or of God? Or am I striving to please men? For if I were still pleasing men, I wouldn't be a servant of Christ. - Galatians 1:10, WEB

Never settle to what the majority of people say. The popular opinion is not always the right opinion.

Pressure may come when we have to stand up for the truth alone. But then we are not alone if God is with us.

No matter what other people say, let us not be disheartened if we know we are in the right. Remember that you are not alone. God is Truth Himself, and He will defend you from those who want to believe a lie.

People can say so much, but only God has the final say. When we try to please God alone, He will never let us down.

What Does It Matter?

What does it matter what they say,
what they say against you,
or how they look down and judge you?

119

What does it matter what they think of you,
when you know how you are
in the eyes of God?

What does it matter how they see you
or what fault they could find in you,
when you have already found forgiveness
from the One that you love?

What does it matter what they say or do?
You have found mercy and light,
and peace and hope.
You have been saved and destined for good
by the Lord whose words
shall have the final say as regards who you are?

What does it matter what they say?
What matters are the words
God Himself has promised you:
You are His. You are loved. You are etched forever
in the palm of His hand!

April 9 :
Suffering Proves True Love

What kind of love is there that knows not how to suffer for the one it loves?

...Simeon blessed them, and said to Mary, his mother, "Behold, this child is set for the falling and the rising of many in Israel, and for a sign which is spoken against. Yes, a sword will pierce through your own soul, that the thoughts of many hearts may be revealed." - Luke 2:34-35, WEB

I have often wondered why God allows His beloved children to suffer. Why not prevent their tears from ever falling? Their hearts from ever being hurt?

One day however, He helped me realize that it is only through suffering that true love may be found. During happy days, when all is well and we need not sacrifice anything, we may be fooled into

120

believing that contentment is goodness, and that friendship is merely being kind to those who are not causing us any discomfort or trouble.

Almost everyone loved Jesus when He was healing the sick and preaching the Good News. But when He was sentenced to be crucified, almost everyone abandoned Him and few were found at the foot of the cross, staying with Him just when it was darkest and hope seemed bleakest.

Suffering unmasks the true thoughts of our hearts. It enable us to see who really loves us. Suffering reveals what goodness and evil had been there all along.

The people we thought to be our friends may not really be our allies. People who seem righteous may not really be merciful and kind.

We find our true friends when we suffer. They are the ones who are there not only in good times, but those who remain even in the worst of times.

A Little Cloud

A little tear, a little crying,
For not all of life is smiling;
A little cloud, a little rain,
Though the sun is always shining.

A little pain, a little aching,
So our hearts can keep on growing;
A little cross to see the right,
A little night before the light!

April 10 :
    God Is Enough

Many times, it is only when we have lost everything that we find out that God is enough.

The LORD is my shepherd:
I shall lack nothing.

He makes me lie down in green pastures.
He leads me beside still waters.
He restores my soul.
He guides me in the paths of righteousness for his name's sake.
Even though I walk through the valley of the shadow of death,
I will fear no evil, for you are with me.
-Psalm 23, WEBBE

This world is not at all perfect, and I am wounded at times in grief. But God is enough for me. He brings me healing, He fills my hunger, He puts my soul at ease.

Even in the worst of times, and especially in the most trying times, I can count on Him to be there for me. For He watches over me always, there is not a moment when I am ever out of His sight.

And so I cling to Him. With all my might I hold on upon His strong and loving arm.

In the darkest of days He will uphold me. He will protect me from my foes. He will be my shield in the fiercest of storms!

Where I hide from fear, He is my courage. Where I despair from darkness, He is my hope! Where I seek for happiness, He is my joy! Where I fall in loneliness, He is my Spouse.

God is my portion and my strength. In Him I shall ever hope and in hope I shall always believe. God is enough, more than enough. I do not deserve such a Love, but He fills me with happiness and my cup shall always overflow.

April 11 :
They Who Are Brave

God raises up the little ones and they become the most courageous of them all.

"Haven't I commanded you? Be strong and courageous. Don't be afraid. Don't be dismayed, for the LORD your God is with you wherever you go." - Joshua 1:9, WEBBE

When I was young I thought I had much courage. Later however, I found out that was not true. I was not really courageous. It was either I was just strong, or that I was totally ignorant of the risks I was taking.

Having courage takes a lot more than strength. It takes a lot more than being unaware of the dangers around you.

They are not brave who are quite capable of defeating their foes. They are not brave who foolishly enter into battles they know nothing about.

They are courageous who are well aware of the suffering they would go through, but who would face it anyway in order to fulfill a higher call. They are courageous who are in their worst day, fallen and aching, yet willing to rise again and again after each fall. They are courageous who are weak in the bed of sickness but instead of thinking about their pain think of their loved ones and those they may leave behind.

They who are truly brave are not those who are merely confident of their own strength. Those who are truly brave are those who know that there is a God who loves them, a God who will be their Strength when all else fails, a God who will never disappoint them when every source of comfort and hope seems far away.

April 12 :
     A PRAYER OF TRUST

When you don't know what to do or where to go, and when you feel everyone has rejected and abandoned you, do not lose hope. God is still there, and when you trust Him, you will not fall.

Those who know your name will put their trust in you, for you, LORD, have not forsaken those who seek you. - Psalm 9:10, WEBBE

Lord, I do not know how to face this situation. I feel also that I neither have the strength nor the courage for it. By myself, I shall fall. So I entrust to you everything. In your wisdom and strength. In

123

your mercy and love. Help me to face what I'm going through according to your will. Let me do the right thing. Keep me from hurting others or from harming my own soul. I offer to you everything - every pain, every fear, every weakness that I have. I cling to you each moment. May your grace sustain me through it all and may your love ever be before me, a light that shines even through my darkest night.

Don't let your heart be troubled. Believe in God. Believe also in me. - John 14:1, WEBBE

April 13 :
In My Father's House

There is a reason why this world keeps on failing us. It wasn't meant to satisfy us, only God can do that.

He said to them, "Why were you looking for me? Didn't you know that I must be in my Father's house?" - Luke 2:49, WEB

Many times, we feel so troubled because we look for the answers in all the wrong places. We seek it in people who could never love us the way we wanted to be loved. We seek it in things that could never really satisfy the soul.

Why look for answers in all the wrong things and then ask God whether He really loves us?

Whenever we feel we have tried everything and looked everywhere, and still feel unsatisfied, let us try to find time for God's presence. Let's set aside every distraction from the world and seek God in prayer and silence.

God is waiting for us. Let us go then where He may be found.

On Higher Grounds

I've searched for love in funny places
I've searched for love in funny ways
I've searched for love both high and low
I've searched for it in all my days

124

Yet often did I wonder
And often did I cry
Not knowing where the roads may lead to
Not knowing what I'll ever find

'Til I sat in silence along the way
'Til I listened to my heart and prayed
That I realized love was always there
And that love shall always stay

I grasped it and I let it go
I breathed it in and I breathed it out
I tasted it and cherished it
I held it with my trembling palm

For love has been there all along
And love will guide me 'til I'm home
What I have sought I know I've found
And my heart shall rest on higher grounds.

April 14 :
How Much You Are Loved

Were you not looking for someone who could really love you so?

Behold, I have engraved you on the palms of my hands. - Isaiah 49:16, WEB

You are loved. Cast away every doubt and feeling of uselessness. Your worth is not determined by what other people say.

Look not on what you have done or failed to do. Look not on your weakness or your poverty. They tell nothing about how valuable you really are.

Look instead upon the cross, and there, see how Someone gave His life for you. See how much He suffered out of love for you.

If He deemed you valuable enough to be saved by His sufferings, why deem yourself unworthy to be loved?

See His wounded hands and believe. It is with such wounds that your name was forever engraved upon His hands.

April 15 :
Happy Endings

When you start to wonder how things can still work out right, try to look up. God is still there. God watches over you. And heaven's waiting for your "happily ever after" to come true.

I heard a loud voice out of heaven saying, "Behold, God's dwelling is with people, and he will dwell with them, and they will be his people, and God himself will be with them as their God. He will wipe away from them every tear from their eyes. Death will be no more; neither will there be mourning, nor crying, nor pain, any more. The first things have passed away." - Revelations 21:3-4, WEB

We need to believe in happy endings once again. We need to believe that light can overcome darkness and that good will always triumph over evil in the end.

It is not wishful thinking. It is hope. And in times of despair and trouble, hope needs to be rekindled in our hearts.

We have learned much of the valuable things when we were children. We only need to remember once again, to see the world again with eyes that know how to dream and hearts that know how to fight to make such dreams come true.

The world we grew up to may be complicated, but the most important things remain simple, and heaven is always within the grasp of a little child.

Things are not perfect yet but they will be. Times are troublesome, but all such troubles shall end. In God, we never hope in vain.

April 16 :
Our Little Sacrifices

When we discover the fruits of the sacrifices we have made for love, we will realize that they were indeed too small as compared with the happiness it yields for all eternity.

Then Jesus said to his disciples, "If anyone desires to come after me, let him deny himself, and take up his cross, and follow me." - Matthew 16:24, WEB

Sometimes, you have to let go of the little things so you can gain what's truly important. You have to learn to overlook many of your neighbors' little faults as you want them to overlook yours.

We are not perfect yet and even with the best of intentions, we may not please everyone.

Let us learn to be more patient then as we try to see others in their best light.

The little sacrifices we make can add up to a big difference in our relationships. It is like oil that reduces a lot of friction in our daily life. It is like a little seed that will eventually grow into a sturdy tree where we can seek shelter beneath the fiercest storms.

April 17 :
Wait and Believe

Wonderful things can happen at the least expected time. Blessed are those who wait.

Oh taste and see that the LORD is good.
Blessed is the man who takes refuge in him.
– Psalm 34:8, WEBBE

Blessed are those who wait upon the Lord, whose expectations come from Him. They shall not be put to shame, neither shall they be disappointed.

For they have put their trust in Him who alone can be trusted. And they have set their eyes on Him who alone can satisfy.

Despise not the time for waiting. We may not see it with our eyes, but beautiful things happen even while we wait.

MEANWHILE

The rain is pouring
The sky is dark
There'll be no hills to climb today
There'll be no seas to cross

But I'll sip my coffee
and I will be cozy
and enjoy the cool wind
blowing by
meanwhile.

The land is plowed
The seeds are planted
Yet harvest time has not arrived
But I'll watch the sunset
and my fields of gold
and I'll take
a sweet little nap
meanwhile.

Yea for those who wait
for their tomorrows
let none then waste
of their todays

For all is well
and all is fine
for those who pray
and smile
meanwhile.

April 18 :

God's Answer

If we only knew the countless blessings God is waiting to pour down upon us once we are ready to receive them!

For everyone who asks receives. He who seeks finds. To him who knocks it will be opened. Or who is there amongst you, who, if his son asks him for bread, will give him a stone? Or if he asks for a fish, who will give him a serpent? If you then, being evil, know how to give good gifts to your children, how much more will your Father who is in heaven give good things to those who ask him! – Matthew 7:8-11, WEBBE

God's answer isn't always what we expect it to be. It may not even arrive at the time we thought it would. One thing is certain however, that God's answer will always be in response to His love.

He who loves much always wants what's best for his beloved. He cannot turn a deaf ear to her pleas. He cannot delay without reason. He cannot remain silent unless silence is the answer itself. To someone who loves much, it is better to suffer than to see his beloved suffering. It is better to die so he can give life to the one he loves.

God's answers will often astound us. We may not see it now, but we will realize later on how they truly worked for our good. God's answers are far generous than we could ever deserve and exceedingly beyond what we could have ever hoped for!

April 19 :

Not All Is Lost

For all the things that have been denied us, may we never forget the many blessings we are given, grace upon grace that is continuously being showered upon us from one glorious morning to the next, enriching us beyond our expectations, preparing us for untold bliss in a life that knows no end!

Therefore we don't faint, but though our outward man is decaying, yet our inward man is renewed day by day. For our light affliction, which is for the moment, works for us more and more exceedingly an eternal weight of glory; while we don't look at the things which are seen, but at the things which are not seen. For the things which are seen are temporal, but the things which are not seen are eternal. – 2 Corinthians 4:16-18, WEBBE

We all suffer some kind of loss somehow. Few are those who are able to go through life unscarred. Some suffer the loss of a job. Some suffer the loss of health. Some suffer the loss of a dream. Some suffer the loss of relationships. Some suffer the loss of the people they love the most.

It's in the nature of this life to suffer loss. No sooner do clouds form that they lose themselves and fall down upon us as rain. No sooner does the moon shine that it suffers the loss of night and it gives way towards a brand new sunrise for all of us. Even a seed loses itself and gets buried deep into the ground to give way for a growth that allows it to rise higher than it could ever think it could.

We are not the only ones who suffer some kind of loss. But we are also not the only ones who are continuously been given opportunities to gain something else. Another job perhaps, another dream, or other friends who can embrace us and share both our deepest griefs and our highest joys.

Not that anything else can replace what we have lost. Not that we could ever fill the emptiness the important people have left in our hearts. But that in time, our hearts are healed and we increase in our capacity to receive other valuable things in our lives. In time, we begin to understand God's great design where things are lost but for a moment, to give way for all the other things that will bring us happiness for all eternity.

April 20 :
   Seeds of Love

You can always plant seeds of love. But you must leave the harvest to God.

Let's not be weary in doing good, for we will reap in due season, if we don't give up. - Galatians 6:9, WEB

Let us make it a habit to plant seeds of love and kindness wherever we may go. Let us plant some in our workplace and in our travels. Let us plant some where we meet our neighbors and where we praise and worship God. And let us never forget to plant some in our homes, within our family circle and our friends, and ask God to bless such seeds which only He can help to grow.

We may not see too quickly the fruits of the good we do, but let us continue to believe that we never labor in vain. For true love and charity takes root deep within the heart and changes the soul. It grows unseen until it blossoms from grace known to God alone.

April 21 :
How Do I Love True?

If you desire to love true, give your whole heart to God and He will make yours just like His. You will know what true love really means.

A new commandment I give to you, that you love one another. Just as I have loved you, you also love one another. – John 13:34, WEBBE

I do believe that if we really learn to love another person truly, we would eventually learn also to love God. Why do I think so? Because when we learn to love another person with all sincerity, we begin to do all we can for their sake. We try our best not to hurt them. We give them everything in our power to make them happy. And if we remain honest with ourselves, we find out that the only way to do all these is to seek God's help. By ourselves alone, we hurt the ones we love most. Left to our own powers, we can't shield them from every want or pain.

We may see ourselves as good people. We may even consider ourselves as loving and kind. But are we kind enough? Is our love always far from our own selfishness and insecurities? If we truly love another, we can only find true hope and assurance if we can entrust them in God's loving, all powerful and merciful hands. We can only avoid hurting them if we allow God to heal us from our own pain, if we let Him change us more into His own likeness.

Only with God's love in me can I love you unselfishly and unafraid. Only with God's love can I love you with a love that you deserve, a love that can truly make you happy!

April 22 :
A Prayer of Gratitude

If I can only keep one true moment of love, I'd have enough to live in joy for all eternity.

For what thanksgiving can we render again to God for you, for all the joy with which we rejoice for your sakes before our God... - 1 Thessalonians 3:9, WEB

I thank you Lord, for all the moments filled with love that you have blessed me with throughout my lifetime. Thank you for filling my heart with incomparable happiness. Thank you for allowing me to see what's truly beautiful and pure.

I have not yet reached heaven, but even here, you have given me a glimpse of my true home. You have allowed me to see a reflection of your face. You have loved me, and you gave me a chance to love you back. May I never waste a single moment of grace, and may I always treasure all your gifts within my heart.

April 23 :
Words That Hurt

Be careful that your words do not cause wounds you cannot heal.

Let no corrupt speech proceed out of your mouth, but only what is good for building others up as the need may be, that it may give grace to those who hear. - Ephesians 4:29, WEB

There are words that can easily hurt us. Those who say it may not even have any intention to offend us, but we are offended just the same. Such words cut through the heart, makes its way uninvited, and leaves much pain and tears.

They may open up past memories we'd rather forget or wounds we thought were already healed. They seem to say how broken we really are, and how unworthy we are to be accepted for who we really are.

When these words come, place them at once upon God's hands. Only by passing through His merciful hands can the pain they caused bring healing, forgiveness and peace. Only by letting Him cast His light upon them can we see what gifts they bring beyond the tears.

May God show us what wounds still need healing. May He strengthen us so that instead of bitterness, we may have more compassion on those who weep. May we clearly see how by His love, we become worthy, beloved and whole.

April 24 :
   To Suffer With Dignity

Only in heaven shall we know the lofty honor of all suffering united with Christ crucified.

Surely he has borne our sickness,
and carried our suffering;
yet we considered him plagued,
struck by God, and afflicted.
But he was pierced for our transgressions.
He was crushed for our iniquities.
The punishment that brought our peace was on him;
and by his wounds we are healed.
-Isaiah 53:4-5, WEBBE

Our dignity does not come from our own strength or from our own power. It is not lost with sickness. It isn't lost with poverty or persecution or even the insults of men. It isn't lost with suffering or even death.

133

God gave us this dignity, the dignity of being made into His own image.

One day He is going to complete the good work He has begun in us and we will finally see Him. We will also know fully our great dignity of being His children.

Here on earth however, we suffer from our weaknesses and from the sins of others. We also suffer from our imperfect physical bodies and from various emotional and spiritual struggles. Many times, we suffer involuntarily. At times, we suffer for the sake of those we love. But through all these, we are assured, that for as long as we suffer with the love of God, we do not suffer in vain.

On the contrary, when we suffer with love, our dignity is raised, and we reach our true dignity as human beings created in the image of God. When we suffer in love, we become like Jesus Himself, who offered His own life in order to save many. Can there ever be a dignity greater than this?

April 25 :
Our Silent Heroes

Some friendships are proven by one great storm or difficulty. Others are tested through the passing of time, by endurance and lasting faithfulness.

A friend loves at all times; and a brother is born for adversity. - Proverbs 17:17, WEB

It isn't only one great trial that tests a friendship. Perseverance and lasting faithfulness prove also how true and precious our friendships are.

It is the daily and constant devotion to our relationships that make it strong through time. It is the little patience and constant forgiveness that builds it up and fastens it with a bond that cannot be easily broken by any storm.

We often fail to notice such deeds. But throughout our lifetime as we look back, we'd be most grateful for people who walked with us

134

in all the phases of our journey, whether it be fun or dragging, in sunshine or in rain. We'd find out how blessed we are with those people who silently provided their hearts to us, enduring all the many trials of daily life, never giving up but constantly being concerned and ready to give a helping hand.

Let us never forget such people. They are the silent heroes God has sent our way to bless and guide us in this journey called life.

FRIEND

I may not always be by your side,
but my prayers will be with you.
I may not always help you,
but deep inside you know I want to.
I may not always do what you like,
but I will do the best I can.
I may not always understand,
but we can still walk hand in hand.
I may not be the perfect friend,
I may not be the best out there,
but in spite and despite all these,
you can be sure somebody cares!

A Prayer For My Dear Friend

Dear Lord, bless my friend who came from Thee
Save her from every harm
Rescue her from every evil and pain.
Guide always her path
And provide her with your Light,
That she may not stray,
And always find her way back home.
Protect her thoughts oh, Lord,
That she may not be anxious
But have the assurance that comes from Your Grace.
Surround her heart with your strength
That she may live in love
And thereby live a meaningful life
Wherever she may be.
May she never forget our friendship
And find in it a treasure that does not fade.

May she remember that there is a person she can lean on to
In times of need,
In times when she may cry.
And even in those times when I can't be there
To hold her hand,
May she always know she's not alone
For You are there, O Lord,
The One who has given us this blessing of friendship,
The One who will protect its joy forever more.

April 26 :
Be Happy Dear Soul

When we are happy in God, we have a happiness that could never be taken away from us.

Therefore you now have sorrow, but I will see you again, and your heart will rejoice, and no one will take your joy away from you. - John 16:22, WEB

How can you not be happy dear soul, when Jesus has loved you so? How can you not be joyful when He has chosen you, and rejoiced over you as a lover rejoices over his beloved one?

How can you not be happy dear soul, when heaven is waiting just for you? And when mansions have been prepared for you even before you were born?

How can you not shout in praise for Him who cared for you and protected you? For Him who pursued you long until you can be found?

This world may yet be filled with darkness and difficulty. It may yet cause you to cry. But let not your sufferings take away your happiness. Let not the darkness take away your love.

No pain on earth could ever match the joys of heaven. No trial could ever take away God's peace. Light shall always prevail. Love shall always be triumphant! Tell me then, how can you not be happy dear soul?

April 27 :
He Who Loves You So

Rest now and stop your weary wandering. Here is healing. Here is peace. Here is happiness. Here is the God who loves you so!

The LORD, your God, is amongst you, a mighty one who will save. He will rejoice over you with joy. He will calm you in his love. He will rejoice over you with singing.
-ZEPHANIAH 3:14-17, WEBBE

The world has failed you, lovers have hurt you, friends have turned away. Why continue seeking love from whom it could not be found?

It isn't that we are meant to be alone. It isn't that we are not to be channels of love to one another.

But if we do not allow God's own love to fill us, our hearts would be so empty that no human being could ever love us the way we yearn to be loved.

Only God's love does not fail. Only such a love can fill us to the full!

Until when must we turn our eyes to someone else? Until when must we keep Him waiting, the only One who truly loves us so?

April 28 :
God is Real

It would make a whole lot of difference once we really believe that GOD IS REAL.

Jesus said to him, "I am the way, the truth, and the life. No one comes to the Father, except through me. If you had known me, you would have known my Father also. From now on, you know him, and have seen him." - John 14:6-7, WEB

God is a real person. He moves, He thinks, He sees. He watches over you. He knows your name. He hears, He feels, He loves. He

137

cares about you more than anybody ever did, more than anyone ever could.

Why turn away when He speaks? Why ask for other things when you can have all things in Him?

He knows your every tear. He shares your joys. He is aware of your highest dreams.

You don't have to live your life alone for He is there. You don't need to carry your burdens on your own for He is more than happy to share it with you.

Whenever you feel tired or deserted by everyone, know that you could always go to Him. He is real. He is closer than you could ever imagine Him to be.

April 29 :
In Your Darkest Night

Someday we will see, how God had been closest to us just when we thought it to be darkest. We were not alone, we were safe, we were loved.

Even though I walk through the valley of the shadow of death, I will fear no evil, for you are with me. - Psalm 23:4, WEB

Never think that God is only with you when things go well. He is not a fair-weather friend who gets frightened when things start to fall apart. He does not leave us alone just when we need Him most.

On the contrary, He is closer to us when it's darkest. He stays with us through the most difficult times.

When all else walks away, we can count on Him to be there for us, comforting us and strengthening us, guiding us until we can find our way back into the light again.

In your darkest night, you can count on God to be there for you. It is there when you can know Him better. It is there when you would realize how much He truly loves you so.

April 30 :
God's Friend

That the Highest should also be the Warmest and the Friendliest to me, what a great marvel, what a bliss, what a treasure I do not and cannot ever deserve!

No longer do I call you servants, for the servant doesn't know what his lord does. But I have called you friends, for everything that I heard from my Father, I have made known to you. - John 15:15, WEB

What does it take to be someone's friend? Common interest perhaps? An attractive personality? A good sense of humor? Similar hobbies?

For some people, it takes a certain social standing before they accept you in their circle. To others, what is needed is talent or intelligence. Still to some, physical strength and a passion for adventure is needed to be considered as a good company.

But what about God's friendship? How do you become friends with Someone who is the Creator of the moon and the stars? How do you approach Him who rules over the earth and to whom the angelic beings bow down and give their allegiance?

Unfathomable as it may seem, all that is required is our humility and faith.

There is no person on earth no matter how poor he may be who cannot achieve friendship with God. There is none who truly desires His friendship and His love who would ever be rejected and cast away.

Each person can be His friend. Each one accepted and loved.

It doesn't matter what your past may be. It doesn't matter how weak or frail you are. Young and old can come to Him. Sinners can be forgiven. Those who are broken can be healed and made whole again.

It is the tenderness of God's compassion that caused Him to reach out to us all. Even when we were not even looking. Even when we knew not we could be found.

Blessed is the man who looks at last to Him who is faithful and true! He shall have One True Friend forever who will never let Him down.

MAY

May 1 :
    Our Best is Enough

If God ever expects us to do something, it's because He knows we can do it. We can never fail Him as we do our very best because our best would always be sufficient in His eyes.

Every way of a man is right in his own eyes,
but the LORD weighs the hearts.
-Proverbs 21:2, WEBBE

People can often set up standards we could never meet. Even if we do our very best, and even if we have the best of intentions, everything would still be inadequate for them and all the work we do would be unappreciated and unrecognized.

Not so with God. It is our intention that is important to Him. Whether we fail or succeed in doing what we ought, we can find confidence in God's pleasure if we have done everything we could to do His will.

God knows what we can and cannot do. He does not expect us to do something beyond what we are capable of. If ever He intends to use us to accomplish things beyond our power, He will give us all the power we need and fill whatever is lacking in us.

Praise be the Lord of compassion! Praise Him who knows us well and recognizes all our efforts to please Him. Blessed indeed are those who serve Him because He understands our weaknesses and supplies all the strength we need to accomplish His will.

I AM A TREE

I am a tree
sprouting forth and reaching out
for the glorious sunny sky
strengthening my stance
drawing forth life
from the warm womb of the ground
bearing forth what fruit

i may offer to all
giving my shade
to those who may want to rest awhile
Not all men may notice me
when they pass by
not all may taste the fruit
that i have whole-heartedly offered
nor avail of the shade
of my embrace
and yet i stand
and yet i stand
for a tree remains to be a tree
though no one comes to rest in thee
its arms remain wide open
its fruit renewed always in their season
its gaze always before the sky
smiling
knowing
standing firm
where God has appointed thee

May 2 :
God's Silence

God's silence is as full of love as His replies.

If you then, being evil, know how to give good gifts to your children, how much more will your Father who is in heaven give good things to those who ask him! - Matthew 7:11, WEB

Be not discouraged by God's silence. Think not that love has vanished just because it could not be heard.

For God's love is ever constant. He who watches over us night and day knows truly what we're going through.

Even in times when He is silent, He is accomplishing for us much more than we could ever understand. For He is there. He is supporting us with unseen hands.

How difficult it is to hold back our answers from those we love the most! What strength is needed to keep ourselves from giving in too soon, lest we spoil the best gifts we desire to bestow.

But God is strong. And God is kind. His kindness is more than our own kindness. His silence is as beautiful as His replies.

May 3 :
With Empty Hands

It is those who hunger most that shall receive most. We don't need hands that our full but empty hands, ready to receive all that God is giving us.

Blessed are those who hunger...for they shall be filled. - Matthew 5:6, WEB

God has not come to seek those who are already full. He came to find those who have nothing more to offer than their poverty. He came to heal the broken, to find the lost, to fill those who thirst for love.

Blessed are they who are empty. They can still be filled. They can cry out for mercy, and they can receive with open arms.

For what do we possess but that which God has given? What good can we do but that which God has blessed?

We come to Him not with fullness and pride. He draws us like little children, and He carries the humble upon His arms.

May 4 :
Treasures in Heaven

In the end, we keep only the things we place upon God's Hands.

...but lay up for yourselves treasures in heaven, where neither moth nor rust consume, and where thieves don't break through and steal;

143

for where your treasure is, there your heart will be also. - Matthew 6:20-21, WEB

How many times have we lost things we wished we could keep forever? How many times have we grieved for something so beautiful that has suddenly been taken away from us?

What inconstancy there is indeed in this life. We strive so much to possess the things our hearts desire and as soon as we get them, we lose them, never to find them again.

If only we could place them somewhere safe, somewhere hidden from everything that could destroy them or steal them away from us.

In the end though, we discover that the only things we get to keep are the things we have placed upon God's Hands. What we surrender to Him we shall have forever. What we learned to entrust upon Him we shall forever possess.

May 5 :
Let Jesus Fulfill Your Desires

If God has given you this good desire, shall He not fulfill it?

If you remain in me, and my words remain in you, you will ask whatever you desire, and it will be done for you. - John 15:7, WEB

Deep within our hearts, we have desires that may have remained hidden through the years. We have almost forgotten them. We rarely allow them to speak to us because somehow, we are afraid.

Not once have we been disappointed while dreaming our dreams. Not once have our desires been put down by others who didn't believe in them.

So we buried those desires deeply, into that place where none can see them anymore, where none can judge us or mock us, telling us we're not even worthy to imagine such things.

But what if Someone comes along who believes in them? Someone who is able to see pass through your masks, uncovering the true cry of your soul?

Will you allow yourself to believe once again? Will you honor the dignity God has placed within you?

Jesus comes knocking. He knows you through and through. Finally, here is Someone who will treasure your deepest yearnings, who cares so much about you He wants to fulfill your heart's desires. Will you let Him? Will you trust again knowing that there is Someone who trusts in you?

May 6 :
Being Who You Are

You are not being called to be somebody else. You are being called to be who you truly are. You are most beautiful when you are able to be the the unique person God has wanted you to be.

"Before I formed you in the womb, I knew you.
   Before you were born, I sanctified you."
-Jeremiah 1:5, WEB

One of the most difficult things to do is trying to be someone you're not. No matter how you try to, you'd merely end up with a lot of heartaches because you're trying to be who you're not.

Let no one pressure you into being someone else. Let no one make you believe you are not beautiful as you are.

God loves you, not because you're perfect, but because you are His. It is within His power to one day make you perfect in every way, but only as you really are, not as a copy of someone else.

There are gifts which He has given to you alone. There are strengths which only you can fully harness. Why not bless the world by being the person God has wanted you to be?

Trust in the One who made you, the One who loved you for who you really are.

145

May 7 :
What I Care About

Why put so much care on the words of those who do not care for you?

"Blessed are you when people reproach you, persecute you, and say all kinds of evil against you falsely, for my sake. Rejoice, and be exceedingly glad, for great is your reward in heaven." - Matthew 5:11-12, WEB

Why should I care about what others say? You make me happy, I'm satisfied. Let them tease, let them shout. It doesn't matter. Such words don't count. What matters is Your presence now.

You are, O, Lord, my all. For You I surrender all. Let the crowds mock me. Let them judge me. I don't care. All I care about is who I am before Your Eyes.

You know me through and through, what I can and cannot do. Still You have called me Yours. You pursued me and found me. Without my mask, You loved me. And now my only joy is to love you back!

May 8 :
Set Your Eyes on Christ

We can never go wrong if we set our eyes upon Christ.

...looking to Jesus, the author and perfecter of faith, who for the joy that was set before him endured the cross... - Hebrews 12:2, WEBBE

Set not your eyes on your righteousness, it will lead you to pride, and soon you will fall. Set not your eyes on your weaknesses, it will lead you to despair, and you will lose hope. For it is not upon ourselves that we should set our gaze upon. It is not upon our works or our many sins.

Consider the Justice of God. All our righteousness shall fall short when we think of His Holiness. What then can we boast about?

146

On the other hand, consider God's Mercy. Shall not our sins be washed away as we repent of them sincerely and seek for God's Compassion?

Set your eyes upon Him alone for in Him is all purity and mercy and truth. He will lift you up from your weakness. He will guard your heart so you won't fall.

May 9 :
Change Begins Within

We can never change the world around us if we do not begin to change from within.

"I have sworn by myself," says the LORD, "because you have done this thing, and have not withheld your son, your only son, that I will bless you greatly, and I will multiply your offspring greatly like the stars of the heavens, and like the sand which is on the seashore. Your offspring will possess the gate of his enemies. All the nations of the earth will be blessed by your offspring, because you have obeyed my voice." -Genesis 22:16-18, WEBBE

There are times when we become disheartened as we look at what is happening around us. We hear how the world is losing its faith. We encounter people who make it more and more difficult to believe how the future could still be brighter and happier.

Let us keep our courage however. Though we think we are alone, we are not at all on our own. Though we think we can do so little, God can still do so much as He makes us instruments of His love.

Change can begin from within ourselves. It begins when we refuse to lose hope no matter how dark things seem to be. It begins when we forgive and when we become channels of mercy to those around us.

We may not see now how our little deeds can change the world. But let us trust God. He is the One who multiplies five loaves of bread so it can feed thousands. He is the One who receives every little sacrifice we make so He can bless so many others along the way.

May 10 :
We Are Not So Different

God made you, and God made me. We are not so different, you and I.

"Don't judge, so that you won't be judged. For with whatever judgement you judge, you will be judged; and with whatever measure you measure, it will be measured to you." – Matthew 7:1-2, WEBBE

We are not so different, you and I. From the outside it would seem we are not so similar. But if we could only see from within, we can see that we are not so different at all.

In many ways, we are vulnerable to the same pain, to the same sufferings. Who among us have not felt alone at times? Or who among us have not lost a person we loved so much?

If we judge another person for one instance of sin or weakness, we may in truth be judging and condemning ourselves.

Before we pass judgment on others, let us try to know them better. Maybe we'd realize that we were not so different from them after all.

May 11 :
Loving Jesus More

There is no greater joy than to know and to love Jesus more!

At this, many of his disciples went back, and walked no more with him. Jesus said therefore to the twelve, "You don't also want to go away, do you?" Simon Peter answered him, "Lord, to whom would we go? You have the words of eternal life. - John 6:66-68, WEB

To love Jesus is to know Him and to accept Him as He is, not as we wanted Him to be.

148

For surely there will be times when we will find it hard to understand everything about Him. We may not always agree with what He says. We may not always understand His ways.

But let such things never discourage us. Let it challenge us instead to know Him more!

Is this not love? To grow in our knowledge of the other from day to day? To let challenges draw us closer instead of drawing us apart? To discover more beautiful things once we overcome what seems to be difficult at the start?

Love Jesus, the real Jesus. Only by knowing Him fully can we Love Him without being afraid!

May 12 :
No Small Gift

My gift is so small that I am ashamed, but Jesus takes it as though it's the most precious thing in the world, and I am filled with joy!

Jesus sat down opposite the treasury, and saw how the multitude cast money into the treasury. Many who were rich cast in much. A poor widow came, and she cast in two small brass coins, which equal a quadrans coin. He called his disciples to himself, and said to them, "Most certainly I tell you, this poor widow gave more than all those who are giving into the treasury, for they all gave out of their abundance, but she, out of her poverty, gave all that she had to live on." - Mark 12:41-44, WEB

Never let the measure of others hinder you from giving what you can. Give of your all. Give to everyone you desire to help. God will never belittle your gifts. He honors every sacrifice done out of love.

If He wanted to receive great gifts only, why has He chosen to be among the poor? If He wanted to praise fine offerings only, why has He chosen to be born as a helpless child?

He became poor for us. He became little for us. Even a small child that needs His mother's care!

149

There is no small gift to Him who sees the purity of one's heart.

May 13 :
God Waits For Us

We are not the only ones who wait. Someday we'll find how how long God has waited for you and for me.

Behold, I stand at the door and knock. If anyone hears my voice and opens the door, then I will come in to him, and will dine with him, and he with me. - Revelation 3:20, WEB

Who am I that the Lord who made the heavens should wait for me? Who am I that He who made the mountains and the seas should stand at the door as I linger on, frightened to accept His call?

Yet He waits. He knocks. He calls.

Day after day He stands unmoved, His love undiminished.

He knows that I need Him. He knows that deep within my soul, I thirst so much for His love.

God grant me the grace to have an open heart that I may finally listen. God grant me true humility that I may finally see how lost I am without Him. God grant me faith that I may believe He is truly there, waiting all along for me.

May 14 :
Power in Patience

We can only wait if we truly believe that it's all going to be worth it in the end.

For the vision is yet for the appointed time, and it hurries towards the end, and won't prove false. Though it takes time, wait for it; because it will surely come. It won't delay. - Habakkuk 2:3, WEBBE

There is power in patience. Without patience, we lose so many things that could have been ours. We fail to reach so many dreams. We fall short of accomplishing our heart's deepest desires.

It is patience that helps us not to settle for lesser things. It is patience that helps us decide in choosing the wiser path. Without it, we choose things that can't really make us happy. We regret being lost and we lose more time trying to make things right again.

When we wait, we show how strong our faith really is. We also prove the depths of our love.

When we wait, we allow God to work in His own time. The seeds grow. The flowers blossom. And the trees bear fruits full of sweetness and of love.

May 15 :
   The Eternity of Beauty

The things of beauty are truly doors towards eternity.

He has made everything beautiful in its time. He has also set eternity in their hearts… - Ecclesiastes 3:11, WEBBE

Whenever we see true beauty, there is a desire deep within our souls to keep it. We want it to last. Such is the power of beauty. It transcends time and sends us forth towards eternity.

Somehow, there is a part of us that protests against something beautiful fading away. It just doesn't seem right for a beautiful thing to die.

Why must something beautiful be brought to decay? Why must something that took us away from our sorrowful pre-occupations be lost forever, never to be found again? Where is comfort to be found?

When we see eternity in the beauty of a rose, we find comfort in knowing that though the rose itself may wither, its beauty remains forever in our hearts. And with this we wonder that perhaps there could really be an immortal soul. For if the soul itself cannot contain all memories of the beautiful, where must all such beauty go?

May 16 :
Grief and Joy

What's the difference between happiness and joy? Happiness is afraid of sorrow, but joy is not. Joy can live amidst sorrow, joy befriends even sorrow and makes things even more meaningful, more blessed and more beautiful than we could ever imagine them to be.

Therefore you now have sorrow, but I will see you again, and your heart will rejoice, and no one will take your joy away from you. – John 16:22, WEBBE

To really grieve for something is to have truly valued it, for if we grieve not for a thing lost, we have not found that thing at all.

We can console ourselves by saying that what's truly important is the journey, and the time of togetherness, but deep within our hearts, we ask, "What good is our time of meeting if sooner or later, we must part?"

Those who say it is but sufficient to love for a moment have not truly loved, for love always desires to last forever. It isn't enough to have loved for a single day. It isn't enough to love for a lifetime. It isn't enough to love for ten thousand years. If we truly love, we want to love without end for only in love is there life.

Grieve if you must, for it has shown that you have loved. We grieve as much as we have been made happy. We grieve as much as we have been made alive.

Grief is our bridge towards joy – joy that has passed, and joy that is to come. Only those who grieve desire to hope, for hope is our only consolation in our time of parting. With God, we know that we do not hope in vain for time shall surely come when our grief shall turn to joy again and that joy can never ever be taken away!

152

May 17 :

When God gives you big dreams, know that it's time for Him to give you bigger wings.

I will instruct you and teach you in the way which you shall go. I will counsel you with my eye on you. - Psalm 32:8, WEB

Do not be disheartened if you feel that your powers are less than God's dreams for you. By ourselves we can do nothing, but with God's grace, all things are possible.

Let the awareness of your limitations bring you closer to God's providence and love. He is ever compassionate and true. It is by His power that you will accomplish everything.

You may not know how. You may not see each step of the way. But you know whose Hand it is that leads you. It is a strong and kind hand.

Let Him lead you then. Believe in His dreams for you. Listen well and walk with joy as you walk closer and closer to your heart's deepest desires.

May 18 :
Fear and Courage

Only the man who fears God can be truly brave!

If your right eye causes you to stumble, pluck it out and throw it away from you. For it is more profitable for you that one of your members should perish, than for your whole body to be cast into Gehenna. If your right hand causes you to stumble, cut it off, and throw it away from you. For it is more profitable for you that one of your members should perish, than for your whole body to be cast into Gehenna. – Matthew 5:29-30, WEBBE

Fear is a natural response to something that might destroy us. Courage is our God-given ability to face our fears when it is more beneficial to fight rather than to run away.

What's wrong with us is to fear the wrong things and to not find courage for the things worth fighting for.

We fear being lonely, but we're not afraid of being with someone who disrespects us. We fear sickness, but we're not afraid of death. We fear losing our pride, but we're not afraid to lose our dignity.

We have to know what to fear and what to fight for. We have to know when to run away and when to keep on holding on.

Don't be afraid of being responsible for your actions. But fear betraying others just to satisfy your desires. Don't be afraid of making a sacrifice for the ones you love. But fear your own selfishness and using other people just to feed your pride. Don't be afraid of suffering that comes naturally in this life. But be afraid that your heart loses compassion and your soul loses its very life.

May 19 :
An Ear and a Voice

There is a time for everything. A time to listen, and a time to speak.

One who corrects a mocker invites insult.
One who reproves a wicked man invites abuse.
Don't reprove a scoffer, lest he hate you.
Reprove a wise person, and he will love you.
-Proverbs 9, WEBBE

How often have we found ourselves talking and explaining things only to find out that the person we're talking to isn't really listening but trying to figure out what to say in reply?

How many times have we found ourselves doing our very best to win an argument to prove our point only to find out that even after we win, our opponent would merely cling stubbornly to his own point of view?

154

Why not reserve your explanations for someone who really wants to understand?

Why not reserve your efforts for someone who really wants to listen?

We cannot change someone who doesn't want to change or make people believe in something they don't want to believe in.

But we can be ready instruments to those who are ready to discover the truth. We can await God's timing, and then we can speak where others may start walking in the light.

May 20 :
In God's Image

God does not love the crowd, but the person within the crowd. He knows your name, and had you been the only person who needed to be saved, He would still have died on the cross for you.

God created man in his own image. In God's image he created him; male and female he created them. – Genesis 1:27, WEBBE

We were created in God's own image, you and I. We were made holy, pure and beautiful. We were made to be so full of love.

How much of that image can we see in each other? When we look at another person, are we able to see what's truly valuable in him or in her?

Quite often, we let people pass us by without even noticing. Who cares who they are? Who cares where they came from?

But each of these people has their own story. Each one has struggles. Each has victories similar to our own.

If we can only learn to look deeply, we'd be able to see through all the masks that people wear. We'd be able to see the true beauty that remains within one's soul. A soul that can appreciate what's lovely and good, a soul that can laugh and weep, a soul that can search for wisdom and truth, a soul that can have compassion on another, a soul that has a capacity to love.

Let us learn to value a person not because of his riches or power or physical attributes. Let us learn to value a person because of his soul and his great capacity to love.

May 21 :
Through The Fiercest Storms

It is through the most difficult trials that God often brings the sweetest discoveries of Himself.

He himself was in the stern, asleep on the cushion, and they woke him up, and told him, "Teacher, don't you care that we are dying?" He awoke, and rebuked the wind, and said to the sea,"Peace! Be still!"The wind ceased, and there was a great calm. He said to them,"Why are you so afraid? How is it that you have no faith?" - Mark 4:38-40, WEB

God will be with you not only through sunshine and happy days but even in the darkest night, and especially through the fiercest storms.

Our God is a victor who overcomes. He is the Light that overcomes darkness, the Good that overpowers and vanquishes every evil and sin.

Think not therefore that the only way He could save us is to keep us from going through any difficulty or trial. Think not that the best way He could ever show His power is to keep us from every storm.

On the other hand, it is through the fiercest of storms that He shows His might. Right there, through the wind and rain, in the valley of the shadow of death, He gives courage that overcomes, hope that vanquishes despair, light that overpowers all darkness.

His presence is not one that is afraid of suffering, nor is His strength one that fades with trials. It is such that can endure even the sorrows of the cross.

156

He is with us, always, especially through the storm. Never think that you're alone or that you have been forgotten. God is with you, even in the eye of the fiercest storm.

May 22 :
In Rest and In Hope

To be still is to rest in the heart of God.

For thus said the Lord GOD, the Holy One of Israel, "You will be saved in returning and rest. Your strength will be in quietness and in confidence." - Isaiah 30:15, WEBBE

It is not always in doing something that we advance. It is not always in fretting about that we gain victory.

Many times, what we really need is a place to rest and to be still, and in that stillness, to gain the strength we need.

We can't win by always focusing on our troubles and seeing how big and terrible they are. We need to see hope. We need to see how God is bigger than all the problems that trouble us.

In that place of rest, we begin to see light again. We are able to focus more on our source of strength and thereby gain courage to face the challenges coming our way.

We need to see God's beauty and might, His majesty and His mercy. We need to be assured that everything will certainly work out in the end because we have a God who can be trusted, a God of justice and of love.

We are not alone. Though we falter, we can rise again. Though we fear, we can renew our courage. We need only to rest awhile and in that rest, find our hope again.

What Stillness Means

Stillness doesn't mean that your problems are already solved
and that you have nothing more to worry about.
Stillness doesn't mean that you are already content

with everything that you have.
Stillness doesn't mean that you have no regrets.
It doesn't mean you no longer have questions
hanging at the back of your mind.

Stillness on the other hand, is that point
where you take a deep breath
to pause for a while,
and to find some rest,
amidst your days of toil.

Stillness is recognizing that you have your problems,
but worrying about them now
will do no further good.

Stillness is hoping to find your hopes again,
and to find answers
beyond those that didn't work.

Stillness is opening up one's heart
to find that deep silence within,
in that secure place
untouched by raging storms.

Stillness is a plea for help.
It is a hand surrendered in prayer.
Stillness is an invitation for mercy
so that one may find its way to peace.

May 23 :
    God Lives!

God manifests His love uniquely to each person. His love is not merely an idea or a formula, His love is true, intimate and very personal for God is a person, a person we know fully in Jesus Christ.

"'They will know that I, the LORD, their God am with them, and that they, the house of Israel, are my people, says the Lord GOD. You my sheep, the sheep of my pasture, are men, and I am your God,' says the Lord GOD." - Ezekiel 34:30-31, WEBBE

The Lord lives! Why must we go on fretting as though He were not alive? The Lord has risen! Why must we despair?

We are not orphans without a Father. We have One always watching over us, pursuing us in love, seeking our eternal good.

We are not without hope. We know that all things will work out in God's wisdom and power. Justice will be rendered, evil will be vanquished for good.

We are not without a friend. While we were yet sinners, Jesus died for us. He considered us His friends and revealed Himself to us.

God lives! He is not a myth nor a story from our own imaginings. He is as real as the air we breathe, the sun that rises each morning, the majestic mountains towering towards the sky.

Everything else will fade in this life, everything that we see and believe as real. But God will remain, God who is real forever - from times ancient and old, towards the infinite future, and in the present moment right where we are.

May 24 :
A Letter to a Child

Life is not a series of consecutive triumphs, but a winding path of ups and downs, of happiness and tears. God leads us every step of the way, especially when the journey becomes tough and we feel too tired to go on. Through it all, what upholds us is the love of Him who alone gives us the strength to carry on.

...for I have learned in whatever state I am, to be content in it. I know how to be humbled, and I know also how to abound. In everything and in all things I have learned the secret both to be filled and to be hungry, both to abound and to be in need. I can do all things through Christ, who strengthens me. - Philippians 4:11-13, WEB

Dear child, when you go forth in this world, remember that not everything would work out the way you wanted to. In fact, most

159

things would be flawed and far from ideal. Many things would bring you pain.

This is not to discourage you or to keep you from dreaming great things. But you need to know these things so you can be brave and so that you may not be easily dismayed. You need to keep your feet firmly planted on the ground like a tree that will never be shaken by the strongest wind. But you need to keep your gaze up in heaven so you may never forget where you will one day take flight to your true home.

But while you are in this life, remember that many things will try to bring you down. There will be times when the weight would be too much that you'd fall. When that happens, remember that the most important thing is to not remain fallen for far too long. Learn your lesson, then get up quickly and move on.

Remember also that people will never easily fit inside a neat box or a sure formula. You can understand better by experience, but many times, people will do things you'd never expect or imagine, and this both for the good and the bad.

Many people don't really think that much. They may say things that hurt you all because they failed to think about what they ought to say. Don't presume that people always say and do things intentionally. Many of the things people do, especially the bad things, are done out of ignorance, or weakness or fear.

Sometimes though, even people you thought were bad would surprise you by doing something really good, even heroic. Thank God then, for there is still that spark of God's light within the soul that is trying to make its way felt and known.

There is goodness indeed in this life, though often mixed with pain. Find it! Let it lead you ever closer to God's grace. God has not given up on this world, why should you?

You have but very little time to gather in it eternal treasures that will never fade, never waste a moment of it! One day, everything will make perfect sense, even the smallest of things would have its story. Have patience then and be strong!

Remember most of all that God watches over you. He is the strength in your weakness, the consolation in all your troubles, and the hope that will never let you down. God loves you and you need never be alone.

May 25 :
To Love Yourself

There are times when we hurt others not because we wanted to, but because we have failed to love ourselves first.

"You shall love your neighbor as yourself." - Matthew 22:39, WEB

You must love your neighbor. This is something we know. But do we also remember that we must love ourselves as well?

In order to take care of other people, we must also know how to take good care of ourselves. We must allow love to grow within our own hearts, and with that love, we can be more capable of helping other people.

God has loved us so much, should we not love ourselves, too? God has offered us His forgiveness, must we go on refusing to forgive ourselves?

Let love be that seed that grows gently first upon your own heart. Take care of it, let it grow strong, and when it bears fruit, let it be as a fragrant flower blessing others with genuine concern and compassion.

May 26 :
Love is in the Ordinary Life

Whoever said we cannot live a beautiful life by living a simple life?

He has made everything beautiful in its time. – Ecclesiastes 3:11, WEBBE

Love is in our daily mess of living. In our small talks and in our household chores. In our daily meals and in our leisure hours. In our busy mornings and in our late night chats.

Love is there as we go about our work and our play, as we shop for our groceries, as we teach the kids their homeworks, as we care for our sick folks, and as we talk about our plans for the future.

Love survives our times of crisis and our moments of pain. It remains hopeful in moments of misunderstandings and in times of hurt.

Love is in a million words of kindness and in countless acts of goodwill, sacrifice and sharing. It is not just a word or a promise made in time. It is a way of life that we choose to walk daily as we show up everyday with all our triumphs and losses, our laughter and our tears.

Love is in the ordinary, in the steady flow of life which leads us ever closer and stronger than before. We may fail to see it for what it really is, but as we look back, we can recognize that extraordinary thread that has kept us together and that has certainly made life worth living for.

May 27 :
> Fix Your Gaze on Jesus

Let us fix our gaze on Jesus. Look to no other. Do not be swayed to turn either to the left or to the right. Do not be disheartened by the many voices that move you to be anxious and afraid. Keep your eyes on Christ for only His loving gaze can help you.

Peter stepped down from the boat, and walked on the waters to come to Jesus. But when he saw that the wind was strong, he was afraid, and beginning to sink, he cried out, saying, "Lord, save me!" Immediately Jesus stretched out his hand, took hold of him, and said to him, "You of little faith, why did you doubt?"
-Matthew 14:29-31, WEBBE

Many times, we become tempted to look at things that rob us of courage and take away our peace. We become curious to look back at the things of the world, at the problems that threaten us, and instead of holding on to hope, we become so immersed in it we could hardly turn away.

Never make the mistake of lifting your eyes away from Jesus. Never think that by your own strength you can defeat the foes that surround you or the darkness the looms ahead.

Looking at our troubles often magnifies them and we do not see them for what they really are. But when we look at our Lord, we see how much bigger He is than all our problems and sufferings altogether. We find strength when we look at Christ. In Him is our hope and our peace.

Therefore let us also... lay aside every weight and the sin which so easily entangles us, and let us run with patience the race that is set before us, looking to Jesus, the author and perfecter of faith, who for the joy that was set before him endured the cross, despising its shame, and has sat down at the right hand of the throne of God. - Hebrews 12:1-2, WEB

May 28 :
> Change The World

You can't do everything but you can do something. You can give your life to God, and God can start to change the world through you.

But God's grace is much greater, and so is his free gift to so many people through the grace of the one man, Jesus Christ... So then, as the one sin condemned all people, in the same way the one righteous act sets all people free and gives them life.- Romans 5:15,18, WEB

Never think that you can't do anything to change the world. You can always do something, and you can always start where you are.

Sometimes we tend to think that only the big people can change the world – the rich ones, the influential ones, the powerful ones.

163

But you have power deep within you. Power from above which no one could ever take away.

You can do something. You can change from within you and be that spark of hope you wish to see.

Remember that it took but one Man to overcome death forever and save all mankind. It took but one Man to restore paradise and blot out sin forever.

Wake up from your slumber and make an offering of yourself. Do everything you can. And leave the rest to Him who can still make miracles happen.

May 29 :
Choose Goodness

Don't choose the lesser evil; choose the greater good.

Finally, brothers, whatever things are true, whatever things are honorable, whatever things are just, whatever things are pure, whatever things are lovely, whatever things are of good report; if there is any virtue, and if there is any praise, think about these things. - Philippians 4:8, WEB

It is dangerous whenever we get ourselves used to the idea of choosing the lesser evil. At the end of the day, evil does not become less. Evil grows, and it grows in proportion to the consent we give it whenever we think we have no other choice.

There is always an option for good. If that wasn't so, God wouldn't have commanded us to avoid sin.

Always choose goodness. Even if it were just a tiny spark or a small flame. By choosing what is good, we allow that flame to grow strong. That flame enlightens another, and soon, many are blessed with its light and warmth.

May 30 :
Love Begins at Home

It often doesn't take much to love the world. We can always start by loving our family.

But the man from whom the demons had gone out begged him that he might go with him, but Jesus sent him away, saying, "Return to your house, and declare what great things God has done for you." – Luke 8:38-39, WEBBE

Sometimes it is easier for us to serve other people than to serve those in our own homes. It is easier for us to join groups for a cause or to donate funds for various institutions caring for the poor than to really take a look at those close to us and ask what they really need.

Love begins at home. It starts with parents caring for their children and for children loving their parents back. It is in being there for each other at the end of the day, sharing stories, heartbreaks, victories. It is caring for our sick folks and for our old grandparents. It is in teaching the kids and in playing with them, letting them know how precious they are because we give them our precious time.

Many times, we don't need to look very far in order to find someone who needs our love and attention. Let us begin to look in our own families and see what we can do to make our homes the kind of refuge that it should be.

May 31 :
The Gift of Your Presence

We can give people so many things and still give but a little. In order to give much, we must not give things, we must give something of ourselves.

In your presence is fullness of joy.
In your right hand there are pleasures forever more.
-Psalm 16:11, WEB

165

There is something in your presence that just couldn't compare with anything else. It is not merely the words you say. It is not merely the things you do. It is who you are that is there – body, mind, heart and soul, all of you that the other person gets to sense and witness, even before you say a single word.

And this is just what a lot of people need today. Presence. Availability. Time.

You can give another person all the money in the world, but it could never compare to the gift of your presence.

Remember this whenever you feel that you have nothing worth giving. You always have something to give, a very valuable gift indeed. Consider giving people the very gift of your presence.

JUNE

June 1 :
　　To The Very End

How far are you willing to go with the one you love? If your love is true, you are willing to stay up to the very end!

But standing by Jesus' cross were his mother, his mother's sister, Mary the wife of Clopas and Mary Magdalene. - John 19:25, WEB

There are days when it's easy to stick to one another. Days full of gladness and joy, full of dreams and hopes for the future. On the other hand, there are trying days. Days too difficult to hide our own tears. Days we hardly know if we could still make it through.

During such days, are we still willing to stay together? Are we still able to hold firm to our beliefs?

True friends walk with each other not only in good times, but especially through the bad. It is the storms of life that bind us stronger, it is the night that brings us closer to each other's arms.

June 2 :
　　God's Joy

It was only when I knew You, O God, that I knew what it is to be truly happy.

Most certainly I tell you, that you will weep and lament, but the world will rejoice. You will be sorrowful, but your sorrow will be turned into joy…. Therefore you now have sorrow, but I will see you again, and your heart will rejoice, and no one will take your joy away from you. - John 16, WEB

We must always hold on to God's joy. Even in dark times. Even in the most painful of moments. Therein only is our peace and our strength.

In this world, we cannot always see that good triumphs over evil. Many times, we see just the opposite, and we weep for all the injustice and suffering we see.

But let us not lose our hope. Let us await God's promise of help and trust in His great mercy. For what He has promised He will keep, and whomever is His, He will never lose.

We suffer but for a moment, we endure but for a night. What awaits us is a new day that will never end. A day of joy and triumph for all that is beautiful and pure and good!

Where Is Your Joy?

And you will hear a little voice within you saying:

Your joy is not in your sadness nor in your confusion.
Your joy is not in the darkness where you are.
Your joy is not lost.
Your joy is not broken.
It is stored somewhere safe,
protected against all harm.
God Himself protects it!
God keeps it secure,
where not even the most piercing grief could touch it.
Your joy is in GOD'S LOVE
and God's Love is always upon you.
LOVE NEVER FAILS.

June 3 :
The Lord's Hand

Are you so down you think you never reached that low in all your life? Take heart! That's just the place where God's Hand can finally carry you.

And after the thousand years, Satan will be released from his prison, and he will come out to deceive the nations which are in the four corners of the earth, Gog and Magog, to gather them together to the war; the number of whom is as the sand of the sea. They went up over the width of the earth, and surrounded the camp of the saints, and the beloved city. Fire came down out of heaven from God and devoured them. - Revelation 20, WEB

Just when you think all is lost, God will have His way. Just when you think evil has triumphed, goodness shall prevail.

No matter how greatly outnumbered you think you are, no matter how strong the enemies seem to be, do not lose hope. There is an unforeseen Hand making its way through the darkness, ready to take the enemies by surprise!

And what a surprise it will be. For in boasting and confidence, evil thinks itself indestructible. In deceit it has worked and deceived many. And in i's vast strength, it thought it could overpower Him who rules the heavens.

But just when its triumph seems near, just when it think it could never be defeated, Divine Intervention overcomes all foes with a mighty victory, God's Hand acts and it shall not act in vain.

June 4 :
Power Comes From God

Your Heavenly Father knows, He sees. He still reigns on high and He will see you through.

Pilate therefore said to him, "Aren't you speaking to me? Don't you know that I have power to release you, and have power to crucify you?" Jesus answered, "You would have no power at all against me, unless it were given to you from above. - John 19, WEB

There are times when we may feel overwhelmed by the things happening around us. We feel helpless as things become out of our control. We do our very best, but things still don't seem to work out the way they should.

Times like that, don't be disheartened. For though we may not see now why such things happen or why God has allowed it so, God knows what He is doing and He is still in control of everything.

Power does not rest upon man. It comes from God! Therefore God gives and God takes away. If He ever allows certain things to happen, it is only to bring about a greater good.

One day we shall see. But today, we must trust. We trust though we cannot see. All we can be certain of is that God reigns. He is Lord of heaven and earth, and He is a Just and Merciful God.

June 5 :
Abounding Grace

God's grace is everywhere, waiting for us, pursuing us, seeking us even in the darkness, blessing us in ways we can never possibly deserve.

The LORD says to his anointed, to Cyrus, whose right hand I have held, to subdue nations before him, and strip kings of their armour; to open the doors before him, and the gates shall not be shut:
"I will go before you,
and make the rough places smooth.
I will break the doors of bronze in pieces,
and cut apart the bars of iron.
I will give you the treasures of darkness,
and hidden riches of secret places,
that you may know that it is I, the LORD, who call you by your name,
even the God of Israel.
For Jacob my servant's sake,
and Israel my chosen,
I have called you by your name.
I have given you a title,
though you have not known me.
-Isaiah 45, WEBBE

God's abounding grace pursues us in our paths, seeks us in our darkness, finds us and embraces us, and will never let us go. It is His grace alone that enabled us to even know we were lost. Without His grace, we could never be found.

For who were even worthy to know Him? Who could ever begin seeking Him without God's grace first reaching His soul?

170

In our blindness, all we could ever do is grope in the dark. Try as we might, we could never find our way.

God's grace alone can reach us where we are. He goes to us for we could never go to Him. He gives us every good we do not deserve, and in His great love, we are changed, we are healed, we are found.

June 6 :
Sacred Tears

How unworthy am I O Lord, that you should bless me with your tears.

"You number my wanderings. You put my tears into your bottle. Aren't they in your book?" - Psalm 56:8, WEB

Sometimes, when all just seems to be painful, just let it go and cry. God understands you. He is not afraid of your tears.

He knows how difficult it is to live in this land of exile. We are not yet home, and many days, all we meet are strangers who don't seem to care for us at all.

Just let it go. Pray with your heart. Words are sometimes insufficient to express the depths of our hurt, but tears will always know how to find a way. God bless the tears that cleanse the heart and bring us closer to Him who hears all our cries.

Jesus wept. - John 11:35, WEB

June 7 :
Far Better Than The Past

As long as we hold on to God, the future is always bright and life is always beautiful.

"There is hope for your latter end," says the LORD. - Jeremiah 31, WEBBE

171

When something bad happens we often feel that things can never be the same again. How could they? How could things ever go on like they used to?

We know what things have changed. We feel the ache of the things we've lost. We could no longer go back.

But though this be so, let hope not be so far from us. For though the past could never be restored, we do have a future that awaits.

Yes, we couldn't undo the wounds that have been inflicted upon us, but we can hope for their healing. We could no longer be the same, but we can be better, far stronger than before!

God can use all things for our good, even the darkness and the storm. He will bring out a far better future than the one we have dreamed of. He will not restore the past, but He will bring a victorious tomorrow, a day of gladness that shall never ever end!

June 8 :
   It Is Not The End

God has prepared for you a beautiful life, an eternal life. Your future is safe with Him and in Him, all your greatest desires will come true!

"For I know the thoughts that I think towards you," says the LORD, "thoughts of peace, and not of evil, to give you hope and a future." - Jeremiah 29:11, WEBBE

Do not worry if you cannot see how things can turn out well. It is not for us to take care of everything, it is sufficient for us to trust.

Trust though you can't see. Trust though you can't understand. Trust even if all you could see is darkness and uncertainty. You are not trusting in what you can see or understand, but upon God whose wisdom is invisible and whose power is beyond our comprehension.

There is a future for you, an eternal one. Even if this life would fail terribly in making your dreams come true, all is not yet the end.

Always have that hope within you, for you are after all, a child of eternity. This life is too short for you. This world is too small.

June 9 :
Never in Vain

No sacrifice done out of pure love is ever in vain.

But I said, "I have laboured in vain.
I have spent my strength in vain for nothing;
yet surely the justice due to me is with the LORD,
and my reward with my God."
-Isaiah 49:4, WEBBE

Quite often, we cannot see instantly the fruits of our labors. We may even think that nothing is happening or that things are getting worse. But we must continue to believe that all things will work together for good if we trust in the will and power of God.

God's power and love often work in secret, hidden from the scrutiny and judgement of men. But God never labors in vain.

The seed planted beneath the ground may appear to be dead, but soon everyone will see that life was working and growing steadily within it until all the world finally witnesses and becomes amazed at how it has sprouted and grown miraculously one day.

Do all that you can therefore. And let God's power work out its miracle in its own beautiful time.

June 10 :
Fleeting Trouble, Eternal Bliss

Only he who has ever known sorrow could ever know joy - true joy, deep joy.

For our light affliction, which is for the moment, works for us more and more exceedingly an eternal weight of glory... - 2 Corinthians 4:17, WEB

There are times when we may wonder if God is ever fair as we consider the suffering of many in this life. Is it fair that some are rich while others barely have something to eat? Is it fair that some are strong while others linger in a bed of sickness and pain? Is it ever fair that others enjoy the love of special people in their lives while others remain utterly cold and alone?

Indeed, if all that we have is this earthly life, everything would seem to be unjust. But in the light of eternity, we can see things in a whole new way.

Not that our knowledge of heaven could ever take away earth's wounds today. But that this small light can give us hope, some consolation and strength, and faith to rise again each day.

There is one day we can look forward to. A day of justice and mercy. A day of fullness, of joy and of love.

In that day, it is those who have hungered who shall be filled. It is those who have grieved that shall shout unceasingly with joy!

Only then can we truly say that we have suffered but for a moment, we have been alone but for a day. And every wound our hearts have suffered have each carved out more space for happiness for us, happiness that far far outweighs all our tears and pain.

A certain beggar, named Lazarus, was laid at his gate, full of sores, and desiring to be fed with the crumbs that fell from the rich man's table. Yes, even the dogs came and licked his sores. The beggar died, and he was carried away by the angels to Abraham's bosom. - Luke 16, WEB

June 11 :
Faith That Overcomes Fear

The darker the night, the greater the faith we must have in the morning.

Don't fret because of evildoers,
neither be envious against those who work unrighteousness.
For they shall soon be cut down like the grass,
and wither like the green herb.
Trust in the LORD, and do good.
Dwell in the land, and enjoy safe pasture.
Also delight yourself in the LORD,
and he will give you the desires of your heart.
-Psalm 37, WEB

There is a kind of night that frightens us, a night without the the light of moon nor stars, a night so cold we almost lose faith in the morning.

And in our great fear, we become angry. We may think this anger is righteous, but many times, it is not. For an anger that comes out of fear is an anger that comes from lack of faith, faith in the goodness and power of God!

Let us take heart then and not let darkness enter our hearts. Let us trust instead in God who is in control of everything, as He has complete control of the sun, the moon and the stars.

Can God ever fear of evil? Can God ever suffer loss?

God knows that the days of evil are numbered. He sits confidently on His throne, His Hands full of justice and of love.

Never will He fail His little ones. Never will darkness have its victory.

God has a plan that overcomes all evil plots. He holds the day of our redemption, and even now, He is already in that glorious future with us. That bright day where we stand triumphant and full of happiness and peace.

175

June 12 :
Prolonging The Pain

There comes a time when we must find the courage to face the pain we fear so we can have the healing we desire.

You will know the truth, and the truth will make you free. - John 8:32, WEB

Many times, we'd rather hold on and suffer what we deem as lesser pains than let go and be devastated by a far greater suffering. Thus, we hold on to situations and things that slowly sap the life out of us. We hardly notice the bitterness that grows within us each day. We close our eyes to the truth and we build for ourselves cages that keep us from being truly happy and at peace.

Why do we allow ourselves to die slowly when we can be healed? Why go on in a pointless battle headed towards defeat when we can start over and hope for a far better day and a far better life?

Closing our eyes never makes our problems go away. Ignoring our wounds never gets them healed.

Find the courage today to face your fears and to be free from them. Let go. Try again. Gather up your strength for battles that are worth fighting for!

June 13 :
When You Face the Wicked

There is no sin that God cannot forgive for a truly repentant heart.

You shall love your neighbour as yourself. - Matthew 22, WEBBE

It is always a challenge whenever we encounter someone who acts in a blatantly wicked way. We know that there is something terribly wrong and yet, the sense of our own guilt hinders us from being too quick to judge. For aren't we all wicked also in many ways? Aren't we all struggling to overcome our inner shadows?

176

On the other hand, merely tolerating such wickedness puts us at a no better place. For when was it ever right to consent to what is wrong?

When we encounter someone who acts wickedly, let us try to treat him as we treat ourselves. In the first place, we shouldn't condemn ourselves when we make mistakes. There is no hope in that, neither is there any good in it. God Himself does not condemn us, why would we condemn ourselves?

On the other hand, we must not excuse ourselves or ever justify the evil we have done. Evil is always destructive, and if we allow it to reign over us, we would eventually destroy ourselves as well.

Let us do then what God would have us do. Let us seek forgiveness and let us forgive ourselves, casting our hopes not upon our human frailties but upon the infinite mercy of God. At the same time, let us cast away all evil, not tolerating the smallest sin we see, knowing that God is holy, and only the pure can ever see Him face to face.

June 14 :
Love and Anger

If we must be angry, let us be angry because we love, and be certain it isn't selfish love but true love, authentic and unselfish love.

The LORD said, "You have been concerned for the vine, for which you have not laboured, neither made it grow; which came up in a night, and perished in a night. Shouldn't I be concerned for Nineveh, that great city, in which are more than one hundred and twenty thousand persons who can't discern between their right hand and their left hand; and also much livestock?" -Jonah 4:9-11, WEBBE

It is hard to imagine how God, who is Love Himself can ever be angry. But I guess, this is precisely the answer... Love. We often err in our anger because we do not love as God loves. Only by having that kind of love can anger ever be truly righteous.

Let us note further how love is the very source also of that anger. God becomes angry when people sin because they become what they should not be, they hurt themselves and they hurt other people. Love only wants what is best for those it holds dear, what can make them truly happy for all eternity.

Let us compare it with our own anger. How many times do we get angry because of love and not because of envy or pride? Is our love as strong as our anger? Or is it so faint it almost falls into nothingness?

June 15 :
The Lord's Will

Here is the test of faith, that we surrender to God's will whatever it may be.

Whether it was two days, or a month, or a year that the cloud stayed on the tabernacle, remaining on it, the children of Israel remained encamped, and didn't travel; but when it was taken up, they travelled. At the commandment of the LORD they encamped, and at the commandment of the LORD they travelled. They kept the LORD's command, at the commandment of the LORD by Moses. - Numbers 9, WEBBE

There are many times when we each have our own plans we desire to accomplish. We think of the good they could do, both for ourselves and for others. We think that if only God could bless those plans and make them happy, all shall be well and good.

When they don't happen however, we are filled with all kinds of doubt. We wonder why God didn't listen to our prayers. What could God be planning all along?

The Lord's will may not be always visible to us, and we may not always understand. But we can be certain by faith, that God always desires what is best.

Let us make it a habit then to discern first of all our Lord's will before trying to make our own plans. No matter how good we think they are, they could never match the greatness of God's own desires.

178

June 16 :
A Little Positivity

It isn't a sin to be happy.

...rejoicing in hope; enduring in troubles; continuing steadfastly in prayer... - Romans 12, WEBBE

A little positivity helps. While it is true that it is good to be careful, sometimes being too careful leads to worry and lost of hope. No matter how we plan things, there is no assurance that they will turn out as we envisioned them to be. There will always be things that will surprise us, things that will be beyond our control.

And that is where a little positivity helps. The ability to look at things in a better light gives us strength to deal with the problems we face along the way. It gives us courage. It is like a lubricant that lessens much friction along the way.

This Is My Moment!

This is my moment!
This is my now.
I live in it,
I breathe in it,
I move,
I sing,
I dance.

This is life,
this is forever –
the rain now pouring over me
will never be the same again,
so I cry
I hope
I laugh like a little child.

I look at the sunrise as though it is my first,
as though it will be my last,
I pray
I smile

179

I love!

I taste the fresh air
as though I'm born again,
I smell the rose
as though an angel gave it to me.
I am here,
I am loved,
I am seen.

This is my moment,
this is the very moment
I BELIEVE!

June 17 :
The Habits That Bind Us

Bad habits always seem to be too small until the time they grow so big we can hardly defeat them anymore.

Therefore let's also, seeing we are surrounded by so great a cloud of witnesses, lay aside every weight and the sin which so easily entangles us... lest there be any sexually immoral person, or profane person, like Esau, who sold his birthright for one meal. - Hebrews 12, WEBBE

There is something about bad habits that keep us bound to them. Aside from the pleasure we derive from them, it is the thought that we can control them and that at any moment we desire, we can break free from them.

We think that we can set boundaries to bad habits that can ensure our safety. We convince ourselves that we would only allow ourselves to taste a little now and then and that there can be no harm to these things that we do.

Sooner or later however, we find out that we become more addicted to its pleasures. We sink deeper and deeper, craving more and more until what desired to control has eventually gained control over us.

180

Do not be ensnared from the very beginning. It is a deception to think we can overcome such a great fire when we are already burning through and through. Every fire begins with but a spark. Let us extinguish it before it grows into a flame we could never put out.

June 18 :
Grace To Change

Even if it's painful, may you always have the courage to change your life for the better, to be the kind person God meant you to be.

...that you put away, as concerning your former way of life, the old man that grows corrupt after the lusts of deceit, and that you be renewed in the spirit of your mind, and put on the new man, who in the likeness of God has been created in righteousness and holiness of truth. - Ephesians 4, WEB

There are times when we think we are so lost we could never find the way to happiness anymore. There are times when we have tried so very hard only to fail again and again, and we no longer think that change is still possible, that there is still hope for us.

Do not be discouraged. Even if you feel so weak you can't even get up on your own. Even if you see all your weaknesses and you can't see how you could possibly be the person you wanted to be.

God has a plan for you. From the very beginning, He has thought of you and loved you. It is not by your own strength that you can do it, it is by God's power.

Change will not be easy. But it is worth it. God can give you the grace. What seems impossible will be possible. When all else fails, God will carry you!

June 19 :
Every Perfect Gift

Let us ask more and more for things of lasting value and infinite worth.

Don't be deceived, my beloved brothers. Every good gift and every perfect gift is from above, coming down from the Father of lights, with whom can be no variation, nor turning shadow. - James 1, WEBBE

There are some things in this life that give us happiness for a moment, and after which, they leave us with a far greater pain and emptiness than we had before. There are some things that seem good at the start yet little by little we discover the darkness that they hide underneath.

Let us not fall into the illusion of such things. They only appear good for a while, but beneath them all is something that will keep us away from true happiness and peace.

Let us consider God's gifts instead. God's gifts are the ones that give true joy and lasting peace. The good that they contain is pure. There is no shadow of illusion in them, and the light that they bring us is not tainted by any kind of evil.

We were not made for things of fading beauty or diminishing good. We were made for eternal wholeness, purity and perfect joy. Expect nothing less, receive nothing of lesser worth.

Life's Fleeting Happiness

Every joy,
every laughter,
every form of happiness
in this life is fleeting
and borrowed
and would soon give way to sorrow,
except for the love of God
which remains
and which gives back life

182

to all the other joys
that spring forth from it.

If you are hurting,
or grieving,
or struck down
with a wound of longing
for a joy that you have lost,
take comfort in God's gentle heart
which has grieved the most
and from which flowed forth
comfort and healing
and joys far greater
than those that we have lost.

June 20 :
    Living Water

God's grace will never run out, they are new every morning, blessing us always with providence, protection and love.

"Don't remember the former things,
and don't consider the things of old.
Behold, I will do a new thing.
It springs out now.
Don't you know it?
I will even make a way in the wilderness,
and rivers in the desert."
-Isaiah 43:18-19, WEBBE

There are days when we'd rather go back and dwell upon the past than face the future or live in the present moment. It seems all the good things have happened already, and none of the things that can still happen could ever surpass our previous bliss. All that we seem to have is a great void for the present day, and a looming anxiety for approaching days.

Everything that seems to be worth having is already gone. Every plan that seemed to be worth taking is suddenly lost. How could we ever go on?

But we remember the promise given us. And we can't shake it off our minds even if we can't see yet with our eyes or feel them with our hearts.

We were promised not only the past, but the future, and all the blessed days in between. We were promised eternity, and grace for each moment that comes.

We may think like we're walking the barrenness of the desert. Our souls thirst and ache, and our hearts are filled with doubts.

But let us not let go of our hope. And let us hold firmly to the promise given us. Even if we walk the driest land, God can give us streams of living water there. He will provide. He will make all things new. He will not only meet our expectations, He will surpass even our greatest desires!

June 21 :
  Loving His Wounds

To love a person for his crown isn't rare, but to love a person for his wounds is to realize what true love is all about.

He has no good looks or majesty. When we see him, there is no beauty that we should desire him. He was despised and rejected by men, a man of suffering and acquainted with disease. He was despised as one from whom men hide their face; and we didn't respect him. - Isaiah 53:2-3, WEBBE

It is not great matter when we love a person for his beauty and for all the wonderful things we can see in him. Such a love pleases us and makes us glad. And many times, what we feel for that person may seem so strong we think we have already learned the depths of a true and lasting love.

All such things enable us to care for another person other than ourselves. It is no longer our own beauty we see but that of another. It is no longer just our own good that matters, but that of our beloved one.

184

But all these are but the surface of the kind of love to which our souls are capable of. If we really desire to reach the depths of it, we must learn to love not only our beloved's strengths but his weaknesses as well. We must cherish not only his crown, but his wounds.

It is only when we are able to love a person at his worse that we can draw upon the very greatness of the love we seek to have. For it is here that we care about not only our own happiness or pleasure, but the good and wholeness of the one we love. Herein only can we love without condition, without any trace of selfishness, without measure, without fear, and without end.

June 22 :
It's the Little Things

Many times, it is the little things in life that make a difference, it's the little things that can make or break our lives.

He who is faithful in a very little is faithful also in much. He who is dishonest in a very little is also dishonest in much. - Luke 16, WEB

In our day to day work, we often find that it's the little things that can annoy us and make us lose our temper. It's the little things that can slowly exhaust our strength and make us lose our hope.

On the other hand, it's also the little things that can suddenly inspire us and give us strength. A little act of kindness, a little word of thoughtfulness, a little gesture of love.

It is up to us how to treat such little things. We can either fill our lives with the little things that drag us down. Or we can fill our days with the little things that can spur us on to reach our biggest dreams.

June 23 :
Love Creates

Just for today, try to create something just for the sake of making something beautiful, something that will reflect the beauty of your own soul.

185

For by him all things were created, in the heavens and on the earth, things visible and things invisible, whether thrones or dominions or principalities or powers; all things have been created through him, and for him. - Colossians 1:16, WEB

Evil can never truly create something good. All it can accomplish is to destroy what is valuable. It tends to corrupt what is pure. It goes forth to darkness and to its own destruction.

To be able to create something good and beautiful is always a power that comes from love. When we love, we overflow in joy and in every sort of goodness. This goodness overflows and extends beyond ourselves. It seeks to express itself, to communicate its affection, and to render all things capable of receiving the same light it has found.

June 24 :
The Desire for Beauty

Things of real beauty do not merely please the eyes, they satisfy the heart.

You are all beautiful, my love.
There is no spot in you.
- Song of Solomon 4:7, WEBBE

We do not live merely to survive. We live to seek that which is beautiful, and if possible, to remain in it for as long as we could. Because only in finding the beautiful do we also find our true selves. We find that which we have lost, what we have been made for from the very beginning of the world.

Along the way, we have filled our hearts with other things, things like wealth or fame or worldly power. We have filled our souls with things that could never satisfy the depths of its desires.

Somewhere along the way, we remember. When we see something so beautiful it captures our very soul, we are reminded of what we really are and what we really need – we are eternal souls longing for incomparable beauty, such beauty that we can find only in God!

June 25 :
A Work of Beauty

We can work without love or we can work with love. We can make beautiful things, or we can make things beautifully.

And whatever you do, work heartily, as for the Lord, and not for men… - Colossians 3:23, WEBBE

Many times, the routine of working takes away what's really valuable in one's work. We work only to earn or because we have nothing better to do. We work with our hands, but we fail to use the heart and the soul.

Let us not waste the opportunity to gather blessings each day. When we work, we can be blessed if we offer our labors to God as we work with diligence, a spirit of self-sacrifice and joy.

In such a way, our work helps us discover what's good and beautiful within us. We are no longer slaves but masters. We are no longer mere tools but artists creating a masterpiece worthy of eternal rewards.

June 26 :
The Way of Mercy

Let no person, no matter how well intentioned he may be, prevent anyone from approaching the Mercy of God.

Whoever will cause one of these little ones who believe in me to stumble, it would be better for him if he were thrown into the sea with a millstone hung around his neck. -Mark 9:42, WEB

There is a simple solution to many of our troubles - MERCY. Mercy alone mends the heart that hurts. Mercy alone keeps us from despair. Mercy alone gives us the freedom to forgive.

Through mercy, God sends us hope, and our faint hearts are revived. Through mercy, our understanding and compassion for others is extended, and we are relieved from the wrath that poisons us from within.

Man has made a very great fall. But there is no fall so great that the cross could not remedy. By God's mercy, even heaven and earth are bridged and reconciled, and the people living in darkness are able to see light.

June 27 :
Forgiveness, Love and Sacrifice

Forgiveness is not forgetfulness, forgiveness is healing.

For while we were yet weak, at the right time Christ died for the ungodly. For one will hardly die for a righteous man. Yet perhaps for a righteous person someone would even dare to die. But God commends his own love toward us, in that while we were yet sinners, Christ died for us. - Romans 5:6-8, WEB

No matter how people try to explain forgiveness, there will always be a part of it that is hard to understand. Forgiveness is never an easy thing. It is not resolved through a given formula. It is not achieved by sheer willpower and strength.

For people who have been terribly hurt, forgiveness will always beg the question for justice. When an offender is forgiven, who will pay then for the damage he has done? It is this element that often bewilders our hearts and our minds. Must forgiveness mean the absence of justice for the one who has been hurt?

But justice must never be missing. It may remain invisible to our eyes, but it is there. In forgiveness, it is a justice that is veiled in mercy, a mercy that comes from love.

In its highest ideal, it is love itself that pays. It is love that makes the necessary sacrifice.

June 28 :
Forgiveness and Healing

We can either seek the ruin of the person who hurt us, or we can seek for healing, consolation and peace.

Man cherishes anger against man;
And does he seek healing from the Lord?
- Sirach 28, WEBBE

Forgiveness is not only for the person being forgiven, it is also for the one who is able to forgive. It is in forgiveness that one begins to let go of the past so that one can finally face the future. It is in forgiveness that one can stop dwelling upon the pain in order to begin the process of healing.

For we are not healed by revenge or by holding on to our resentments no matter how justified we think we may be. We are not healed by forever repeating the tragedies we've been through. We are healed when we seek our wholeness where it can truly be found.

Our healing is not within the power of our offender. It is in the power of Him who heals all hearts, in Him who heals both body and soul.

By always looking back, we deprive ourselves of the chance to look to Him who can lift us up, who alone can restore all that we have ever lost.

It is never easy. But we need to make that necessary exchange – to let go of our bitterness to receive the sweetness of peace; and to offer up all our miseries to receive the healing we're yearning for.

June 29 :
Forgiveness and Compassion

If God ever asks us to forgive, it is because we, too, have also been forgiven.

189

Jesus said, "Father, forgive them, for they don't know what they are doing." - Luke 23:34, WEBBE

It is very difficult to see the good virtues of people who have just hurt us. At the moment of pain, all we can see is the evil they have done, an evil for which we may suffer our whole lives through.

But if we can only see through the eyes of compassion, we may begin to see that behind the frightening masks, there are people like you who have also been hurt. People who may not even know what they are truly doing because they are so lost in their own darkness and pain.

This is not to lessen the weight of their sins nor to ignore our own suffering. But to be able to find compassion for those who have hurt us is to help us release much of the wrath that weighs us down.

To see a brother or a sister instead of seeing an enemy is to find a place for love. It is in this very place where we can begin to find a ray of hope for our own healing and peace.

June 30 :
Stop Counting the Cost

We know we found something of infinite worth, when for the sake of it, we stop counting the cost of our efforts and we start to give everything else away.

Again, the Kingdom of Heaven is like a man who is a merchant seeking fine pearls, who having found one pearl of great price, he went and sold all that he had, and bought it. - Matthew 13, WEBBE

Recent times have taught us to weigh the cost of almost everything. We invest something in order to get a desired profit. We give in order to receive. We love in order to be loved.

But is this really what true love means? Is love something we can weigh or measure in any way?

For if we truly love, why do we count each effort that we do for love? And why do we continue to keep a record of wrongs?

190

In counting the cost of everything, we fail to find that which could never be counted. In seeking what is visible, we fail to find what exists beyond what the eyes can see.

If we truly desire to find love, let us try to reach for something beyond what we can count or measure, something beyond what we can command or control. Sometimes, it's when we seem to lose everything that we gain what's truly valuable. It's when we empty ourselves that we are truly filled.

JULY

July 1 :

July 1 :
   Surrender in Love

To love is to surrender, and in that surrender, we find true freedom and happiness.

But the father said to his servants, "Bring out the best robe, and put it on him. Put a ring on his hand, and shoes on his feet. Bring the fattened calf, kill it, and let's eat, and celebrate; for this, my son, was dead, and is alive again. He was lost, and is found." -Luke 15:22-24, WEB

We have often imagined love to be something we must pursue, something we could hardly grasp no matter how much we persevered. Yet in another sense, love is something to which we must surrender to, something we must allow to take hold of us. It is that point when we finally stop running and let ourselves be grasped, to finally stop searching and let ourselves be found.

Let love find you and take hold of you. Surrender, and taste what true freedom means, what true joy feels like. It is no longer running, no longer trying to escape or flee. It is finally being where you're supposed to be. It is being able to rest in knowing you have been sought, and you have been loved all along.

"Therefore behold, I will allure her,
and bring her into the wilderness,
and speak tenderly to her.
I will give her vineyards from there,
and the valley of Achor for a door of hope;
and she will respond there,
as in the days of her youth,
and as in the day when she came up out of the land of Egypt.
It will be in that day," says the LORD,
"that you will call me 'my husband,'"
-Hosea 2:14-16, WEBBE

July 2 :
God's Light

We hate seeing evil, but we often look so long at it that we, too, are consumed by the evil we see.

For you will light my lamp, Lord. My God will light up my darkness. - Psalms 18:28 WEBBE

Our eyes are not made to focus on more than one direction at a time. We can only focus on one.

The same is true with spiritual things. We can either focus on the bad and be driven down, or we can focus on the good and be lifted up.

When we try to focus on evil, our spiritual eyes find nothing but darkness. No matter how justified we feel we are, dwelling upon the thought of sin pulls us down. It sooner or later infects our hearts as with a poison. It blocks our view of the light of God, which is our joy and our peace.

July 3 :
Do It For Love

Much could be truly accomplished if more and more things are done out of love.

Let all that you do be done in love. - 1 Corinthians 16, WEB

There are many reasons why we do the things we do.

There are things we do because we have a duty or a moral obligation to do them.

There are also things we do out of fear. We're afraid that certain things might happen if we do not perform certain actions so we act out of our need to address our fears.

We can also add to this the things we do out of guilt. There may be some people who can hold our hearts hostage and we do what we can not to disappoint them or cause them pain.

It would be hard to create a sure formula to determine the things we must and mustn't do. We all need God's wisdom to show us the way. There will also be times when we must do those things we take no liking or pleasure in.

But through it all, let us not forget the most important reason for our actions, which is LOVE.

More than fear or guilt or duty, may we find ourselves doing more and more things out of love.

July 4 :
    Love Who You Are

We can only be really loved if we are loved for who we truly are.

For you formed my inmost being.
   You knit me together in my mother's womb.
I will give thanks to you,
   for I am fearfully and wonderfully made.
-Psalm 139, WEBBE

Revealing ourselves for who we really are comes with it the risk of being unloved.

When you reveal your heart and open yourself, you may be accepted, or you may not. You may be loved or you may not be loved.

But unless you give yourself and others the chance to love you as you are, all the affection you would ever feel will only be superficial and skin deep. This is because you know that what other people love is not the core of your being but the mask you wanted them to see. Do you really desire to be loved as somebody else and not as you really are?

July 5 :
Only God's Light Saves

There is but One True Light, God's Light, and it is the only Light that heals, that saves, that loves without measure or end.

He who walks in darkness, and has no light, let him trust in the Lord's name, and rely on his God. Behold, all you who kindle a fire, who adorn yourselves with torches around yourselves; walk in the flame of your fire, and amongst the torches that you have kindled. You will have this from my hand: You will lie down in sorrow. - Isaiah 50:10-11 WEBBE

We live in a world where we are constantly told that we can believe our own truths, and no matter what that may be, we can fight for it as a right that ought to be given us. We are taught that the world revolves for our sake alone, and that the only thing we must value is what can give us pleasure in this short life that is ours. We have been robbed of faith. We have been deprived of hope.

Must we be surprised then that we find no true meaning to life? Must we be perplexed that we can find no lasting joy in all the pleasures and desires we have sought? Must we be amazed that we feel so worthless even if we exalt ourselves to be the children of a great and vast universe we live in?

I tell you, we mustn't be surprised at all. For this universe we boast about isn't something that could love us and know us as we are. These rights and pleasures we seek are not the things we really need so we can be found. Though we boast of our strength, it will fail. Though we exalt our knowledge, it cannot understand. For we have blinded our eyes to the Truth. And we have preferred darkness because we are afraid of the Light.

July 6 :
Empty Enough To Be Full

When God gives us something, may our hands be empty enough so we can receive His blessings to the full!

195

I am the Lord, your God... Open your mouth wide, and I will fill it. - Psalms 81:10, WEBBE

Oftentimes, we wonder why God hasn't answered our prayers, why He hasn't given us what we desire. We were taught that we only need to ask to receive and that we only need to seek to find, but we have asked so many times and sought for so long, but we still fail to find what we were looking for.

Could we have forgotten something else? Could God have forgotten our prayers?

Many times, the answer is not whether God is willing or not to give us what we need, but whether or not we are ready to receive His many blessings.

Could we be asking for all the wrong things that won't do us any good? Could we be refusing greater blessings because we just couldn't let go of what we think we want?

God is more than willing to give us great things, He desires it for us much more than we could ever desire them for ourselves! But He is waiting for us to open our hands and receive them. He is waiting for us to let go of what little we think we have, so He can bless us with more, to finally be empty enough to be truly full!

July 7 :
In God's Ways

To decide to do good things without God is to accomplish just the very opposite.

Don't be wise in your own eyes. – Proverbs 3:7, WEB-BE

Many times, we think ourselves to be doing a good thing. We do things our own way and not ask for God's grace or wisdom. We see ourselves as righteous and holy, unable to make mistakes like the people around us. What happens is that instead of accomplishing something good, we may even cause harm because we have relied upon our own goodness alone.

196

What can possibly happen when we fail to allow God to guide us? We may start to preach in eloquent words that are empty of true power, power that can touch and change hearts. We may start to reprove our brothers and sisters with more hatred than love in our tone and therefore make them lose their hope in God. We may start out on a grand mission where God does not want us to go, and so we become unequipped for the challenges that could come in the days ahead.

We must be very humble, even when we think we are doing good things. For it is not in the external act alone that gives value to our works. It is in our sincere and humble desire to be able to accomplish God's will.

"For my thoughts are not your thoughts, and your ways are not my ways," says the LORD. "For as the heavens are higher than the earth, so are my ways higher than your ways, and my thoughts than your thoughts.
-Isaiah 55:8-9, WEB-BE

July 8 :
My Burden Is Light

This world often tires us so. Why not come to Him who alone can give us rest?

"Come to me, all you who labor and are heavily burdened, and I will give you rest. Take my yoke upon you, and learn from me, for I am gentle and lowly in heart; and you will find rest for your souls. For my yoke is easy, and my burden is light." - Matthew 11, WEB

There are many times when we just feel so tired and exhausted. We were told to do our best and we did, but there still seems a very long way to go. We were told to give our all and we gave everything, but we have reaped nothing for all our years of labor and pain.

In times like that, we can look to Him who knows how hard we have already tried. To Him who has compassion upon us. To Him alone who can refresh us and give us rest.

197

O, weary one, you need not carry your burden alone. You need not feel you're on your own. For you have a Father who cares for you, who is ready to catch you when you feel so weak that you'd fall.

Rest upon Him and let Him carry you through. Let His love empower you. Let His kindness soothe your every ache and pain. Upon His strong and loving arms, your burden becomes light and even your bitterness becomes sweet.

TIRED

There are times when I feel tired…
tired of hoping
tired of trying to make things happen
to make sense of things
to make sense of where I am
right now.

And when nothing works
I go back to where I was
to places I had been
and I try to bring back
the happy memories
times when I was
where I was supposed to be.

But sometimes memories are not enough
to feed one's heart,
for soon I also get tired
of remembering
tired of looking back
tired of not being able
to bring back
the happy days before.

And in my tiredness
all I could do is rest –
one step at a time,
one breath,
one thought,
one heartbeat,
that is all that I could do,

and I guess that's enough
for a while,
until I get my strength back,
my will,
my meaning,
my life.

July 9 :
Anger and Hope

Let us use our anger to build rather than to destroy, to defend what's right rather than to pursue what's wrong.

I sought for a man amongst them who would build up the wall and stand in the gap before me for the land, that I would not destroy it; but I found no one. -Ezekiel 22:30, WEBBE

Anger need not always be destructive. Anger can be useful if it pushes us to defend what is good and right.

We need not remain as mere observers of all the wrong things in the world. We can be angry about it and we can do something to make a change for the better.

Those who accept the evil around them sooner or later experience a depression in their souls. Depression comes because hope is lost.

We can regain that hope and do something instead. We can find the courage to make a difference, to make things good again.

Many times, it takes but a few men of courage to make a great change, men who are not afraid to stand up for what is right and to fight a good fight while not succumbing to the darkness around them.

July 10 :
Love Will Make a Way

Let us be patient in love, it will accomplish the good it was meant to do in its own time.

For as the rain comes down and the snow from the sky, and doesn't return there, but waters the earth, and makes it grow and bud, and gives seed to the sower and bread to the eater; so is my word that goes out of my mouth: it will not return to me void, but it will accomplish that which I please, and it will prosper in the thing I sent it to do. - Isaiah 55:10-11,WEB

Let us not grow weary if our efforts of love do not bring us quickly the fruits we desire. Love has its own time, its own course. It may seem slow in accomplishing its task, but we must never lose faith in it. It is still our best option, and many times, our only chance. For though we may not see how it works, it will certainly act in favor of good. It alone can change and touch the human heart. In its own beautiful time, it will accomplish more than we could ever expect it to do, creating miracles along the way and moving even mountains to make way where we thought there could never be a way.

July 11 :
Forgiveness is the Bridge to Heaven

Heaven is forgiveness. Being forgiven. And being able to forgive. Forgiveness brings peace. Forgiveness unites us and builds bridges where we once built walls. Forgiveness allows us to lay down our burdens, our guilt, our anger. When we finally find healing and wholeness, we find forgiveness as well. Forgiveness is what we call as heaven.

If we say that we have no sin, we deceive ourselves, and the truth is not in us. If we confess our sins, he is faithful and righteous to forgive us the sins, and to cleanse us from all unrighteousness. - 1 John 1:8-9, WEBBE

Forgiveness may be one of the most difficult things we need to do in life. It is never easy. Quite often, we may even think it to be impossible to do.

Yet for as long as we hold on to our grudge, we also hold on to our pain. We desire to have justice, but it flees from us. We want to be happy again but all we could ever feel is our pain.

200

We need forgiveness to find healing and to be whole again. We need to forgive all of those who have hurt us, and we need to forgive ourselves as well.

There is no citizen of heaven who has ever reached it without having forgiveness in his or her heart. In heaven, we are set free from everything that hurts us, and we look to the present bliss instead of holding on to the past. In heaven too, we accept the forgiveness of Him who saved us and kept us from despair. We look no more to our sins but to His infinite mercy and love.

Whenever you stand praying, forgive, if you have anything against anyone; so that your Father, who is in heaven, may also forgive you your transgressions. - Mark 11:25, WEBBE

July 12 :
The Beautiful and The Mysterious

May God give us eyes that see what is beautiful and good and true.

Finally, brothers, whatever things are true, whatever things are honorable, whatever things are just, whatever things are pure, whatever things are lovely, whatever things are of good report; if there is any virtue, and if there is any praise, think about these things. - Philippians 4:8, WEB

In the midst of the monotony and dullness of life, we discover that it is beauty that saves us. Wherever we find the beautiful, we also find the eternal, and we learn that though not all things can be defined, they can be felt, and their awe can reach the deepest parts of the heart.

It is in that awe for the mysterious that our thoughts are lifted higher and we come to realize the desires of our own souls. Desires we never even thought we had.

It is the desire for the greatest good, the highest sanctity, the purest love.

It is the longing for our true dream, for a lasting and unshakable happiness penetrating our very bones!

July 13 :
Our Spiritual Battle

It is not our job to tell whether the enemy is stronger than us. It is only up to us to fight and to trust in the God who is stronger than all our many foes.

"See now that I myself am he. There is no god with me. I kill and I make alive. I wound and I heal. There is no one who can deliver out of my hand. For I lift up my hand to heaven and declare, as I live forever, if I sharpen my glittering sword, my hand grasps it in judgement; I will take vengeance on my adversaries, and will repay those who hate me. I will make my arrows drunk with blood. My sword shall devour flesh with the blood of the slain and the captives, from the head of the leaders of the enemy. Rejoice, you nations, with his people, for he will avenge the blood of his servants. He will take vengeance on his adversaries, and will make atonement for his land and for his people."
 - Deuteronomy 32:39-43, WEBBE

There are times when you don't know how to carry on as you see the number of odds against you. As the enemy advances from every side, you are tempted to give in to fear. You see their stature and their great number and you are tempted to despair. Everything seems to point out to a losing battle and your hopelessness seems to sap your strength away.

Deep within you however, you know you can't just give up. To retreat would be to accept immediate defeat. To surrender is to give up fighting for a cause that is higher than even your own life.

So you go on, and you fight. And you entrust everything to Him who alone can determine the true victors of the battle. You look up to Him and you give everything that you have. It doesn't matter anymore no matter how small or weak you think you are. The battle belongs to God and it is His unfailing strength that will carry you through.

July 14 :
Goodness and Wisdom

Wolves seem strong by themselves, but that is their very weakness. The sheep can defeat them because the sheep have a Master who will never let them down.

Behold, I send you out as sheep amongst wolves. Therefore be wise as serpents, and harmless as doves. - Matthew 10:16, WEBBE

Much of the world is covered with darkness because those who are good are often afraid to shine their light. While wicked men plot about evil, good men fall into indifference. While those who are evil commit every sort of injustice, good men keep silent as though it is a sin to speak against what is wrong.

Tolerance of evil is never a virtue. Neither is cowardice something to be strived for. Good men should be wise men who are not easily deceived or abused.

While it is true that we are called to forgive, to love and to be patient, we are also called to be courageous, to be strong and to overcome evil.

Let us be meek as doves indeed as we strive not to cause harm to others. But let us also be wise and discerning, able to distinguish between right and wrong, and ever prepared to fight for what is right.

July 15 :
Evil is Deceitful

Great evil first comes in small doses.

But evil men and impostors will grow worse and worse, deceiving and being deceived. -2 Timothy 3, WEB

Evil is really powerless against goodness. But it works through malice and deceit. It works by pretending it is good and attractive and beautiful until you fall for it and lie to yourself that darkness is

203

light and light is indeed darkness. Evil works by manipulation, by hiding in the shadows while whispering its many temptations until you let yourself off your guard. And after everything it has done to you, it leads you to think all is hopeless until you believe more in your misery that in the power of God's mercy.

Never let evil triumph over you by letting it lure you to its many tricks. Always be vigilant! Never let it talk you into giving up what is truly precious and good.

And if in times you fall and succumb to its darkness, never lose hope. It is not in despair that you can find solace but in the infinite love and mercy of Him who has always loved you and who always will. No misery is greater than His love. No darkness is ever powerful enough to put out His Light!

July 16 :
Examine Your Heart

God is everything that's good and beautiful, but in order to see Him we must first desire Him, and who can desire Him but they whose hearts are pure?

The heart is deceitful above all things
and it is exceedingly corrupt.
Who can know it?
"I, the LORD, search the mind.
I try the heart,
even to give every man according to his ways,
according to the fruit of his doings."
-Jeremiah 17, WEBBE

Our hatred for evil is different from our hatred for something good.

Our hatred for all evil things stem from our natural desire for goodness. It is supported by our conscience and our sense of justice. It is remedied by compassion and mercy for our fellowmen who fall.

But our hatred for goodness is warped and unnatural. It is a form of envy and makes us lie to ourselves, to who we are supposed to be.

204

What remedy is there to satisfy those who hate good men when the only desire of that will is to see good men fall?

Some good men may indeed fall. But by God's grace they can rise again. Goodness always has a way to triumph in the end.

Let us therefore examine our hearts and pray that God may purify our thoughts and our desires. We are weak and sinful. But with God's mercy, we can be healed. We can be whole. We can rise again!

July 17 :
How Long is Sorrow?

When we finally see God's face, it wouldn't matter how long we've ever waited. In that moment, all that would ever matter is our endless joy!

How long, LORD?
Will you forget me forever?
How long will you hide your face from me?
How long shall I take counsel in my soul,
having sorrow in my heart every day?
How long shall my enemy triumph over me?
Behold, and answer me, LORD, my God.
Give light to my eyes, lest I sleep in death;
lest my enemy say, "I have prevailed against him;"
lest my adversaries rejoice when I fall.
But I trust in your loving kindness.
My heart rejoices in your salvation.
I will sing to the LORD,
because he has been good to me.
-Psalm 13, WEBBE

There are times when we ask ourselves how long must sorrow last? How long must the poor and helpless suffer? How long must those who hunger yearn for bread? How long must orphans ache for a Father's love?

205

We look around us and all that we can see is suffering. There is injustice everywhere. There is pain. There is grief we cannot even put into words.

We then look towards heaven and we wonder how far indeed could it be? When will that blessed day come when heaven finally comes down upon us? When those who thirst shall thirst no more? When those who are misjudged are condemned no more? When those who have fallen rise again and walk into the arms of a Father who will wipe away all of their tears?

We don't know how long, and many times, all we can do is sigh. But we must believe that it will never be too long. God knows our pain and our cries. He will never come too late for those whom He loves.

July 18 :
Blessed Suffering

When Jesus walked the earth, it was the poor, the sick and the suffering who came to Him. They were the ones who found Him. They were the ones who were truly blessed!

Blessed are those who mourn, for they shall be comforted. -Matthew 5, WEBBE

Blessed are those who mourn, those who walk the valley of tears and have no one to lean on to when they cry.

Blessed are those whose hearts are broken, who have been failed by those whom they held dearest in their hearts.

Blessed are those who fall and have no more strength to carry on.

Blessed are those who have searched for so long and found nothing in the world to fill the emptiness of their souls.

Blessed are you. Blessed indeed is your sigh!

Blessed are you because there is a God who hears, a God who won't turn you away when your cry.

206

Your heart has been left desolate of worldly happiness, and it is now empty enough for the King of Kings to fill.

You have been failed by many lovers and now you stand ready for Him who is Most Compassionate and True.

Your strength has left you, now you can be refreshed with power that knows no end.

Blessed are you, blessed is your sorrow. For it has made way for eternal joys to come and dwell in you!

July 19 :
Our Biggest Regret

Never regret that you have loved.

"But I tell you who hear: love your enemies, do good to those who hate you, bless those who curse you, and pray for those who mistreat you. To him who strikes you on the cheek, offer also the other; and from him who takes away your cloak, don't withhold your coat also. Give to everyone who asks you, and don't ask him who takes away your goods to give them back again." - Luke 6, WEBBE

At the end of our lives, we'd be surprised at what our biggest regrets shall be.

Our biggest regret won't be that we have been kinder than we should have been.

Our biggest regret won't be that we have forgiven someone who did not deserve our mercy.

Our biggest regret won't be that we have allowed our hearts to trust someone who will only hurt us in the end.

Our biggest regret shall be that we have been less kind than we should have been.

Our biggest regret shall be that we have not forgiven someone who has sought for our mercy.

Our biggest regret shall be that we have not loved, and that we have hurt those whom God has sent our way to be loved.

July 20 :
   You Are Special

We learn to love each other when we begin to realize how truly unique and wonderful we are. Like seashells along the shore, no one is entirely alike, each is crafted with an imprint of God's hand, each one different and special, each one valuable and loved!

Don't be afraid, for I have redeemed you. I have called you by your name. You are mine. - Isaiah 43, WEBBE

We all want to be special in one way or another. It is not enough that we are taken care of, we must be seen. It is not enough that we are loved, we must be known and loved for who we really are.

In our desire to be special, however, we try to imitate those who are well admired. We do all we can to be just like them, and along the way, we forget our own uniqueness and beauty.

God has given to each one a special beauty that only he or she can exude. We need not be dismayed that we are not like the ones people praise. In order to shine, we should only be true to who we really are.

Where I Fit In

I can't help it at times, if I trip when I walk
Or I sing some notes out of tune.
I am not like ones you've seen
on movie scenes –
Lovely, witty and sweet.
I am not the shy underdog
with a heart of gold,
or that daring adventurous girl

full of charm.
I fall short trying to fit in,
where I cannot fit in,
trying to be beautiful,
trying to be good.

I look at me
and I cannot see
what He sees,
how someone could love
the likes of me.
But as I look into His eyes
all I know
is that I am loved,
every bit of me – loved.

And I fall for Him,
fearfully yet joyfully,
I fall…
I let myself surrender all –
my hurts, my doubts,
my anger, my insecurities.
And they all vanish
at the sight of Him.

I am moved,
I am thrilled,
I am healed,
every bit of me –
accepted and made whole.

Without even trying to,
He changes me.
Into His own likeness,
He fashions me.
And I sink deeper
into His affections,
where I lose myself
without truly being lost,
where I discover another me,
the one I've always
been meant to be!

And it doesn't matter anymore
that I could never fit in
anywhere else,
for there I've found my place,
for there I've found myself,
the one He sees,
the one He truly loves!

July 21 :
No One Like You

God loves no other person in the very same way that He loves you.

"Before I formed you in the belly, I knew you. Before you came forth out of the womb, I sanctified you." - Jeremiah 1, WEB

No person can ever be replaced. Not even the smartest nor the most beautiful person in the world can ever match the essence of who you are. You are here because God willed you to be, because no one in the whole universe can ever substitute for the likes of you!

And that is why each day that you are in this world is a treasure. For none can ever put back the hours that you walked upon this life.

You may have failed to notice it, for you thought all that you ever did were simple things. Nothing extraordinary, it seemed.

Yet how could the days you spend not be special? How could each breath you take not be more precious than gold?

This present time that you are here is that special time when people can see you dance, can hear laugh, can watch you walk, can listen to what's going on within your beautiful soul.

No one else is just like you. Be who you really are!

July 22 :

Burdens and Wings

Sometimes, God gives us burdens so He can give us wings.

"Come to me, all you who labor and are heavily burdened, and I will give you rest. Take my yoke upon you, and learn from me, for I am gentle and humble in heart; and you will find rest for your souls. For my yoke is easy, and my burden is light." - Matthew 11:28-30, WEB

I tried to escape your burdens, Lord. From troubles, I tried to flee. Little did I know they would strengthen me. Little did I know they would set me free.

For the burdens you give are sweet, Lord. They are sweet because You carry it with me. And the burdens you give are light, Lord. They are light because you turn them into wings to carry me!

He gives power to the weak. He increases the strength of him who has no might. Even the youths faint and get weary, and the young men utterly fall; But those who wait for the Lord will renew their strength. They will mount up with wings like eagles. They will run, and not be weary. They will walk, and not faint. - Isaiah 40:29-31 WEBBE

July 23 :

Do It In Secret

Deeds are not of lesser worth just because they were done in secret.

When you pray, you shall not be as the hypocrites, for they love to stand and pray in the synagogues and in the corners of the streets, that they may be seen by men. Most certainly, I tell you, they have received their reward. But you, when you pray, enter into your inner room, and having shut your door, pray to your Father who is in secret, and your Father who sees in secret will reward you openly. - Matthew 6, WEB

211

There are some good things we must do openly so that men may see and praise God. There are deeds that must be done in the light so we can reach those who are in the dark.

But there are some deeds that are better done in secret, good deeds that need to be seen by the holy eyes of God alone. For it is in being hidden that their value is preserved and their purity is unstained, and they become worthy of God's reward and praise.

July 24 :
Secure in His Love

Only love can heal our desire for vainglory because only by being secure in God's love can we finally stop from seeking the praise of men.

Woe, when men speak well of you,
for their fathers did the same thing to the false prophets.
- Luke 6, WEBBE

Criticism from other people may cut through our heart even more painfully than physical wounds. Hurtful words echo long after they have been spoken. And the hurt they cause remain long before we are healed.

Humiliations can cause us terrible sufferings in that they remind us of the shame we feel within. Shame for our weaknesses. Shame for all our wrongdoings.

No wonder then that we often try to cover up our imperfections so we can avoid being shamed again. We try to lift up our self-esteem, to gain the praise of men, to convince everyone that we are worthy of approval and honor.

Sadly, such attempts only last for a while. Sooner or later, someone says a careless word and all the glory we have sought instantly disappears. As we were brought high, so were we cast down ever more painfully.

We need to find true healing for our lack of self-worth and our desire to be accepted and loved. And the solution is not so much as to pretend to be who we are not, but to know that God already loves us for who we truly are.

It is not our self proclaimed righteousness and perfection that would claim for us the affection we desperately want. We need only to look at the One who has compassion for our weakness, and who alone can lead us to gain the beauty we desire.

July 25 :
God's Tenderness

Love has a certain element of tenderness, which alone pierces through the heart and binds us more intimately than any force in the universe ever can.

"Therefore behold, I will allure her, and bring her into the wilderness, and speak tenderly to her. I will give her vineyards from there, and the valley of Achor for a door of hope; and she will respond there, as in the days of her youth... It will be in that day," says the Lord, "that you will call me 'my husband,'... I will betroth you to me forever. Yes, I will betroth you to me in righteousness, in justice, in loving kindness, and in compassion.
Hosea 2, WEBBE

It isn't violence that can break through our hearts. It isn't force that binds us and keeps us together. Only tenderness has the power to accomplish what the fullness of love desires to do. Tenderness that approaches us little by little, and handles our feelings with the deepest affection and delight. Tenderness that is willing to wait for the right time until we are ready and we are no longer afraid.

O, the great tenderness of God that seeks and that patiently waits for His beloved. The kind of love which alone can touch us in our frailty and in our brokenness, mending our wounds, healing our deepest pains.

God's love is quiet, yet it is strong. And its strength moves in its tenderness that never fails.

213

July 26 :
Like a Mother's Love

God's love is not only strong, it is also tender, as tender as a mother's love for her children.

Jerusalem, Jerusalem... How often I would have gathered your children together, even as a hen gathers her chicks under her wings, and you would not! - Matthew 23, WEB

God's love can also be likened to a mother's love, a mother that cares deeply for her children and would do everything in her power to protect them.

It is a love that is willing to give all and to sacrifice all for the sake of her children. It is a love that will never give up no matter what the cost.

Who can truly understand the depths of a mother's love who bore her child in her own womb? Who can feel her anguish when her child is lost and away from her love? To a mother, the most painful suffering is not her own but of her child's, and the greatest disappointment is whenever any of her children refuses to receive her love.

July 27 :
Cast The Accuser Away

God is not accusing you, He is pardoning you. God is not condemning you, He is saving you. Whenever you are tempted to despair, remember who God really is. He is not your Enemy, but your Kindest and Truest Friend.

I heard a loud voice in heaven, saying, "Now the salvation, the power, and the Kingdom of our God, and the authority of his Christ has come; for the accuser of our brothers has been thrown down, who accuses them before our God day and night. - Revelation 12, WEB

Who is it that accuses and brings false charges against you? That troubles you and wearies you and points out every wrong and imperfect thing he could find in you? That brings before you again and again your past disgrace, your every folly, your bitter shame? Who is it that wants to humiliate you and discourage you and suck out every breath of hope that is still left in you? Who is it that wants you to be damned?

Certainly, not God.

For though God is just and holy, and has nothing to do with any wickedness or sin, He loves you and desires only your good. He came not condemn, but to save and to give hope, to give light where there is darkness, life where there is death.

He is the voice of justice, but He is ever also the voice of mercy and infinite love! Our repentance is not one therefore that should bring us to despair, but to hope, and to trust in the One who never gives up on His children.

Whenever you hear the voice that curses you to despair, cast it away! Go forth at once into the presence of Him whose mercy is boundless and whose love for you knows no end.

July 28 :
Clothed With Dignity

We have sinned in shame, but God clothes us again with dignity. The Father waits for you to love you and to welcome you back into His arms.

The scribes and the Pharisees brought a woman taken in adultery. Having set her in the middle, they told him, "Teacher, we found this woman in adultery, in the very act. Now in our law, Moses commanded us to stone such women. What then do you say about her?" - John 8, WEBBE

To be caught guilty and worthy to be condemned is different from being falsely accused. When we are accused falsely, we at least have our conscience on our side, and we have faith that God Himself would defend us as His own.

215

But there are times when the accusations against us are true. We may have made some mistakes, we may have made some selfish decisions that have hurt others along the way. And when we are accused of such things, all that we can feel is utter shame and guilt for the wrong we have done.

It's as though we are being dragged naked and without honor for all the world to see our disgrace. We may want to hide and run away, but we are bound. We want to change our awful past, but the harshness of those who accuse us want to crucify us to that very moment when we are most ugly and detestable.

During such times, let us look towards Him who understands all our misery and pain. Like the woman caught in adultery, let us humble ourselves at His feet and await His compassion. For He is not Lord only of the past but of our eternal destiny. He is not Justice only but Love and Mercy itself.

Reach out to Him who understands that we are but dust, to Him who suffered rejection from men, despised, afflicted and considered a plague.

He will cloth you with dignity and wash away your sins. He will take away your shame. He will heal the wounds of your soul and restore you to everlasting life!

He has no good looks or majesty.
When we see him, there is no beauty that we should desire him.
He was despised
and rejected by men,
a man of suffering
and acquainted with disease.
He was despised as one from whom men hide their face;
and we didn't respect him.
Surely he has borne our sickness
and carried our suffering;
yet we considered him plagued,
struck by God, and afflicted.
But he was pierced for our transgressions.
He was crushed for our iniquities.
The punishment that brought our peace was on him;

216

and by his wounds we are healed.
-Isaiah 53, WEBBE

July 29 :
Consumed By Love

To love is to be the most beautiful we can ever be.

Greater love has no one than this, that someone lay down his life for his friends. - John 15, WEBBE

To love is to find happiness, that kind of happiness that could never be bought. It is to live beyond the self, to be set free, to find who you really are.

When you love, you become less and less afraid, and more and more courageous. You find the courage to do the things you never thought could ever be done.

You become so full of life that you can't help but overflow with joy! You become a vessel of the Most High and a channel of His grace.

Soon, you notice the change within you as your wounds begin to heal and as every dark and bitter part of your soul become filled with light. Love transforms you into light and you become like a candle glowing for others to see.

You know the cost, but you burn ever more fervently. You offer everything that you are. Love consumes you and you know that there could never be anything more beautiful than that!

July 30 :
Our Time Is Short

The shortness of time reveals that we are made only for eternity.

He has made everything beautiful in its time. He has also set eternity in their hearts... - Ecclesiastes 3, WEB

Time Is Always Short

Time here below
is always short
it will never
be long enough.

Long enough to laugh,
long enough to dance,
long enough to touch,
long enough to love.

No matter how long
no matter how well lived,
a lifetime will always
be not enough.

It isn't enough,
it never will be,
for the human soul,
for the human heart.

For there is something
in our spirit
that longs for more,
infinitely more.

We long
for something
that knows no limits,
that knows no end.

And maybe even that
is a clue
in knowing who
we really are.

We were not meant
to be bound by the limits of time
We were not meant
to die.

For everything here below
will fall short
of the glory and bliss
that only heaven can provide.

July 31 :
Sacrifice and Love

When we sacrifice for love, we gain more than we could ever give away.

"This is my commandment, that you love one another, even as I have loved you. Greater love has no one than this, that someone lay down his life for his friends." - John 15, WEB

Sacrifice and Love. Two words that will always go together. Two things God Himself has taught us with His life.

By this we know what true love is. By this we see what's worth finding and what's worth dying for.

Many times, we fail to understand the depths of its meaning because we see it from afar. We see saints and heroes who willingly offered their lives in martyrdom, things we supposed we'd never need to do in our own lives.

And yet, were we not all called upon to carry our own cross? It's in this very cross that we can render the offering of the self for love.

The opportunity is there for us each and every day. It is when we choose to help someone even if there is nothing we'd get back in return. It is when we forgive those who cannot even ask for forgiveness. It is when we let go of our own comforts for the sake of those we love. It is when we forego the little mistakes, the small offenses, the minor irritations we encounter in or daily lives.

Without sacrifice, we end up letting each other go and giving up on one another. Without sacrifice, we sacrifice love itself, and we end up losing that which matters most in life.

219

AUGUST

August 1 :
   The Illusion of Evil

Evil done to another is never a triumph, it is always a harm done to your own soul.

But each one is tempted when he is drawn away by his own lust and enticed. Then the lust, when it has conceived, bears sin. The sin, when it is full grown, produces death. - James 1, WEBBE

No matter how victorious and attractive evil may seem to be, let us always remember that it could never triumph in the end. For it is in the very nature of evil to destroy itself. It is in the very nature of sin to lead to death.

Evil merely hides behind an illusion, an illusion that it could somehow survive, that the good it offers can somehow be sustained. This illusion entraps us and make us believe in a lie.

Darkness cannot even preserve itself. No matter how small we think the sin we give excuses for, it harms us, and it will eventually lead to our own destruction.

August 2 :
   Worry is Useless

Instead of fretting about, pray. Instead of worrying, trust in the God who can do all things.

"Which of you, by being anxious, can add one moment to his lifespan?" - Matthew 6:27, WEB

What use is worrying? If things do not turn out according to your desires, can your worrying do anything about it? Or what if things turn out well after all? What if you've worried yourself so much only to find out things have turned out far better than you could ever control or imagine them to be?

It is useless to worry. Reserve your strength for far better things like dealing with whatever will happen.

If things do not work out in your favor, you will have no other choice but to accept it and to move on from there. Start over if you must. Cry if the grief is too hard to bear. Do everything that is possible to overcome your troubles and trust in the God who cares for you and watches over you.

If things turn out to be far better than where your own thoughts could ever take you, raise your voice in thanksgiving and praise Him who has made all things beautiful in His time.

Fear Not, My Child

Fear not my child
Fear not.
Rid yourself of useless anxieties,
There is more that you can do at rest
than you can ever do fretting about.
Let everything that you do
be done out of love
pouring out of a peaceful heart.
It is not how many ideas
that run through your mind
that matters.
It is the way that you believe.
It is the way that you surrender
to everything that is good
which heaven is showering you
in every moment.
Fear not my child
Fear not.
There is no need for you to hurry
nor for your hands to tremble.
Time stops for love
and love alone.
And I want you to enter
the door that leads to forevermore.

August 3 :
You Will Be Stronger

No man is weak when He is strong in the Lord.

There is no king saved by the multitude of an army.
A mighty man is not delivered by great strength.
A horse is a vain thing for safety,
neither does he deliver any by his great power.
Behold, the LORD's eye is on those who fear him,
on those who hope in his loving kindness...
-Psalm 33, WEBBE

There are times when we feel anxious about the problems we're going to face. We feel our strength is not enough to face them. We don't know how we'd ever make it through.

But take heart! It is not your strength now that will determine your victory. It is not by your own power but by God's strength that you will overcome the challenges coming your way.

Stronger

I'm going to be stronger
By God's grace I know I shall be!
I have my fears but I'll face them
I won't let them get the best of me

I'm going to be stronger
I may be broken, but I'm gonna mend
God is my Healer, my Beloved Friend
I'll trust where He takes me though I can't see the end

I'm going to be stronger
there is no sense in despair
For God is my Refuge, my Armor and my Shield
He will certainly help me as I rise again!

August 4 :
Beyond Expectation

We can never prepare ourselves enough for the happiness God has prepared for us in heaven.

But as it is written, "Things which an eye didn't see, and an ear didn't hear, which didn't enter into the heart of man, these God has prepared for those who love him." - 1 Corinthians 2, WEB

What is heaven? It is something we can never quite grasp here on earth. Maybe something we can sense or desire, but never something we can fully imagine or understand.

What is God's love like? It is something that touches us and changes us, something that moves us far beyond what we thought we're capable of. It is like the wind that comes and goes where it will, gentle and strong at the same time, giving us life.

All our lives, we have dreamed of many things, we have desired many loves. Quite often though, something touches us that we have not expected at all, and we realize that it is this very thing that we have been looking for all along.

Keep your faith then. Believe even though you cannot see. God moves always, and He always moves out of great power and compassion.

You may not know it now, but He is constantly pursuing you, doing every good thing to draw you closer and give you joy. A joy beyond everything you have ever possessed and beyond all things you could ever hope for.

August 5 :
Forsaken by Love

We love only when we bleed.

"My God, my God, why have you forsaken me?" - Matthew 27:46, WEB

Love is happiness, yet it is also sorrow. Love is fullness, yet it is also being empty. Love is light, yet it is also darkness.

For no one loves for good times only, but loves the more when bad times come. No one loves to receive only, but shows one's love is true by giving one's all.

The one who knows how to love has fully lived, and because one lives, one is prepared even to die. For love is an offering not only of what one has. It is a complete surrender of the self, reserving nothing, holding nothing back.

It is in being consumed to the very end that love proves its true power, a power that conquers all pain and all darkness, rising yet again for it can never truly die.

August 6 :
Our Thirst for Love

It is not the one who thirsts for love that lacks love, but the one who cannot even look, who does not really care to be found.

I will get up now, and go about the city; in the streets and in the squares I will seek him whom my soul loves. - Song of Solomon 3:2, WEB

Broken hearts, hearts that grieve, hearts overcome with painful and unfulfilled longing. These may yet be nearer to love, these may yet possess it! They are not the ones who truly lose what's precious. For even in their pain, love lingers. Is love not the true reason behind each tear? Is love not the reason for the wounds of the heart?

Let those who thirst for love know that love has found them even before they began to thirst for love. Love itself has carved out that space, which only love can fill.

After this, Jesus... said, "I am thirsty."- John 19:28, WEBBE

August 7 :
Love Waits

He who cannot wait cannot truly love.

Therefore the LORD will wait, that he may be gracious to you... -
Isaiah 30, WEBBE

Love waits. Love is willing to wait because true love can never be
replaced. We can love others, it is true. But we can never love
another in the same way that we have loved before.

In the same way, God waits for us, for our love. In God's heart,
there is a place which only you can fill, and He IS waiting for you
there.

I WAIT

I wait for you, my love
I wait...
I will not open my heart
to another.

For who is there
who can ever be like you?
Who is there
that can ever take your place?

In my heart is a space
that is so sacred
and none can enter in
but you.

And I shall wait for you
though it takes forever,
though my heart bleeds
and my all consumed.

I wait because I love you
And love waits
for the only one
that it loves.

225

August 8 :

The Silence of Love

The sun rises each day without need of trumpet or sound, but it blesses the whole world as it makes the seeds grow and the flowers blossom, giving warmth and life to all.

Why do you stand far off, LORD?
Why do you hide yourself in times of trouble?
-Psalm 13, WEBBE

There are times when all that we could hear is the silence of God. We want Him to tell us what to do. We need Him to answer the many questions we have. We desire to hear His voice of comfort, telling us we need not worry or fret. But all that we hear is His silence.

Why does He not speak? Why does He not tell us He is going to answer our prayer? Why does He seem so far away?

In times when we cannot hear, may we listen to faith, and may we hold on to hope.

God's silence does not mean He does not love us. God's silence does not mean He doesn't care.

But His silence is love itself, wisdom itself. It is to work in us something that can only be accomplished without noise.

August 9 :

Shine Your Light

And where there is darkness... shine!

You are the light of the world. A city located on a hill can't be hidden. Neither do you light a lamp, and put it under a measuring basket, but on a stand; and it shines to all who are in the house. Even so, let your light shine before men; that they may see your good works, and glorify your Father who is in heaven. - Matthew 5, WEB

226

Darkness can never be extinguished by complaining about it or by saying how terrible it is indeed! It can never be conquered if we fear it or if we give in to despair. There is only one thing necessary. In order to overcome the darkness, we need to give out LIGHT. Courageous light. Joyful Light. Loving Light.

Your light must be greater than the darkness around you. Your beauty must be far more alluring than the deceiving attractions that lure the world away from the True Light.

And as the world makes its way further and further into violence, continue to sow peace. As the world grows in pride, seek out humility. As men grow in hate, grow more and more in Love.

August 10 :
  Christ In You

And when people see you may they be blessed because they can see Christ in you.

The chalice of benediction, which we bless, is it not the communion of the blood of Christ? And the bread, which we break, is it not the partaking of the body of the Lord? For we, being many, are one bread, one body, all that partake of one bread.- 1 Corinthians 10, WEB

The love of God can never separated from the love of other men because each of His children are called to be a reflection of Christ Himself. When we are able to truly love another, it is God also that we love.

We often complain that we do not see God, that we do not know how to love Him. He is there in our neighbor and our friends and our family. He is there among the sick, among the beggars, among those who walk in the darkness. We may not see clearly now, for Christ is hidden still in many. But one day we shall see when the fullness of light has dawned upon us all. In heaven we shall always see God because He is truly there wherever we may look. You will see Him in me, as I will see Him in you!

227

August 11 :
Love Without Equal

It is always a blessing to love another. But let no blessing take you away from the One who loves you without measure, without equal, and without end.

You shall love the LORD your God with all your heart, with all your soul, and with all your might. - Deuteronomy 6:5, WEBBE

There is so much goodness in the love of another person. So much beauty and so much light! At times we think we have already caught a glimpse of eternity as we love another person wholeheartedly and without reserve.

But O, what pain when betrayal comes! What bitterness and anguish. How could the very person we loved break our hearts apart?

Have we not given it our all? Have we not excluded everybody else so we can give that person everything we ever had? Have we not emptied ourselves and looked to him or her as a god that must be served and adored?

Ah, but that is what we have forgotten. That though the love of another person is good, it can never equal the love of God. That no matter how beautiful it may be, it is still a love given to a fragile being, weak and vulnerable as we ourselves are.

A Beauty That Never Fades

I have seen so much beauty in this life,
I have felt overflowing love,
I have been happy,
I have been filled with so much joy!

But O, I have also seen so much hatred
and violence and apathy,
I've felt so much sorrow
that almost drained my eyes of tears.

228

I have seen how something so beautiful
could suddenly be corrupted, twisted,
decayed and left to waste.
I have seen how something so wonderful
could suddenly end,
and how something so precious
could suddenly be taken away from you,
tearing both your heart and soul.

What is this life worth then?
What does it all mean?

Why must darkness spoil the light?
Why must love be filled with pain?

Is there a way to restore everything
back to wholeness?
Is there some chance that good
might not end in evil things?

Only God holds the key.
From everlasting to everlasting,
the One who changes not,
whose Light has never grown dim,
and whose beauty never fades,
He alone can save
and keep what's good and beautiful and true.

Left to ourselves we grow weak.
We turn love to hatred,
we hold something beautiful
and it soon withers away and dies.

With God however, all things are kept,
cleansed and made whole.

Sorrow turns to joy,
Suffering turns to strength.

We approach in ignorance,
and we leave with wisdom;
We approach in fear,

and we leave with courage.

We live forever in LOVE!

August 12 :
Only Beauty Remains

And if beautiful things can be seen in this world, how much more in heaven where God dwells?

Bless the LORD, my soul...
He covers himself with light as with a garment.
He stretches out the heavens like a curtain.
He lays the beams of his rooms in the waters.
He makes the clouds his chariot.
He walks on the wings of the wind.
He makes his messengers winds,
and his servants flames of fire.
-Psalm 104, WEB

What is beautiful? It is something which words rarely could explain, but which tears so often reveal so easily. Tears that come from the heart, and the heart, which alone can see.

Beauty moves us, changes us, redeems us. It allows us to have a glimpse of Him from whom all goodness could ever come.

We can't help but be still when beauty comes to us. We have to be still. Beauty moves us, but beauty also captures our soul in a moment where everything is sacred, and where we want everything to remain as they are. They are perfect as they are!

It is beauty alone that gives us true humility, because before it, all other lights fade away and we remain in awe and in gratitude for Him who has allowed us to see His face.

August 13 :
He Hears Your Prayer

Silence does not mean we are not being heard.

You number my wanderings. You put my tears into your bottle. Aren't they in your book? - Psalm 56:8, WEB

Someone is listening to your prayer. Someone who knows you. Someone who cares for you and watches over you.

You may not know it yet, you may not even believe, for in His silence you may think He isn't there.

But He hears. He catches your every tear.

And He weeps with you. With His whole heart He goes with you where all is painful and dark.

And when everything seems too heavy and impossible to bear, just when you feel you cannot make it through, He carries you. Silently but powerfully, He bears the burden you cannot bear. Your wounds become His, and by His wounds, you are healed.

August 14 :
Love Receives Gladly

If you really love me, come take my hand and receive my love.

"Rise up, my love, my beautiful one, and come away." - Song of Solomon 2:10, WEBBE

Love on earth will always be a struggle. Even with a perfect Spouse, one does not get away with tears, for the imperfect one will often misunderstand the other. How does one ever begin to understand the Lover who gives and gives no matter the failings of the other?

Oftentimes, all we need to do is to accept everything with love and we cannot even do it! We feel ashamed, we back out, we focus on

231

our woes instead of focusing on the One who loves us. Do we think that love is always counting the cost and demanding of us something for everything we are given?

Far from it! Love does not count its gifts. Love is happy in giving, and it is grieved whenever we block its course, thinking it is always an exchange, something we should deserve.

If I really want to deserve love, I need only to recognize its generosity, its kindness, its desire to satisfy the beloved. I must not lift myself high, but allow myself to bow down low. I am loved. My Lover desires to bestow light upon my darkness, joy upon all my misery, beauty upon all the unloveliness I see in me. Is it not enough to lean with trust and to receive with gladness all that is given me?

August 15 :
With Eyes Of Faith

Faith needs a new kind of eye to see, an eye that sees in the light of love.

Jesus said to him, "Because you have seen me, you have believed. Blessed are those who have not seen, and have believed." -John 20:29, WEB

There are times when we experience a lack of faith. We start to have questions. Doubt creeps in and we begin to want solid proofs to what we profess to believe.

Why do we believe Him in the first place? Why do we believe even if we do not see?

But when we come to think about it, we can turn this question the other way. Why should we not believe? Can we have more solid proofs that our faith isn't true? That He doesn't really exist? That He isn't the most beautiful thing we could ever desire and have?

Believing in God is much like falling in love. You can't have all the evidences and assurance you want. But somehow, what you have is enough to know that it's worth taking the risk, and if you let go of your chance, you will forever forfeit the most beautiful thing you can ever have. You would gladly sacrifice everything because nothing can ever make sense again without it. You would gladly risk it all because without doing so, you know you have already lost everything.

August 16 :
Breathe

Sometimes, all that you can do is to carry on... and breathe.

The LORD will fight for you, and you shall be still. - Exodus 14, WEBBE

Sometimes, we don't need great explanations, profound truths or deep insights. What we need are just simple things to hold on to and to help us make it through another day.

Sometimes the aroma of a freshly brewed coffee will do. Sometimes a song that soothes the soul. At other times, it's a book that calls to be read again, the innocent smile of a child, or a cozy blanket to snuggle into.

There will be a time for big things and big thoughts. But for now, I guess that it's enough to breathe.

August 17 :
Seasons of Healing

Not all wounds are mended in an instant, but with God's grace we trust they shall be completely healed.

But you are a God ready to pardon, gracious and merciful, slow to anger, and abundant in loving kindness, and didn't forsake them. Yes, when they had made themselves a moulded calf, and said, 'This is your God who brought you up out of Egypt,' and had committed awful blasphemies; yet you in your manifold mercies didn't forsake them in the wilderness. The pillar of cloud didn't depart from over them by day, to lead them in the way; neither did

233

the pillar of fire by night, to show them light, and the way in which they should go. - Nehemiah 9, WEBBE

Quite often, I wonder why God doesn't transform us immediately into perfection the moment that we believe in Him and truly desire from within our hearts to be His forever. Why couldn't we be good once and for all so that we may finally avoid hurting other people and making so many mistakes? Why couldn't we overcome our bad habits at once? Why couldn't we be relieved from our suffering of being sinful, of being the cause of darkness instead of being a channel of His light?

I've realized that though God can well do so, He sometimes allows many of us to be perfected through many seasons of trial and healing. In this way, our humility is established, and we know more who we are by ourselves without His grace. In this way also, we get to know more about the patience of God, how He bears with us, forgiving our many trespasses and blunders, and waiting patiently for that day when we shall finally be like Him, holy, loving faithfully, and pure.

August 18 :
   Set Free by God

Do not despair. God comes to heal, to save, to set you free!

He has sent me to heal the broken hearted,
to proclaim release to the captives,
recovering of sight to the blind,
to deliver those who are crushed...
- Luke 4, WEBBE

Any bad habit associated with intoxicating pleasure is difficult to overcome due to the intense sensation felt by the person every time he engages in such a habit. During such a time, everything else seems to fade away, even right thinking, even far reaching consequences in the future, even loved ones.

Afterwards, when the pleasure or sensation has left, one can begin to see the damage it has done to himself and to others. In a way, one repents, and desires to leave behind such a harmful vice. But

234

one's resolve quickly breaks as soon as the sensation starts to creep in again and lays hold upon him, becoming its slave. The cycle never seems to stop until there is full destruction of a life bereft of every good.

But is there hope? Can one be free?

The answer may seem too simple, but the answer is Him who sets prisoners free and heals those who are wounded, both in body and in soul. It is grace that can empower us, grace that can assist us when even our very best is never enough.

This does not mean however that we do nothing. Grace is strength, but we must use that strength that is given us. God opens the prison doors, but we must choose to walk outside so we can truly be free.

The struggle for many may not be instant. It can be a daily battle where one rises and where one falls again. But the important thing is to always get up, never letting go of God's Hand, God's strong yet gentle Hand that will always be there for us, guiding us, until all that is lost has found its way again.

August 19 :
Prayer and Sacrifice

Will God not hear a prayer borne out of sincerity and a love that's willing to offer all?

"You mute and deaf spirit, I command you, come out of him, and never enter him again!" Having cried out, and convulsed greatly, it came out of him. The boy became like one dead; so much that most of them said, "He is dead." But Jesus took him by the hand, and raised him up; and he arose. When he had come into the house, his disciples asked him privately, "Why couldn't we cast it out?" He said to them, "This kind can come out by nothing, except by prayer and fasting." - Mark 9, WEB

We often encounter frustration not because there is lack of support from God, but because we have relied upon inappropriate instruments.

235

There are things we cannot accomplish by force. There are arguments we cannot win by mere eloquence. There are souls that cannot be won over by words.

But what force cannot achieve, gentleness often can. What arguments fail to prove, friendship often can express. And what words cannot win, the witness of our lives often can.

Yes, it is true, there is much evil in the world today. Evil holds dominion over worldly affairs, over earthly riches and positions of power. It holds sway over channels of communication and influence.

But there is a far greater power that often remains untapped. It is the power of the spirit. And that power can only be access by much prayer and the unselfish sacrifice of our lives.

August 20 :
The Tears We Hide

We cant always be strong, but sometimes, we have to risk trusting others with our tears so they'd have the chance to wipe them all away.

The LORD is near to those who have a broken heart, and saves those who have a crushed spirit. - Psalm 34:18, WEBBE

The most terrible thing to feel in the world is not to be weak. The most terrible thing to feel is to know that even in your strength, even in your riches, even in your possession of power, you are alone.

Therein is our poverty, therein is true anguish. And in that poverty, there is nothing we can do but to risk ourselves all the more and make ourselves vulnerable. No one can join us while we are enclosed. No one can see us while we remain hidden.

By opening ourselves to others, we risk getting hurt more. But it is only by this risk that we also invite others to come and to be the friend of our souls.

236

Why do we hide our tears from the world?

We hide our tears –
because we don't want to appear weak
because when we appear weak, other people would avoid us
because they don't want to be affected by our weakness
and when they leave us, we just become even lonelier than before

We hide our tears –
because we don't want to lose our credibility
with the people who trust us and depend on us
because when they see us crying, they'd think we're crumbling
and when we crumble, they'd have no one to lean on to anymore

We hide our tears –
because we don't want to appear hurt
because when our loved ones see how hurt we are, they'd get hurt as well
and we don't want to see them hurt
because we'd only get hurt the more

I've hidden my tears for quite a while, 'til there came a time when I surrendered, and I set them free – I let them overflow, and I've realized, I don't want to hide my tears anymore.

I don't want to hide my tears anymore –
because I want to show others how much I understand their tears,
and in so doing, help them feel they're not alone;
because I want to show one doesn't have to be perfect all the time,
just so you can be strong;
because I want others to understand me,too, in my hurts,
trusting they can also be strong, and that they could also love me for who I am,
not for who I could be or pretend to be.

August 21 :
  Listen With Your Heart

Must we say that we love when we cannot even listen?

So, then, my beloved brothers, let every man be swift to hear, slow to speak, and slow to anger... - James 1:19, WEBBE

We have always wanted people to listen to us, to really listen. To listen not only with their ears, but with their heart.

Yet few are those it seems who know how. Few are those who can look beyond our words, beyond our tone, beyond our outward arrogance and anger.

How fortunate indeed to find one who can listen even to our silence, even to the words we fail to say. They see not only the words we wanted to say, they see our souls, they see who we really are.

If I Didn't Listen

Forgive me if I didn't listen well,
If I didn't hear you when you spoke.
Forgive me if I blocked and hindered
The thoughts you wanted to share.

I was more occupied with my thoughts
Than with your thoughts,
I was more concerned with my feelings
Than I was with yours.

I was not able to hear
What you truly wanted to say.
I was not able to know you better,
I wasn't able to value who you are.

Forgive me for I should have shown more compassion,
I should have respected you.
I should have opened up my heart,
So you could have opened yours.

Forgive me for I have made you feel more alone,
I have not listened to your fears or to your pain.
I was so absorbed in my own defenses,
In my own hurts and fears.

Forgive me for I have not listened well,

238

I should have known we're not so different after all.
If I had only listened,
I may not have felt so alone.

August 22 :
Loving Our Scars

It's when I fall that I get learn who will be there to catch me.

There is no fear in love; but perfect love casts out fear, because...
He who fears is not made perfect in love. - 1 John 4:18, WEBBE

It is easy to be confident when one knows one is beautiful. It is easy then to believe one deserves to be loved. And maybe that's why we often desire to present only our very best to others. Maybe that is also why we're afraid to show the imperfections we try to hide.

For how could anyone love us once they see how broken we really are? How could anyone love us once they see the many faults we hide inside?

But Oh, how we need others just to do that! How we need to be loved not only for our best but even for our very worst.

We can disbelieve most people who claim they love us for our beauty. But how can we doubt them who love us despite all our scars?

me and YOU

I am so small,
and You're so BIG,
how can I ever love YOU
the way You love me?

Sometimes I hate myself
for just being me,
yet how wrong am I
to think that way.

239

For I am me
because of You,
and You gave up part of You,
so I can be me.

Please help me Lord,
to live with gladness;
Knowing that I am me,
and believing that each moment,
I shall be more of You!

August 23 :
Loving Too Much

We only love too much when we love too little.

"Come to me, all you who labour and are heavily burdened, and I will give you rest." - Matthew 11:28, WEBBE

There is a certain fear in trying to love too much. It is the fear of being rejected. The fear of not being good enough to be loved.

We do not always see it. We hardly realize it's there.

But we feel it in the hurt when our love is not returned. We feel it in the exhustion of giving everything and receiving too little, of doing everything and not having anyone to lean on to when we're tired.

You know then that you have loved too much. Too much and too little. For though you have given much, you had so little left to withstand the pain.

For who has not loved and not touched pain? Knowing all the we shall ever love shall never be faultless, and not all shall return the love we have given them?

Loving Broken People

We cannot exempt ourselves from the world
while we are in the world,
and while we are in it

240

it is our lot to love broken men.
Yet how can we do it
when we are ourselves are broken,
and need to be assured
that we are loved
that we are accepted
for being the broken people that we are.
We cannot love a person
with an all accepting, transcending and encompassing love
without being hurt somewhat,
without being disappointed,
without being failed
of our expectations.
We cannot love
without being broken,
yet we cannot continue in love
without being stronger
than our brokenness.
It is only in Jesus
where we can find healing and strength
so as to continue in this love,
so as to continue suffering again and again
yet rise again and again
in a love that is far above
any expectations,
in a love that does not retreat
from any hurt
or any frustration,
but in a love that dares to dare
in a love that dares to dream
in a love
that never ever fails!

August 24 :
    The Gift of Faith

Faith is not seeing with our eyes, but seeing with our hearts.

"He said to him, 'If they don't listen to Moses and the prophets, neither will they be persuaded if one rises from the dead.'"- Luke 16:31, WEBBE

There are times when we may wonder why Jesus did not simply show Himself and His miracles to all who did not believe.

But then another question quickly comes to mind: Would people believe then?

When Jesus still walked the earth with His disciples, He did many miracles. He even brought a dead person back to life! Aside from this, He healed the blind and many who are sick. He multiplied bread to feed thousands. He stopped a storm. He turned water into wine!

But did everyone believe in Him? No! But these even made those who did not believe to become even more stubborn in their unbelief. They plotted for His death! Will not the same thing happen today as it did then?

There is a different miracle that is needed - the miracle of the heart. It is being open to God's true kingdom, which is love. We may not see Jesus now, but God can grant us the gift of faith.

Jesus said to them, "If you were blind, you would have no sin; but now you say, 'We see.' Therefore your sin remains."- John 9:41, WEBBE

Salvation

God was there
from the very beginning
but I knew Him not
and I turned away
I looked at the world
and beheld its splendor
til that same splendor
snatched me
and I was thrown
amidst its cold brightness
and I yearned for the warmth of home
In despair I wept
and I cried out to my God:
Rescue me for I desire not these things

242

and I will have none of this beauty
if only to be back in your arms
And my God heard me
and ran to me
and snatched me away from the world
and took me even
within His heart
Therein only
did I find joy
and peace
and LOVE
atlast!

August 25 :
Love Endures

What kind of love is there that cannot endure the darkness?

Love... bears all things, believes all things, hopes all things, and endures all things. Love never fails. - 1 Corinthians 13, WEBBE

To love another is not always to experience days of elation and happiness. It is not a constant feeling of romance, of starlit nights and roses, of endless sweet nothings, of chocolates and champagne and lovely sunsets spent in each other's arms.

In this life, to love another is to be able to accept everything and bear everything for the sake of that love. It is both living in joy as well as living in sorrow. It is both in bearing the storm and in rejoicing as the sun shines again. It is sharing days filled with adventure as well as days filled only with silence. It is keeping that flame of love alive both in days with your beloved and in days of waiting while he or she is gone.

Love is in life, but it isn't fearful of death. Love is in health, but it isn't weakened by sickness. Love is in wealth, but it isn't conquered by poverty.

For love is beyond death or sickness or poverty. Love has health and wealth and life of it's own. It endures everything and triumphs always in the end. In truth, if love be true, there really is no end.

243

Only times of waiting and of silence, until it comes and revives us all again.

August 26 :
Joy in Humility

Humility is in the gratitude of the heart.

Abraham answered, "See now, I have taken it on myself to speak to the Lord, although I am dust and ashes." - Genesis 18:27, WEBBE

The life, strengths, and challenges God has given me, I've realized, were there to make me ever grateful and humble. To know how much I have received and how much I ought to give in return, and realize how little I am able to do so. To know how high a standard I must observe, and to constantly fall, unable to rise without holding on to His Hand. To be given a vision of what one can do, and to bear the inability to do them. To see others accomplish what I could never do. To be content with what little acts of love I am capable of. And to be the beloved of Him who is all perfect and pure despite my lowliness. Such great reasons for humility and for unutterable joy!

August 27 :
Humility in Love

No joy must be lost when we think well of our neighbor.

If therefore there is any exhortation in Christ, if any consolation of love, if any fellowship of the Spirit, if any tender mercies and compassion, make my joy full by being like-minded, having the same love, being of one accord, of one mind; doing nothing through rivalry or through conceit, but in humility, each counting others better than himself... - Philippians 2, WEBBE

It is never those who boast that draws our hearts. It is never those who are proud.

But we are drawn to those who never think too highly of themselves. Those who can always seem to think of something good in others around them.

244

It is not lack of confidence. It isn't low self-esteem.

But it is in a soul that doesn't even need to lift oneself up or to gain the regard of others. It is in that kind of confidence that doesn't even need to think of oneself too often or too much.

Instead of focusing on themselves, they are intent on finding the good in others, too. They are keen to see their beauty.

They are those who are not afraid to praise other men, those who are not afraid to admit that someone can be better in this or that skill, or in this or that virtue.

Love occupies their hearts so much that there isn't room for that kind of fear. What's present is much room for thanksgiving and appreciation, and much room indeed for trust in God from whom all good things come from.

August 28 :
The Light of Faith

The intellect fails to understand many things when it fails to see in the light of faith.

All things were made through him. Without him, nothing was made that has been made. In him was life, and the life was the light of men. The Word became flesh, and lived among us. We saw his glory, such glory as of the one and only Son of the Father, full of grace and truth. -John 1:3-4, 14, WEB

It isn't easy to explain one's faith. But it is like a light that illuminates everything in our life that's dark and cold and bitter. We may not always have the words to describe it, but would we rather lose our faith just because we cannot express it the way the world wants us to?

Would we rather go back to the darkness where we were? To meaninglessness and loneliness, and to hurting the ones we love?

Would we rather live being merely swayed by our passions - without hope, without true love, without purity in our heart?

What kind of life would we rather live? What kind of existence would we rather go back to?

How does one even begin to explain what faith really is?

August 29 :
> I Surrender To Love

To love is to receive everything in joy!

Keep me as the apple of your eye. Hide me under the shadow of your wings... - Psalm 17, WEB

We can spend our lives trying to please people and trying to deserve their love. We can get used to this way of living and loving that we don't know how to receive love anymore. Love that pursues us. Love that doesn't ask anything from us except that we receive it with trust and open arms.

Someone Loves Me Now

I am used to loving
used to giving
used to doing things
for the one I love.

But I have yet to be used
to being loved
to being given everything
by the one who loves me.

How can I ever get used
to receiving so much love?
To being the apple of his eye?

When can I ever get used
to being still, being me,
being happy

even though I know
I do not deserve
all that he is giving me?

But I have to get used to love,
used to his kisses,
used to his warm embrace.

I am not the one
who decides now
how things must happen.
I am not the one
who does everything anymore.

There is someone now
who is there for me,
who sees me,
and who will take care
of all my tomorrows
just as much
as he takes good care of me
today.

August 30 :
   The Reality of Faith

The world doesn't know it. But faith is far more real than the kind of reality many people think.

"For most certainly I tell you, if you have faith as a grain of mustard seed, you will tell this mountain, 'Move from here to there,' and it will move; and nothing will be impossible for you." - Matthew 17, WEBBE

It is faith that helps us see what others fail to see. It is faith that makes it possible to find a way where others find no way at all.

In eternity, we will see better, and we will understand more how faith is indeed tangible, more tangible than the knowledge possessed by the wise. Faith enables us to make sense of things, to value things for their true worth. It sees true beauty. It knows which things are passing and which things truly remain.

Faith is not wishful thinking. It is not a fantasy based on our mere imaginings. For how could our fallen mind even imagine the things of faith? It is like a man born blind trying to imagine the light!

No. We know faith only because the eyes of our spirit have been opened for us.

Faith is more real than we think. With it comes new horizons we could never have dreamt or imagined. With it comes wisdom. With it comes the power even to move mountains into the sea!

August 31 :
  Your Own Cross

Let us give others the chance to grow and to be strong.

For each man will bear his own burden. - Galatians 6:5, WEB

We were never meant to carry the cross of other people. We were meant to carry only our own. When we become overly responsible for others, we fail to love ourselves enough, and we also fail to love others by not helping them to grow and to be strong.

Let us never forget that no matter how well intentioned we may be, we can only do so much. There are some things we can accomplish, and there are some things we cannot. There are some things we are responsible for, and there are some things that are already the responsibility of other people.

In the end, God is the One who bears the burden of the whole world. Even though our strength is often insufficient, even though we make many mistakes along the way, we can have faith in the God who makes the sun to rise each day and who makes all the stars to shine through the night. Nothing will happen without His consent. Not one hair of yours or mine shall fall without His will.

Do not be overly anxious then as though you were the only one who can do something, as though the world would fall without your care.

248

God honors us by giving each one of us a burden meant for us alone. Let us carry it with love and leave all else to Him who has counted the stars and knows each one by name.

SEPTEMBER

September 1 :
   Keeping Love Alive

Great love is often kept alive by small deeds.

He set another parable before them, saying, "The Kingdom of Heaven is like a grain of mustard seed, which a man took, and sowed in his field; which indeed is smaller than all seeds. But when it is grown, it is greater than the herbs, and becomes a tree, so that the birds of the air come and lodge in its branches." - Matthew 13:31-32, WEB

Little Deeds of Love

A glance of kindness
To keep the fire burning
A touch of patience
To keep the love alive

A word of courtesy
A nod of gratitude
A pat of consolation
To uplift the mood

A smile
A quick embrace
A kiss
Never miss one deed.

And you know
That all you need
Are these little things
To keep the love alive.

September 2 :
To Find What's Beautiful

The human heart aches for beauty because we are meant to have it, to find what's beautiful not just outside by moreso within our souls.

Finally, brothers, whatever things are true, whatever things are honorable, whatever things are just, whatever things are pure, whatever things are lovely, whatever things are of good report; if there is any virtue, and if there is any praise, think about these things. - Philippians 4:8, WEB

We live to seek what's beautiful, and once we find it, our desire is to keep it, to preserve it forever if we could.

That's why we take so many photographs. That is why we paint and do sculptures and so many works of art.

We want to capture that moment of beauty where we transcend the mundane and leap at once from time to eternity. We want to enter into that magical realm where we become free at last, where we not only touch the beautiful, but where we become one with it, and in finding the beautiful, we also find ourselves.

Morning Joy

Joy is in cool mornings,
A cool morning breeze when the sun is bright;
Joy is in this feeling,
Of rebirth and delight.

And I yearn to wake up and awaken;
I yearn to walk beneath the light;
I yearn to walk just near the trees,
And watch some little birds in flight.

I yearn to walk just near the shore,
And watch the waves at sea;
There's nothing I could ask for more,
Than earth's enchanting melody.

251

In the early hour of the day,
When night has just passed away;
When all is fresh, and all is beautiful,
When all is brilliant, ever pure.

Joy is in cool mornings;
A stroll amidst a brand new day,
When life is just beginning,
When angels sing and dance and pray!

September 3 :
 The Peace of God

Something happens when we call on to God in prayer - we find hope amidst our despair, we healing amidst our suffering, we find peace where there was no peace.

In nothing be anxious, but in everything, by prayer and petition with thanksgiving, let your requests be made known to God. And the peace of God, which surpasses all understanding, will guard your hearts and your thoughts in Christ Jesus. - Philippians 4:6-7, WEB

You can't control everything. Try as you might, plan as you might, you'd still encounter things that never even crossed your mind.

So don't waste time fretting. Quite often, the things we feared don't happen at all. On the other hand, things happen that we never even feared.

Why waste your strength for what you could never even predict? Conserve your powers so you may have the ability to deal with what you will truly face.

September 4 :

God gives us new joys every morning, if only we have an open heart to receive them.

By the river on its bank, on this side and on that side, will grow every tree for food, whose leaf won't wither, neither will its fruit fail. It will produce new fruit every month, because its waters issue out of the sanctuary. Its fruit will be for food, and its leaf for healing. - Ezekiel 47, WEBBE

When Happiness Flew

I found happiness once
It gave me so much life
that I never wanted it to depart.

So I tried to keep it in a drawer
I had it under lock and key
until the day I opened the drawer
and found that happiness
wasn't anymore there for me.

I cried so hard when I lost it,
until the day when I found it again.
Happiness looked almost the same
yet a bit different
as it called my name.

It warned me never to keep it,
that if I wanted it back,
I have to let it go.

I was tempted to capture it again,
but then I remembered my drawer
and so I watched
as happiness flew.

I thought I've lost it for good,
but it came back from day to day,

253

always the same, yet always different
ever old but ever new.

I wasn't afraid anymore,
and I knew I would never lose it again
because since I let it go,
happiness returned and became my friend.

September 5 :
Pray Like a Child

To reach God, we don't have to be so strong or wise, but we do have to be humble enough like children.

From the lips of babes and infants you have established strength... - Psalm 8:2, WEBBE

We don't need to impress anyone when we pray.

We can pray simply and sincerely, like children usually do.

Pray from the heart. Pray with trust. Pray knowing that your Heavenly Father is listening to you, loving you, and is even more desirous than you are to grant you your prayer, provided that it would be best for you.

The Prayer of a Child

The prayer of a child
is often answered.

It is answered
because it is pure.

It is answered
because it has no fear.

It does not think about the past,
it does not worry about the future.

It is not ashamed to express the truth,

it is not ashamed to express how it feels.

The prayer of a child
goes right up to heaven,
unto the ears of God
who hears it,
because it wants to be heard.

The prayer of a child
is answered
even before it has been uttered.

It was answered
when the child started to pray
with her heart.

September 6 :
Who You Really Are

When we realize the kind of person God wanted us to be, we'd see that we expected not too much but far too little of ourselves.

The LORD, your God, is amongst you, a mighty one who will save. He will rejoice over you with joy. He will calm you in his love. He will rejoice over you with singing. - Zephaniah 3:17, WEBBE

You are not yet who you really are. Others may see but a dim reflection. You may see as with a mirror full of cracks and stain. But that is not the entire essence of who you are.

You must be able to see the person that God sees, the person God Himself has made.

You must see your true beauty and dignity before any shame or sin has ever touched you, before any pain and suffering has ever taken away your light.

Let all stains of disgrace be washed away. Let every wound that has blemished your wholeness be healed.

255

Trust in the One who has made you. Let Him purify you once more and renew you. Let Him reveal to you who you really are.

September 7 :
Loving Yourself

There is something a bit tricky about loving yourself. It's important to be really honest. You also have to be brave. Add to that a touch of gentleness and understanding and as much forgiveness as you could possibly give. Above all, trust in God's love for you.

Behold, you are beautiful, my love.
Behold, you are beautiful.
Your eyes are like doves.
- Song of Solomon 1, WEBBE

There can be times when you will really find it hard to love yourself, to see what good there is in you. Times like that, you can try to think of a person you really loved. What was there in him that you loved? That despite all his faults and shortcomings still manages to shine through?

Surely he wasn't perfect all the time. He wasn't always in his best light. Still, you believed that what was good in him was there. No matter how hidden or clouded it may have been, it can still sprout like a seed coming forth from the ground. And you wanted that seed to grow, every bit of that beauty to fully blossom in time.

Not that you didn't love him for who he was. But that you see something more. Something that was truly in him all that time, waiting to be fully manifested and seen.

September 8 :
A Mother's Love

There is no comparison on earth worthy to depict a mother's love.

As one whom his mother comforts,
so I will comfort you.
-Isaiah 66:13, WEBBE

To what can we compare the great love of a mother? It is a love that is not selfish. It is a love that is very patient! It is a love that never grows tired or disheartened. It is a love that is giving, always giving and could never give enough. It is a love that is gentle and kind. It is a love that is strong, one that would defend her children though it costs her own life! It is a love that is never afraid of sacrifice, but one that would take on every suffering just to be able to save her child. It is a love that lingers long after it has been forgotten. It is a love that never dies.

September 9 :
The Works of God

There's a certain kind of beauty in the works of God. We recognize it when we see it. We know that something has come from God.

God didn't make death; neither does he delight when the living perish. For he created all things that they might have being. The generative powers of the world are wholesome, and there is no poison of destruction in them... - Wisdom 1, WEBBE

There is both grandeur and a certain kind of simplicity in the works of God. There is uniqueness, but it is never out of place. There is modesty, there is space, there is rhythm. There is nothing forced about it. Nothing that is superfluous. Nothing that is without purpose or better end.

The beauty of His works proclaim His glory. It proclaims His power and His generosity.

But it also reflects His tenderness and humility. It shows us He cares for the little things as much as He cares for the great ones.

There is not a tiny detail to life that God has ever forgotten. There is not one stroke of His works that is done without love.

There Are No Squares In Nature

Come to think of it, when have you ever seen the following?

A square leaf
A square fruit
A square tree
A square raindrop

Coming to think of it, nature, unlike man, does not produce

Square moons
Square suns
Square planets
Or square galaxies

There are no square rainbows
Nor square flowers
Nor square heads
that could fit inside a square box

Yet more often than not, that's exactly what we do.

We try to put everything inside a box
We try to make all things black and white
We try to make everything spic and span
as though we could put a square peg inside a round hole
and then congratulate ourselves for the feat we have done

Since the dawn of man-made technology,
we have certainly lived in a world of squares:

square houses
square buildings
square computer screens

We write on square papers using square tables
We sleep on square beds and enter upon square doors

Where has all these taken us?

These square things have made a war with our own hearts
And against all mysteries that enrich and empower us

The next time someone tries to put your immortal soul inside a small box

Kindly remind yourself:
There are no square stars in the Universe.

September 10 :
Time To Change The World

You can change the world. Let it begin by allowing God to change you and make His miracles in your life!

Don't look on his face, or on the height of his stature, because I have rejected him; for I don't see as man sees. For man looks at the outward appearance, but the LORD looks at the heart. – 1 Samuel 16:7, WEBBE

It is time to change the world, your world. Don't think that it's impossible. Think instead that all things are possible for those who believe.

God believes in you, you know. He formed you in the womb and knew you even before you knew yourself.

He has great plans for your life. And if He has not yet revealed it to you, it could be that you would not be able to believe in them for now. You'd think it impossible to reach.

But what is impossible? What is it that God could not do?

God makes His miracles today as He has made them yesterday, and we are His greatest miracle!

Don't think of your smallness, think instead of God's greatness. Don't think of your poverty, think of God's great wealth! Don't think of your fears, think of the courage God can bestow upon you.

It isn't to the strong or to the swift that success comes. Many times, victory belongs to those who are little in the eyes of the world.

September 11 :
   Silent Heroes

What could have happened if the sun didn't shine today because we failed to be grateful? Or if the trees no longer grew because we failed to notice them?

"Be careful that you don't do your charitable giving before men, to be seen by them, or else you have no reward from your Father who is in heaven. Therefore when you do merciful deeds, don't sound a trumpet before yourself, as the hypocrites do in the synagogues and in the streets, that they may get glory from men. Most certainly I tell you, they have received their reward. But when you do merciful deeds, don't let your left hand know what your right hand does, so that your merciful deeds may be in secret, then your Father who sees in secret will reward you openly. – Matthew 6:1-4, WEBBE

We don't have to begin with a lot of noise. We can start quietly and faithfully with our task. Let others boast of their plans. Let them take pride in their bright ideas. But in the end, it is not the noise that matters, but the substance of what we really do.

We do good deeds not to acquire praise or recognition. We do them because it is right, because we are inspired by love. And love does not fade away because it is silent sometimes. Love is always there, and it could be doing more in times when it is silent than in times when it is heard.

God is the same. He gives us every good we do not deserve. He gives us His blessings even without our recognition.

Many times, it is the deeds done in silence that truly counts because they have been done in sincerity. They were the ones done out of pure and faithful love.

September 12 :
In Your Best Light

In times when you can't even face yourself in the mirror, try to find yourself in God's loving eyes.

Therefore God, your God, has anointed you with the oil of gladness above your fellows. All your garments smell like myrrh, aloes, and cassia. Out of ivory palaces stringed instruments have made you glad. – Psalm 45, WEBBE

Try to see yourself in your best light. Not in the way other people have judged you before, or in the way you may have looked down on yourself. But in the way God believes in you, in the way He knows you best of all!

You may not feel so strong now, you may even feel broken. But even your sorrow could never diminish the light God has bestowed upon you. You are not your brokenness. You are the person who is capable of overcoming that brokenness.

See the beauty that God sees in you. See the glory that will last for all eternity.

Throw away any self-pity or despair. Put on hope and faith instead. Put on strength and courage and pure love.

Live your day as though you are nearer each day to your very best self. With God on your side, your hope is never in vain.

September 13 :
Give Better Gifts

It is a great thing to be generous in giving, but it is a heroic task to withhold your gifts so you can give others what is truly better!

"Every good and perfect gift is from above, coming down from the Father of lights, with whom can be no variation, nor turning shadow."
- James 1:17, WEB

It is never easy to withhold ourselves from giving our loved ones what they want. If we could only afford it, we'd give them all we possibly could and never deprive them of anything they could ever ask.

What father could say no to his son if he asks him for a toy he wants? Or what mother could bear the tears of her daughter if she asks to eat her favorite snack?

Even with other people we barely know, we find it hard to refuse anyone who comes to us who are in desperate need for something. Our natural love for others prompt us to be of help whenever we can and to immediately help those who are in pain.

Sometimes though, what could really help other people are not the things we could give them. In fact, some gifts could even make their situation worse!

What can help others at times is an opportunity to learn and to help themselves, a chance to be strong, a season to discover what they really need to be happy.

A good father or mother must never give in to the cries of a child if the child asks for anything that could harm him!

We must have the wisdom to know when it is wise to give and when it is better to wait and to leave things in the hand of God. By doing so, we are able to give others not just what they want but what they really need, we are able to give far better and lasting gifts!

September 14 :

Surpassing a Mother's Love

God's love surpasses even a mother's love, and it is a love that no one could ever take away from us.

Can a woman forget her nursing child,
that she should not have compassion on the son of her womb?
Yes, these may forget,
yet I will not forget you!
– Isaiah 49:15, WEBBE

A mother's love may be the purest and most tender love we know. Whenever we get hurt as children, we run to our mothers. Whenever we feel sad or afraid, we know our mother would be there to comfort us. A mother would sacrifice her all for her children. She would offer up even her own life for their good!

Can we now imagine how tender and pure God's love is? Even if a mother may forget her own child, God promised He never would! Even if a mother may fail to love her own child, God never would.

God's love is a love that can never fail. It is a love that would always remain fervent, pure and unselfish. It is a love that is the source of all goodness, all beauty and all happiness.

September 15 :

Unmerited Grace

You don't have to deserve God's grace, you only need to receive it with an open heart.

From his fullness we all received grace upon grace. For the law was given through Moses. Grace and truth were realised through Jesus Christ. – John 1:16-17, WEBBE

What is grace? It is to receive a favor totally unmerited and undeserved. It is to be loved without condition or any strings attached. It is to be shown benevolence without being asked for anything in return.

To be given grace is to be given a great treasure. It is to be offered help without losing your dignity. It is to be understood and appreciated for who you are, not for what you have or what you can give back.

It is like the sun shining quietly and giving warmth to everyone even if everyone is so busy doing something else. It is like the rain quenching the thirst of the earth for free. It is like a mother taking care of her son, not minding her lack of sleep, not asking for anything but to be allowed to love and to give ever more.

September 16 :
Give Things That Last

To be able to be good givers, we need not only be generous, we need also to be wise.

"For the wages of sin is death, but the free gift of God is eternal life in Christ Jesus our Lord." - Romans 6:23, WEB

We may have experienced giving again and again to someone until we feel so empty and exhausted that we wonder whether everything we ever did was in vain. What have we done wrong? Why is it that others could never seem to be satisifed with all that they have received?

Sometimes, the answer is not in whether we have given enough, but in whether we have chosen well what to give.

There are many gifts that can give temporary happiness. They quickly give excitement to those we give, and they too, may think that our gifts are the answer to their prayers.

Soon however, they feel dissatisfied again and start to ask for other things. This cycle goes on with people really having no clear idea what could make them truly satisfied.

We must pray then that what we give has an enduring value. More than fleeting excitement, it must be able to satisfy the soul. More than material wants, it must be able to heal emotional and spiritual wounds that hinder people from receiving true happiness.

September 17 :

Let Love Change You

It is love alone that can change the human heart.

"I will give them one heart, and I will put a new spirit within you; and I will take the stony heart out of their flesh, and will give them a heart of flesh; that they may walk in my statutes, and keep my ordinances, and do them: and they shall be my people, and I will be their God." - Ezekiel 11:19-20, WEB

We can go on trying to change people by fear, by anger or by humiliation, and we can just go on failing again and again. It is love alone that can change a human heart, and it is love alone that can redeem a human soul.

Without love within, all the external changes we can make will never last.

Without love guiding our way, we are forever lost.

For it is not in what we have or what we do that we can find the meaning of life. It is always in who we are, and we only discover who we really are in LOVE.

When we start to love, we start also to be changed, to be changed for the better and for good!

It may not happen at once, but through seasons of blessed struggle, love finds its way and occupies all of our being.

We finally change because then we become finally free. It is in love that we find true freedom, the freedom to be happy and to be good.

Let love change you. Then, as that love takes over your whole being, let it overflow unto others, changing every heart it blesses along the way.

September 18 :
Find The Answers in God

We often look so long because we fail to look where all the answers could be found: in God.

When they didn't find him, they returned to Jerusalem, looking for him. After three days they found him in the temple… - Luke 2:45-46, WEBBE

There are times when we may feel lost. We try our very best to find our way, but we only end up becoming even more lost than we have been. We ask for directions but none could point us to the right path.

There are times also when we feel helpless. Other people may try to tell us what we ought to do and how, but we are powerless to even begin. None of those we sought could accompany us and give us the strength we need to carry on.

During such times, why not try to find your answers in God? Why not try to ask Him what others have failed to provide you? Why not go to the One who has been waiting for you all along?

September 19 :
In Forgiveness Starts Healing

Revenge can never give true peace.

Confess your offences to one another, and pray for one another, that you may be healed. – James 5:16, WEBBE

It's seem so easy when we talk about forgiveness, but it's never easy when we are the ones hurt. But we can take comfort in knowing that when God forgave us,He also took all the pain and hurt. He doesn't offer us cheap forgiveness.

Whenever Jesus Christ extends His merciful heart to us, we know that such a heart was not a heart that remained safe in a faraway heaven, but a heart that has been pierced, a heart that is gravely wounded and that knows how it is to suffer.

Let us pray that we may know Jesus' mercy more, that we may learn more of His passion and suffering so that we may also learn from Him how it is to forgive.

When we forgive, we stop expecting healing from the person who hurt us. We instead ask for healing from God, the only one who can bind up our wounds and make us whole again.

September 20 :
Too Busy To Be Good?

It isn't enough to be busy doing things. The question is, "What are we being so busy about?"

But Martha was distracted with much serving, and she came up to him, and said, "Lord, don't you care that my sister left me to serve alone? Ask her therefore to help me." Jesus answered her, "Martha, Martha, you are anxious and troubled about many things, but one thing is needed. Mary has chosen the good part, which will not be taken away from her." – Luke 10:40-42, WEBBE

Our busy world seems to tell us that as long as we are busy doing something, we're already busy being good people. But is that the case? Have we thought about how well we're spending our time daily? Have we been so caught up in the hectic schedule of our days that we easily get irritated when we're interrupted or when somebody delays what we wanted to accomplish?

Don't be so busy that you don't have time anymore to be good. Don't be too busy that you don't have the time anymore to lend a hand. Don't be too busy that you don't have time anymore to smile. Don't be too busy that you don't have time anymore to be patient. Don't be too busy that you don't have time anymore to love.

September 21 :
A Deep and Abiding Love

If your love is true, you must not only love deeply, you must also love faithfully.

Many men claim to be men of unfailing love,
but who can find a faithful man?
-Proverbs 20:6, WEBBE

There is a love that has grown slowly yet ever so deeply. This kind of love is not one that arrives with a lot of noise, excitement and thrill. It is not a love that promises much yet fails to live up to its own promises.

Rather, this love is a love that grew little by little. It became faithful from day to day and grew stronger through time. It is a love that was able to hang on in good times and in bad, in exciting times and in seemingly boring days. It is a love that has learned to be patient. And because it has been patient, it has grown deep.

When it grew deeply, this love could not be brought down anymore by any passing storm. Its roots could no longer be torn away by fierce winds. It has become a love that can withstand what's difficult and tough because it is firmly planted in faith, hope and true humility.

This is a love that can truly last: a deep, abiding and faithful love.

September 22 :
Have Faith!

Will the Lord who died for you ever betray you and turn His back on you?

Return to your rest, my soul,
for the LORD has dealt bountifully with you.
For you have delivered my soul from death,
my eyes from tears,

268

and my feet from falling.
-Psalm 116:7-8, WEBBE

You've got to have faith. God has not failed you yet, and God never will!

When you go to Him in prayer, will He not hear you? Will He not have mercy on you? And if He gives you His mercy, will He hold back any good thing from you?

Is God so unloving that He will not provide for the needs of His children? Or is God so weak that He cannot have the power to grant us what is good for us?

Have faith for God is love. Love only desires to give good things. And if He cannot grant us exactly what we asked, we have the comfort of knowing He will give us what is even better!

September 23 :
    What The Future Holds

We should have courage for the future; the God of love, strength and wisdom is already there.

...for it is an easy thing in the sight of the Lord
to swiftly and suddenly make a poor man rich.
The Lord's blessing is in the reward of the godly.
He makes his blessing flourish in an hour that comes swiftly...
In the day of good things, evil things are forgotten.
In the day of evil things, a man will not remember things that are good.
For it is an easy thing in the sight of the Lord
to reward a man in the day of death according to his ways.
The affliction of an hour causes delights to be forgotten.
In the end, a man's deeds are revealed.
– Sirach 11:21-27, WEBBE

Who could tell what could happen tomorrow? Those who are rich could suddenly find themselves poor. Those who are laughing could suddenly find themselves weeping. Those who are proud could find themselves humbled. Those who have many friends could find themselves all alone.

On the other hand, those who are poor could suddenly find themselves rich. Those who are weeping could find themselves able to smile and laugh. Those who are humble could find themselves lifted up by God. And those who are alone may find family and friends who will really love them.

Who could tell what the future holds? Only God can. And we trust the One who holds our future. We trust in His wisdom, in His power, and in His love.

September 24 :
    God as Our Friend

God is our most precious friend. We can find no other. His friendship will last for all eternity. Nothing can ever tear it down.

For one will hardly die for a righteous man. Yet perhaps for a righteous person someone would even dare to die. But God commends his own love towards us, in that while we were yet sinners, Christ died for us.– Romans 5:7-8, WEBBE

God is the most faithful friend we could ever have. He will not lie to us. He will never betray us or let us down. What He could do for our good He will certainly do even if it would cost Him His life. And He has died for us while we were still His enemies, that through His resurrection, we may have true life.

We often boast of our earthly friends. We are proud of our friends in power or those with great wealth. Yet how many of such friends could really be there for us in times of great need? How many can sacrifice their comfort so they can help us? And how many are ready to willingly lay down their lives for our sake?

What Fills My Heart With Joy

My heart is filled with joy because of God's wonderful love for me.

270

Weak and small that I am, He takes notice of me and witnesses my life.
He takes me as I am and fashions me after His own glory.
He takes away my shame and my brokenness.
He heals my wounds.
He makes me beautiful and strong.
I will always look forward for that morning when He makes everything new.
Within my heart shall always dwell His voice, and I shall never be alone.
Wisdom is His constant gift, and respect, an eternal blessing as love.
Who would appreciate my small tokens of love? It is He who does not disregard my smallest efforts and my meekest prayers.
Who has planned the best things for me? It is He who has my welfare in mind for all eternity.
My short life is but a vapor that fades, but He grants me a life that never ends.
I am poor and have nothing, but mansions He has prepared for me where He is.
I cry and He wipes away my tears.
I run in grief, but He pursues me, and He wins me back with His words of love.
He shows me the value of each heartbreak,
the cost of every tear.
He shows me how each sorrow can turn to joy
a joy that never fades.
People may hunger now, but they shall be filled.
People may mourn, but they shall be comforted.
We shall receive far more than what we have lost,
and far more than what we could ever dream about.
He is just, but He is also merciful.
He reigns from on high, yet He is never out of our reach.
He is my Father, but He is also like a Mother who loves her children
each one is valuable, no one is dispensable,
each one loved as though she were her only child.
I have my questions but He answers them one by one,
I have my doubts, but He fills my soul with faith.
Where can I go that He cannot follow?
What wrong can I do that He cannot forgive?
There is nothing that can ever separate me away from Him,

and there is no one who could take away these things that fill my heart with the Joy of Him!

September 25 :
Do Not Despair

Do not give in to despair. There is always hope!

"Behold, I will do a new thing. It springs forth now. Don't you know it? I will even make a way in the wilderness, and rivers in the desert." - Isaiah 43:19, WEB

Even when we think there could never be a way... Even if we feel we could never be happy again... We must go on believing and we must never lose hope.

If ever we are visited by feelings of discouragement and of hopelessness, we must remember that it can never come from God.

What comes from God is always light, and in that light, we start to see a way. Because God Himself is the way. He has made all things and in any moment, He can make all things new!

It is not for us to think how such a way can be made. It is for us to rest in faith and to trust the One who can. It is not for us to close the door and shut ourselves in the dark, it is for us to wait until God Himself walks in and creates the miracle we need!

September 26 :
True Friendship

Do we love God only for His benefits or do we love Him for who He really is?

Greater love has no one than this, that someone lay down his life for his friends. – John 15:13, WEBBE

There are friendships made for the sake of meeting each other's needs. There are also friendships made only for the sake of pleasurable times. A person may consider himself having many friends, but if most of his friends are built only for the sake of getting tangible benefits or deriving fleeting pleasures, can one still say that he has many friends?

True friendship consists of people who desire only the good of the other. True friendship does not count what one gives or how much one could take. It does not live upon our changing wants and passions. Rather, it endures even difficult times and lives long after our initial attractions have passed.

It is the same with our friendship with God. Do we say we are His friends just because He will make things easier for us in this life? Do we want to be His friends because of the gifts He can bestow upon us? Or do we love God for who He really is?

What is our greatest desire? To use God's friendship so we can acquire the earthly things we want? Or to love God Himself, the giver of everything that is good?

September 27 :
    With You All Along

You are never alone. Even when you think everybody else has walked out of your life, even if you think your closest friends have rejected you and forgotten you, have faith still that you are not alone.

"Can a woman forget her nursing child, that she should not have compassion on the son of her womb? Yes, these may forget, yet I will not forget you!" - Isaiah 49:15, WEB

In times when even God seems distant and silent, think not that He has cast you away. For His silence is as near an answer as His promptings. And His veil is as as kind and gentle as His light.

It takes a far deeper love to hide the good that we do so it can work out something better. It takes a far greater mercy to withhold immediate relief so you can offer true healing and recovery.

273

God has not left you. You may not feel His presence, but He is closer to you now, strengthening you in ways only His wisdom and love could ever know.

One day you will finally understand. And when the eyes of your heart has finally been opened, you will see that God has always loved you, that God has always been with you all along.

September 28 :
Our Greatest Longing

If we can only become really honest with ourselves we'd realize that our heart's greatest longing is none other but God Himself.

"…delight yourself in the LORD,
and he will give you the desires of your heart."
-Psalm 37:4, WEBBE

How good is God! How good indeed is He.
While I asked what He desires of me to be,
 He sent the question back to me.
What is it that you desire, He asked.
What is it that you long for the most?
He who is King and who is to be served
is concerned with my heart and asks.
He does not impose.
Rather, He honors our hearts' purest desires,
 for He knows that within it
 is a great good He Himself has made.
He desires for us our greatest joy.
 Shall we have the courage to find out
and to pursue what it is we desire most of all?

September 29 :
God Blesses Our Gifts

God accepts whatever gift we can best offer Him. If it is health, God accepts our health and all that we can do with our labors. If it is sickness, God accepts our sickness and our pain. If it is praise, it is praise He receives with gladness. If it is misery, then it is misery He welcomes with open arms.

They told him, "We only have here five loaves and two fish." He said, "Bring them here to me." He commanded the multitudes to sit down on the grass; and he took the five loaves and the two fish, and looking up to heaven, he blessed, broke and gave the loaves to the disciples, and the disciples gave to the multitudes. They all ate, and were filled. - Matthew 14:17-20, WEB

Whatever state in life we are in, whether we are rich or poor, whether strong or in weakness, God receives from us all that we can offer Him. He honors each gift, each sincere thought, each sacrifice that we do out of love.

We need not be afraid that we can offer Him nothing, because He is the One who provides, and He is the One who blesses all our gifts, multiplying each one in His Grace and in His Love.

September 30 :
Acceptance and Hope

We must accept the times when it is not within our ability to help other people. Let us not despair however, because we have hope in God.

Trust in Yahweh with all your heart, and don't lean on your own understanding.
In all your ways acknowledge him, and he will make your paths straight.
Don't be wise in your own eyes. Fear Yahweh, and depart from evil.
It will be health to your body, and nourishment to your bones.
-Proverbs 3:5-8, WEB

275

True humility calls us into the truth of what we can and what we cannot do. We may sincerely desire to do more, yet our capacities and resources may not allow such to be done. We may want to be of help to those we love most, yet it may not be our help that they truly need.

Once we start to realize the limits of what we cannot do, we also begin to understand what God can do. Instead of trying to do everything on our own, let us put those we cannot handle in God's faithful hands.

Pray and do your very best. And at the proper time, leave all else to God who can make miracles happen before your very eyes!

OCTOBER

October 1 :

    To Love Your Enemies

To love is not to tolerate evil but to seek the good. To forgive is not to forego justice but to find healing.

"But I tell you, love your enemies, bless those who curse you, do good to those who hate you, and pray for those who mistreat you and persecute you, that you may be children of your Father who is in heaven." – Matthew 5:44-45, WEB

To love your enemies is not to consent to evil or to rejoice at the damage it has done. It is not to remain in a state of being abused. It is not to stop seeking from relief. It is not to hinder justice.

To love your enemies is to stop the cycle of pain, hate and suffering. It is to show mercy. It is to guard your peace and to protect the joy in your heart. It is to flee from the stain of sin.

You are not God. You can easily misjudge someone or inflict punishments that are far heavier than the sins committed. You can easily turn to the evil you so despised. When that happens, you will only be shamed, and your suffering much worse.

God does not sleep. No one can escape His justice. Would you rather that you defend yourself or that God Himself defends you?

October 2 :

    Wisdom From Above

We cannot rule wisely without allowing the God of wisdom to rule upon our hearts and minds.

...because the foolishness of God is wiser than men, and the weakness of God is stronger than men. For you see your calling, brothers, that not many are wise according to the flesh, not many mighty, and not many noble; but God chose the foolish things of the world that he might put to shame those who are wise. -1 Corinthians 1:25-27, WEB

277

Our human wisdom could never compare to God's wisdom. We are from below, while He is from above. We see but a little, while He sees all. He sees everything that was, that is and that is yet to come. His eyes can penetrate beyond the outer shells of our defenses. His gaze is like a sword that pierces through our masks.

If we are to avoid disastrous consequences, we should always ask for the guidance of God's wisdom. Without it, we are like blind men groping through various obstacles and traps. We may think we are going towards the right direction, but in truth, we may be headed for a deadend or a place where we do not truly wish to go.

Trust in the wisdom of Him who created the heavens and the stars and who put the mountains and hills where they are. Trust in Him who held back the waves of the seas and who determined the boundaries of the deep and of the earth.

October 3 :
    Where Are You Going?

It is not enough that you enjoy the journey, the more important thing is to know where you are headed for.

Enter in by the narrow gate; for wide is the gate and broad is the way that leads to destruction, and many are those who enter in by it. How narrow is the gate, and restricted is the way that leads to life! Few are those who find it. - Matthew 7:13-14, WEB

We cannot go on living without knowing where we are headed for. Days pass by so quickly and soon we will realize that we have but a little time left. What have we done with the time given us. Have we arrived nearer to where we wished to go?

Let us not be distracted by passing pleasures and short-lived amusements. Some roads may appear attractive, but they may lead us astray eventually. He who is a wise traveller brings with him a map so as not to be lost. He avoids the paths that will deter him from reaching his destination and takes the safest route to arrive where he desires to go.

One day we shall see how our journey has lasted but for a moment. We must never endanger our eternal treasures for fleeting desires.

October 4 :
To Love God Above All

To love God is to finally find happiness.

"You shall love the Lord your God with all your heart, with all your soul, with all your strength, and with all your mind; and your neighbour as yourself." – Luke 10:27, WEBBE

To love God above all does not mean that we love our neighbors less. When we put God above all else, we are able to love our neighbors more. We no longer love them for what they can give to us or for what they can do. We no longer love them because of our own selfish interests, but because of the love we have received from God. Through God, our love is purified; it becomes a holy and healing love. It is not a love that aims merely to please others. It is not a love concerned with temporary comfort or pleasures. But it is a love that desires what is truly good for all. It is a love that is tender, and it is a love that is courageous and strong! It does not depend on men's praise or approval. It does not fade with difficulties or trials. Rather, it is a love that endures, a love that gives true joy, a love that saves.

October 5 :
Our Silent Testimony

Sometimes we say more when we speak less.

In the same way, wives, be in subjection to your own husbands; so that, even if any don't obey the Word, they may be won by the behaviour of their wives without a word… - 1 Peter 3:1,WEBBE

Sometimes, it is the silent testimony of one's life that speaks the loudest. It is not the words we say or preach; it is how we live our lives and how we live out what we are trying to preach.

279

Words sometimes evoke defensiveness upon those who hear. We wanted to say something, but they hear something else. Instead of hearing our love, they hear our rejection. Instead of hearing encouragement, they hear our judgment.

When words are seen as an offense, our silence could be tangible signs of acceptance and understanding. By our mere presence, we can communicate our desire to help. By our smile we can convey our friendship.

Even when we are misunderstood, our silence can mean a lot. Through our silent suffering, we are able to communicate our patience. Through our tears, we allow outbursts of anger to flow as sorrow borne for those we love.

October 6 :
   Judge Not So Quickly

Judge not prematurely. Give others some benefit of doubt. Only God knows all things and all that could ever happen.

Don't judge,
and you won't be judged.
Don't condemn,
and you won't be condemned.
Set free,
and you will be set free.
– Luke 6:37, WEBBE

To refrain from judging other people is not to stop trying to discern or to see things wisely. It is not to refrain from trying to know what is right and what is wrong.

Rather, to refrain from judging others is to prevent forming untimely conclusions. It is to avoid thinking that we already know everything when in so many cases, we know not much at all.

We must stop judging from the external alone because there is so much that we do not see. We must stop judging from our experiences alone because there is so much that we do not yet understand.

280

How can we say that we already know everything about another person when there is so much that we don't even know yet about ourselves?

How can we conclude that a person's life would never change for the better when we can't even guarantee that our lives won't change for the worse?

Instead of seeing ourselves as all-knowing and all-seeing, let us humble ourselves and acknowledge our own smallness. Instead of quickly judging by mere appearances, let us ask God to help us see from the heart.

But with me it is a very small thing that I should be judged by you, or by man's judgment. Yes, I don't judge my own self. For I know nothing against myself. Yet I am not justified by this, but he who judges me is the Lord. Therefore judge nothing before the time, until the Lord comes, who will both bring to light the hidden things of darkness, and reveal the counsels of the hearts. Then each man will get his praise from God. – 1 Corinthians 4:3-5, WEBBE

October 7 :
Love and Courage

Only Love can make us brave!

The LORD is my light and my salvation. Whom shall I fear? The LORD is the strength of my life. Of whom shall I be afraid? - Psalm 27:1, WEBBE

To love is to not be afraid. It is to be braver than you thought you were. It is to be far more courageous than you ever thought you could be.

When you love, you learn to be strong. You may still feel nervous, but you fight the fear and you go on fighting for the one you love. For the sake of your beloved, you forget your own cares. You overcome all else that worries you and troubles you.

All fear starts to fade away once you learn that the only thing you're afraid of is to lose the one you love.

October 8 :
Little Things Matter

Sometimes, it's the small deeds done with great love that can change the world.

Indeed, who despises the day of small things? - Zechariah 4, WEB

We often dream of great deeds that will make our name known throughout the world. We desire to make a big difference in the lives of others. We want to accomplish heroic tasks to prove our worth, and to be a witness that we have lived meaningful lives.

Many times however, it is the little things that can make a big difference. It is the simple lives that can truly count.

In truth, we avoid the little things because it is the little things that we fear. We know that it is the small things that are concrete and real in our daily lives. And it is the small sacrifices we make that can truly hurt.

To forego small offenses and forgive a hurting word, to give courtesy and respect where it is rare, to give attention to someone who is speaking, to do a tedious chore no one else wants to do, to wake up early so you can pray, to not brag about your accomplishment, to not spread false reports, to keep silent when there is nothing good to be said. These are small things, but may we have the courage to do them and thereby live heroic lives everyday.

October 9 :
Hidden in Thy Wounds

There is no safer place to hide than within the wounds of Christ.

He himself bore our sins in his body on the tree, that we, having died to sins, might live to righteousness. You were healed by his wounds. - 1 Peter 2:24, WEB

It is not during the times when we were most confident that we experience the deepest intimacy. It is not when we feel most beautiful that we feel the most loved.

On the contrary, it is during the times when we are most down that we feel the warmest embrace. It is during the times when we feel most repulsive that we feel most accepted and cared for.

Our wounds are quite often the very keys that open the path towards true happiness. It is there when we learn what sincerity is, and what true sacrifice means.

Jesus comes right when we feel we do not deserve His gifts. He carries us in His arms and saves us. In our darkest hour, He provides the light and grants us the happiness we have long been searching for.

October 10 :
Be Happy

Be happy. And let your happiness spread wherever you may go.

My son... treat yourself well... Don't defraud yourself of a good day. -Sirach 14, WEBBE

Sometimes, holiness is simply being happy. It is in being able to live your life with the heart of a child, not burdened by the past or worried about the future. It is being in the moment and being able to find joy where you are.

Many times, we tend to think only of suffering when we think about sanctity. And while it is true that love entails sacrifice, love also means much joy, true joy! The kind of joy the world today has almost forgotten. That happiness that lifts up the soul, that urges one to pray in thanksgiving, and that makes even the heaviest of burdens light and sweet.

283

WHY NOT?

You ask me why I'm happy?

I am happy because I have a great inheritance.
My Father is the King of the Universe,
And I am a daughter of royal blood.

My time never runs out
For my time is forever;
Never will I worry of the moment,
For mine are the eternal reaches of time.

My peace surpasses the understanding of the wisest men
For it is a peace that never shatters
With the most troubling shadows of the night.
It is a peace that comes from the spring of letting go,
Completely letting go.

You ask me why I'm happy?
I ask you rather, why not?

October 11 :
The Power of Prayer and Sacrifice

God is never deaf to the prayer of a sincere heart.

She, weeping, looked up towards heaven; for her heart trusted in
the Lord. -Daniel 13:35, WEBBE

Never think that there is nothing you can do. Your power does not
depend on your strength or your riches. Your power comes from
above, and you unlock that power through prayer and sacrifice.

Through prayer, you come before the very presence of God.
Through sincerity of heart, your spirit is moved by faith and by love.
Faith that can move even mountains. And love that can overcome
all things!

And when you offer your prayer with sacrifice, your love becomes fully manifest. It is no longer a love that is invoked only in words. It becomes a love that is proven by tears.

October 12 :
Don't Forget To Smile

Our happiness must come from the simple fact of knowing we are loved.

You will show me the path of life.
In your presence is fullness of joy.
In your right hand there are pleasures forever more.
- Psalm 16:11, WEBBE

The darkness that we see over the world can sap away our hopes for a better future. Slowly, in the drudgery of everyday troubles and frustrations, we go weary of life. Our strength is exhausted; our hearts are broken with pain.

We almost forget that the sun still shines somewhere, that dark clouds cannot last. We almost forget that we have seen happy times also, and they can still come again.

Through all the difficulties of everyday life, forget not your memories of laughter. Through all the times of solitude, forget not the friendships you have shared.

Even if you think you have not been fortunate enough in the past, cling to the gift that is given you today. You are given life and with that life, an opportunity to find the greatest yearnings of your heart.

Don't forget to smile. Smile for visions of hope, of love, and of new adventures. Smile for all the wonderful things that can still happen in your life.

October 13 :

Our Greatest Triumphs

Our greatest triumphs are not always won in moments when we are strongest or most confident. Many times, they are won when we feel we are weakest or most vulnerable.

Therefore I take pleasure in weaknesses, in injuries, in necessities, in persecutions, in distresses, for Christ's sake. For when I am weak, then am I strong. – 2 Corinthians 12:10, WEB

It is easy to smile when problems don't come our way. It is easy to give something when we ourselves are not in need. It is easy to hope when you are not in despair. It is easy to love for as long as you are also loved.

It is in moments of weakness that our faith is truly tested. It is in moments of pain that our loved is purified as through fire.

When everything seems against us, and when every spark of hope seems gone, and we are still able to choose to believe, it is then that we have reached true triumph. When we get nothing for all the love that we have given, when all we get is silence for all the good we have done, and still we continue to do every good we can for the sake of those we love, it is then that we have become truly human and truly a friend of God.

October 14 :

If You Want To Save Me

It is love alone that saves.

I have come as a light into the world, that whoever believes in me may not remain in the darkness. If anyone listens to my sayings, and doesn't believe, I don't judge him. For I came not to judge the world, but to save the world. – John 12:46-47, WEBBE

If you really want to save another person, save him with you prayer, save him with the silent testimony of your holy life, save him with

286

love. Do not try to save him with your judgments, with your mockery, with your hatred.

For you will hear his answers to your questions and you will never listen with your heart. You will hear his explanations and you will never understand.

You will think you are bringing your light when all that you really bring is your darkness. You will think you are bringing grace when all that you bring is condemnation.

A wounded soul does not need an argument. A wounded soul needs compassion and healing. A blind man does not need an eloquent speech. A blind man needs God's miracle to open up his eyes and see.

October 15 :
The Value of Suffering

For a loving God to ever allow any suffering, there must be something really valuable in it.

It is good for me that I have been afflicted, that I may learn your statutes. –Psalm 119:71, WEB

The value of suffering is quite often invisible to us until suffering has passed and done its work. While we are suffering, all we can feel is the pain, and all that we can see is its darkness. In suffering, we feel so alone, even abandoned. We are like lost souls that do not know how to find its way back.

After suffering has done its work however, we learn how it is able to do for us what we cannot do for ourselves. We can finally see how it has changed us, purified us and even strengthened us. We learn how it has opened our spiritual eyes, how it has taught us much wisdom.

Suffering instills in us compassion for those who hurt, understanding for those who are lost. It helps us see what apathy does. It makes us see clearly what evil can do and how powerless we are against it if not for God's grace.

287

God could have saved the world without suffering, but He chose to save it by undergoing even death itself. He has succeeded not merely in defeating pain but in overcoming it. He has given dignity to those who suffer and He is able to give all those who weep far more happiness than they have lost.

October 16 :
God as the Giver of Gifts

In God is wisdom and power and love and every good thing we can ever have.

Now there are various kinds of gifts, but the same Spirit. There are various kinds of service, and the same Lord. There are various kinds of workings, but the same God, who works all things in all. But to each one is given the manifestation of the Spirit for the profit of all... But the one and the same Spirit produces all of these, distributing to each one separately as he desires. – 1 Corinthians 12:4-7,11, WEBBE

God is the true giver. From Him comes all good things, all that can ever give us happiness. He is the author of life, the source of all created things, both seen and unseen. Without His providence, no being can continue to exist.

God indeed gives us the world and all we need to live. And in addition to this, He gives each of us a special gift, a gift that is unique only to us, to the kind of person we are. He does not give everyone the same gifts, and sometimes, this is why we sometimes ask why we are not given what our neighbors have. Only God, in His wisdom knows what gifts are fit for us, gifts that will bless not only us, but those around us. It is not for us to question His wisdom or generosity. Rather, we should thank Him for His kindness and for His love.

October 17 :
Your New Name

You cannot even imagine how happy you will be when God Himself bestows upon you your heavenly name.

To him who overcomes, to him I will give of the hidden manna, and I will give him a white stone, and on the stone a new name written, which no one knows but he who receives it. - Revelation 2, WEB

We take a lot of time and effort to make a name for ourselves, even to earn titles that will distinguish us from the rest of men. We take great pride in them and we feel offended whenever someone belittles our name, our ancestry or our title.

But what is an earthly title? It is but a vapor that quickly fades, a crown that is easily forgotten, stolen and thrown away.

Even earthly rulers lose their power and those with great names lose their reputation. Emperors have been overthrown and kings have been overcome by other kings.

It is not to such titles as frail as these that we should attach our souls into, but to eternal crowns that will never fade, to a name that cannot be taken away.

One day we shall have new names, ones that we have truly earned, ones that will forever be our reward from Him who knows what names we must bear in His heart.

October 18 :
Great Riches in Small Vessels

Consider not your smallness, but the greatness of your God! Consider not what others see, but what God sees in you.

The bee is little amongst flying creatures,
but what it produces is the best of confections.
 Sirach 11:3, WEBBE

289

There are times when others may look down on us, times when we are measured by our stature, our positions, our influence or our riches. There are times when we may find it hard to believe in ourselves anymore and to believe in the great plans God has for us.

During such times, don't believe the many voices that try to put you down! Rather, listen well to the voice of God who loves you and encourages you. He alone knows what great potentials you have. He alone knows what riches are within your eternal soul.

GOD SEES

There are times when I feel
as though nobody knows
what I'm going through –
how sad it is, how empty
how I struggle with pain
that almost overpowers me.
Yes there are times when I'm tempted
to think I'm all alone,
but GOD SEES.

There are times when
I really thought I was doing something good
for someone I love
but then that loved one
misunderstands
and I feel as though every effort
I've made were in vain.
Yes, it felt so bad
and it seemed all my works were useless,
but GOD SEES.

How often have we wanted
others to see who we truly are
or what's really going on
deep down inside,
but try as we might
we are either rejected
or passed by unnoticed
as though we didn't matter,
as though we weren't there?

For all such times
and for all such hurts
may we always remember
that though people may fail to see
and may fail to know,
there is One who always knows,
who knows us so intimately.
Everyone else's eyes may go blind,
but GOD SEES.

October 19 :
A Time For Rest

You are not alone. Be still and know that you have a God and that He loves you very very much.

"You will be saved in returning and rest. Your strength will be in quietness and in confidence." – Isaiah 30:15, WEBBE

It is not always a time for running and striving. It is not always a time for battles and for spears. There is a time for rest and silence, a time for reflection and renewing of one's strength.

If you cannot carry on, surrender your burdens to God and let Him carry you. Let Him take away your worries. Let Him wipe your every tear.

We have a Father in heaven who cares for us and watches over us. Things do not always depend upon our strength.

Spend some days of quiet and try to hear His gentle voice guiding you within. Listen to the sounds of nature that continue to await the will of Him who brings healing and hope.

Quiet Days

There are times when you have nothing much to say,
when silence is enough to witness your day,
and you need that space just to be
to live

to go on.

You see the world around you
as people go rushing about
to where they ought to go,
and you simply notice
and see
and accept.

Things from the past
are held safely
where they are cherished
but where
they do not disturb
the present moment.

Concerns of the future
are also held safely
where they are thought of
but where
they do not steal
any of
today's joys.

The sun rises
where it ought to rise,
the sun sets
where it ought to retire.
All things happen as they should,
all things happen as they would.

And the quiet in our hearts
surpasses the noise of our times.
We have nothing much to say,
but our hearts are full,
and our souls are filled
with people and things
that truly satisfy.

October 20 :

We cannot receive anything when our hands are always full.

In the beginning, God created the heavens and the earth. The earth was formless and empty. Darkness was on the surface of the deep and God's Spirit was hovering over the surface of the waters. God said, "Let there be light," and there was light. – Genesis 1:1-3, WEBBE

Make space in your life for good things to come in. Open a door. Free up some time out of your busy schedule.

You don't always have to be so full of activities here and there. You don't always have to do the talking.

You can be still for a while and listen. You can allow some space in your heart for new dreams to be born and for God's surprises to take place.

October 21 :
God Works in Mysterious Ways

We are but children in awe of the glory of God!

Where were you when I laid the foundations of the earth …
Whereupon were its foundations fastened?
Or who laid its cornerstone, when the morning stars sang together, and all the sons of God shouted for joy?
– Job 38:4, 6-7, WEBBE

God works in mysterious ways. He turns a simple seed into a mighty tree and a lowly caterpillar into a beautiful butterfly! Who knows what wonders He is accomplishing right now beyond our notice?

There are times when we may grow impatient for we do not see what God is doing. We do not know when He would ever answer our prayers.

293

But God is never idle. In times when we think He is doing nothing, He is already accomplishing something beautiful and great! Quietly He does His work, closing doors that would harm us, paving a way even through the desert to make a way for us, protecting us beyond our knowledge.

Who else is able to collect each drop of water from the sea and make the rain to fall? Who else is able to form the hills and the mountains out of nothing?

Take heart for your answer is coming. It may not arrive at the time or way you want, but if you keep your faith, it will definitely come in the perfect moment. It will not only satisfy you, it will astound you!

October 22 :
God Can Do All Things

Unless you realize how little it is you can really do, you'll never know how infinitely much God can do for you!

Now to him who is able to do exceedingly abundantly above all that we ask or think, according to the power that works in us, to him be the glory in the assembly and in Christ Jesus to all generations forever and ever. Amen. – Ephesians 3:20-21, WEBBE

Do not be discouraged when you learn how little you can do. Learning our human limits and weaknesses should not dishearten us. Rather, it should be the beginning of wisdom and of faith in the God who can do all things.

It is not by our power that we can accomplish much, but it is by God's power. It is not by our strength that we can be confident of victory, but it is by God's strength.

It is not that we should no longer do the best we can, but that even when our best efforts fail, we do not lose hope, because our hope is anchored in God.

Because of this hope, we can persevere. Because of this faith, we can rise again and again even though we may fall.

We know how much God can do. We know how much God loves us! Is there anything He can withhold from those He loves so much?

October 23 :
God Will Provide For You

God will provide for you today. You may not see very far ahead or how this or that problem can be solved in the future, but rest assured God will meet your every need today.

If you then, being evil, know how to give good gifts to your children, how much more will your Father who is in heaven give good things to those who ask him! – Matthew 7:11, WEBBE

It is not always for us to see or understand everything God is doing for us. It is not always for us to know. What we can do is to trust in Him, in God's goodness and in His generosity.

God will provide for you today. He will give you the strength to face your troubles. He will give you grace to avoid evil.

God will provide for you today. He will protect you. He will shower you with His love. He will send you instruments of His comfort and compassion.

God will provide for you just what you need at this very moment. You may not understand yet why He has given you things you didn't ask or withheld some things you prayed for. But one day you will realize how He has only given you what will be good for your eternal destiny.

Have faith! God's providence can never fail.

October 24 :
Stand Firm

Let no one move you from the place God has appointed you to be.

Therefore put on the whole armour of God, that you may be able to withstand in the evil day, and having done all, to stand. – Ephesians 6:13, WEBBE

Sometimes, what we need to do is not to seek new grounds or explore new horizons. Sometimes, we already know the task God has given us to do. We already know where we ought to fight our battles. What remains to be done is to stand firm in the path where we are.

No matter how strong the winds may blow, we must not let our courage be swayed. No matter how dark the night may be, we must not lose sight of the coming dawn.

Stand firmly where God has planted you. Keep your hopes up! Never give up.

God will give you the strength to withstand the fiercest storms. Let Him uphold you and keep you where you ought to be!

October 25 :
Overcome Your Fears

When God tells us not to fear, He will also give us the power and the courage to obey His will.

For God didn't give us a spirit of fear, but of power, love, and self-control. - 2 Timothy 1:7, WEB

Many times, our troubles appear bigger than they really are. From a distance, they look menacing. It's as though they have all the power in the world to defeat us.

Once we gain the courage to face them however, we often see them for what they really are. We begin to see how they are not as frightening as we thought them to be. Sometimes they disappear. And many times, we find out we've already grown much stronger and bigger the moment we gained the courage to face them. We find out we've become capable after all in overcoming our greatest fears.

296

October 26 :
    To Be Gentle

We rarely realize how much power there is in kindness, and how much strength there is in gentleness.

"Behold, my servant, whom I uphold;
my chosen, in whom my soul delights…
He will not shout,
nor raise his voice,
nor cause it to be heard in the street.
He won't break a bruised reed.
He won't quench a dimly burning wick."
-Isaiah 42:1-3, WEB

There are many people whose burdens are so heavy they are like boats full of stones. The weight that they carry is so much already they could hardly stay afloat.

For such people, every additional problem sent their way only makes it harder to carry on. It's as though there comes a time when all it would take for them to sink is just one more painful blow – an insult, a cold shoulder, a harsh word, a rejection.

Think about the burdens other people carry. Let us not be that one more stone that would make their burdens unbearable. Let us not be the final blow that would snuff out what little hope they may have.

Instead, let us be like those who make other people's burdens lighter. Let us be like those who are like quiet stars giving light, giving hope to those who look up to heaven in prayer.

October 27 :
It Takes Time to Heal

God knows our weakness and by His gentleness, He sometimes prefers not to heal us all at once.

...for I am the LORD who heals you. – Exodus 15, WEBBE

It takes time to heal. We may understand things intellectually. We may forgive with our will. But our healing comes in seasons, times of waiting and of rest.

The pain doesn't disappear in an instant. And the things that have been broken and lost are frequently not immediately restored.

When our hearts break, we have to pick up the pieces one by one. We have to start again each day, bearing the pain until we are whole again.

It takes time, but one day, our hearts will finally mend. We shall be stronger, better, more capable of compassion. Take heart! With patience and hope, look forward to that day when you shall regain even more than what you have lost.

I WILL SMILE AGAIN!

I will smile again
Though tears flow from these eyes

I will smile again
And trust tomorrow the sun shall rise

Though darkness may enfold me
Though heavy rain can't help but pour

Though shattered, lost and broken
Though heart could barely bear it all

Though tired and weary and confused
Though badly hurt and bruised

I know that I will smile again
And I will smile again!

October 28 :
Trust in God's Justice and Love

It is because God is merciful that God is also just!

"You shall not take advantage of any widow or fatherless child. If you take advantage of them at all, and they cry at all to me, I will surely hear their cry…" – Exodus 22, WEBBE

We can trust in God's justice because we can trust in God's love. We know He will defend the poor and the oppressed because He is merciful. We know we can let go of our vengeance because He is the One who will defend our cause!

God knows our suffering. He knows how we hurt, how we are beaten up and abused. Trust in Him for He shall not remain silent. He will not tolerate evil nor allow His little ones to be deprived of their due.

The world may not recognize your cries, but trust that God hears. God's heart is so merciful that no tear from His little ones will be beyond His notice. He grieves when you grieve. He weeps when you weep. And when you cry out to heaven, He certainly hears.

October 29 :
We Don't Need Much

There comes a time when we realize we don't really need that much money to be happy.

"You don't have, because you don't ask. You ask, and don't receive, because you ask with wrong motives, so that you may spend it for your pleasures." – James 4:2-3, WEB

How much do we really need to live a joyful life? How much do we really need to live a life of purpose and meaning? Many times, it seems as though we need so many things. But when we come to

299

think of it again in the light of God's providence, we come to realize that we don't really need much.

We only seem to need so many things when we desire what we don't really need. Do we really need such a big house? Do we really need such a luxurious car?

We may not realize it, but we crave for bigger and greater material things because our souls are so empty within. And that is why sometimes, even if we already possess so much, we're still unhappy and unsatisfied.

What do we really need? We need the basic necessities of life. We need enough resources to be of help to others. We need sufficient providence to love. Only by loving can our lives have purpose and joy.

AT THE END OF THE DAY

At the end of the day,
after all the work is done;
At the end of the day,
as we watch the setting sun;

After all the trials,
and after all the pain;
After all the struggles,
to make it through the day;

I thank God for peace and rest,
and for little smiles from you;
I thank God for rising stars,
and for little hugs from you;

For there is no blessing,
such as this I found so true:
It's such a pleasure just walking home
at the end of the day with you!

October 30 :
The Blessings Given Us

There is no room for envy when we realize that our blessings are but gifts to be shared to one another.

Isn't this the fast that I have chosen:
to release the bonds of wickedness,
to undo the straps of the yoke,
to let the oppressed go free,
and that you break every yoke?
Isn't it to distribute your bread to the hungry,
and that you bring the poor who are cast out to your house?
-Isaiah 58:6-7, WEBBE

Your blessings are not for you alone. They are to be shared with others. In the same way, the blessings of other people are not for them alone. They are to be shared with all of those God desires to be blessed.

For this reason, there must be no room for envy. God does not favor one at the expense of another. He gives us gifts that can bless one another. Even the earth is but a gift to be shared by all, to be protected and used as stewards of God.

Let us remember this whenever we have an abundance of blessings from God. Let us not hoard them for our own good alone. But like good stewards, let us share them with all of those who are in need. In keeping a surplus of things we do not need, we deprive others who are in need of them.

October 31 :
To Persevere To The Very End

Perseverance proves the depths of our desires.

Let us not be weary in doing good, for we will reap in due season, if we don't give up. – Galatians 6:9, WEBBE

There are some things we seem to want for a moment. When the next moment comes however, we lose interest in it and we start to pursue other things. What happens is that our dreams vanish just as fast as they have arisen, only to be replaced by other dreams that also fail to be accomplished.

The truly valuable dreams are those that do not disappear quickly. They are those that we pursue even when times are difficult and everything seems to be against us.

It is not that we fail to be realistic, but it's just that deep within us, we know the truth in our dreams. Even when we cannot see exactly how they can happen, we believe that they will. Even when we do not know every step we need to reach it, we have hope they shall be revealed to us in the right time.

We persevere only when something is embedded deeply within our hearts. We do not give up because we know that love never fails.

NOVEMBER

November 1 :

Where Our Loved Ones Go

Herein is our only consolation - that when our loved ones go, they go to Him who is All Love, All Beauty and All Happiness.

Jesus said to her, "I am the resurrection and the life. He who believes in me will still live, even if he dies. Whoever lives and believes in me will never die. -John 11:25, WEB

When we wake up each day, we hardly think about that day when everything will end and this life as we know it will be no more. We may believe in the afterlife, we may even believe in heaven. But when someone we love so much suddenly dies, we wonder if we really believed at all.

Is there really a life after death? Could we possibly see our departed loved ones again? Where could their souls possibly be? How could we be certain they are happy and at peace? All these questions come to mind as we search for answers that our hearts could really believe.

In the end however, our only assurance is the infinite love and mercy of God. It is in His hands that we entrust everything – all that we love, all that we could possibly hope for. In Him who suffered death itself to give us eternal life, we entrust our loved ones. In Him who conquered death and is already victorious, we entrust all our hopes.

Poem of Grieving Loss of a Loved One

Where would you go
that i cannot follow?
for how long must i wait
until we meet again?
what would i do
in times that i miss you?
where would i go
in times when i long to see you again?

How must i spend
the nights without you?
how do i bear
each morning that you're not there?
shall i ever smile again?
will i ever laugh again?
will i ever face the world again
knowing that im not alone?

why must you leave me?
why must i cry these tears
when you're not here
to wipe them all away?
why must i suffer
the empty days without my beloved?
why must i dream
without you by my side?
the days shall never be the same again
i will never be the same again
without you
the life of my soul,
the joy of my heart,
the light in my eyes,
the hope of my dreams,
the comfort of my lonely nights,
without you my beloved,
i grieve and cry,
i grope and stumble in the dark,
i weep with all my soul
i desire with all my heart
i let go of all of me that you took away with you

i keep all of you that is in me,
and will always remain in me
wherever i may go

i wait and pray and hope
i will look forward to each brand new day
thankful for all that i've had and will always have
thankful for the sun that shines again
believing and hanging on
believing that life will go on
it can't help but go on
it shall go on
and in so going
there really is no end
only mornings and evenings
and life that never ever ends.

November 2 :
A Day of Consolation

Our peace comes from believing our loved ones shall one day rise again.

The righteous perish, and no one lays it to heart. Merciful men are taken away, and no one considers that the righteous is taken away from the evil. He enters into peace. - Isaiah 57, WEB

The death of a loved one may fill us with a sense of deep loss and grief. It is a time of parting, a time of looking back and a time of sensing a vacuum in the future. Our hearts may be filled with a mixture of emotions – longing, regret, bitterness, pain.

Yet in all these, it is quite possible to also have consolation. It is possible to still have hope.

For though this day be a day of parting on earth, it is also a day of rejoicing and triumph in heaven. Though this day is a day of emptiness here below, this day is also a day of fullness up there where our loved one finally meets Him who alone can give eternal rest and joy.

Let every parting then be not only a day of loss but of consolation. Let every pain be healed with hope. For in God there is life far better than one we could ever imagine to be. In His arms there is bliss and healing and peace.

The Unbreakable Thread

I cannot understand
how two people
who used to be so close,
whose souls were knit
so tightly together
could suddenly
be parted
and stripped away forever
from each other's arms
mere whispers
used to draw our hearts together,
but now even my loudest cries
fail to bring you back to me
how can it be?
how can you suddenly
be so far away from me?
must I accept your passing
as a fitting end to what we've had?
should I accept that from this moment
there will always be a chasm between us
one that I can never cross
to see you
and to be with you again
not even for a single happy while
have you really gone away
have you really left me
all alone
can't you hear me now as I speak
can't you see me now as I search the skies
for traces of your smile
O how I wish you could see me now
And how I desire that all this time
that I've been praying,
you're really sitting there, listening
gazing at me

loving me
as you've always done before
How I pray
you have not really gone,
that you haven't left my side at all,
not even for a short lonely while
That all the while I have been weeping
you're holding out your hand
catching my every tear
that all the while I have been praying
you're praying with me, too
and with all the angels
in whose company
you now walk amongst
Who knows indeed?
who knows?
maybe you haven't really left
maybe the love we've had
has woven a golden thread
between you and me
a thread that shall remain
as surely as love remains
a thread that shall draw us together
forever
and we'll never ever need
to say goodbye...

November 3 :
Forgiving Those Who Do Not Know

Jesus never accuses us unjustly. He knows that many times, we just don't know what we're doing and so He forgives us and gives us His immeasurable love.

Jesus said, "Father, forgive them, for they don't know what they are doing." – Luke 23:34, WEB

It is never easy to forgive, especially when we have been hurt so much. Even if we want to, how do we do it? Where do we start?

We can start by thinking about Jesus when He prayed for the forgiveness of those who do not know what they are doing.

It may be hard to believe. How can people not know what they are doing?

But in many cases, it is true; we do not know why we have done what we have done. We do not know why we uttered words that could hurt other people. We do not know why we failed to understand those who are dearest to us. We do not know why we failed to be more compassionate and merciful to those who are suffering.

We may be aware of the things we do, but not the entire consequences of our actions. No one may have forced us to do what we have done, but we have failed to reflect on the results of what we did. We often fail to consider other people's feelings. Many times, we regret our actions because we wouldn't have done them had we only known how much hurt and damage they would cause other people.

God is so merciful to us. He knows how ignorant we often are, and He offers us His forgiveness. Let us pray that we may also learn to forgive others who do not know what they do.

And I thank him who enabled me, Christ Jesus our Lord, because he counted me faithful, appointing me to service; although I was before a blasphemer, a persecutor, and insolent. However, I obtained mercy, because I did it ignorantly in unbelief. – 1 Timothy 1:12-13, WEB

November 4 :
   When No One Understands

You always have a True Friend in Jesus.

But he was pierced for our transgressions.
He was crushed for our iniquities.
The punishment that brought our peace was on him;
and by his wounds we are healed.
-Isaiah 53:5, WEBBE

There are times when we feel that no one understands our pain. We tell people how we suffer, but they do not know how deeply we truly hurt.

Where can we find comfort? We feel so alone in the dark that we could hardly believe in the light!

Look to Jesus, the suffering Jesus. Jesus does not merely promise us healing, He shared even our wounds. Jesus does not merely promise us life, He shared even our death!

Before your heart was even broken He knew the depths of your misery. He went before you in the darkness so you will not be alone even there.

Jesus knows your every sigh, your every tear. He has felt your most painful wounds, and He will never leave you alone. He will be right there with you, even when all the world turns away.

November 5 :
   To Find Jesus

When we have at last turned our eyes upon Him, we shall finally see the answer to our prayers. We shall finally know that we were never alone.

"He arose, and came to his father. But while he was still far off, his father saw him, and was moved with compassion, and ran, and fell on his neck, and kissed him." – Luke 15:20, WEBBE

Why must God allow us to suffer without any comfort from men? Why must He allow it that we find no hand to hold us or listening ears to hear our cries?

It is not God's will that we be deprived of family or friends. It is not His desire for anyone to feel alone. All that God desires for us is to be loved, for we are made out of love and for love.

If He ever allows us to feel deserted by people, it is to have the opportunity to have us seek Him and feel His presence. It is to draw

309

us closer to Him, the One who truly loves us most, the One who has always pursued us in His great love!

November 6 :
Refuse No One

If it is Jesus who asks, would you refuse Him?

Come, blessed of my Father, inherit the Kingdom prepared for you from the foundation of the world; for I was hungry, and you gave me food to eat. I was thirsty, and you gave me drink. I was a stranger, and you took me in. I was naked, and you clothed me. I was sick, and you visited me. I was in prison, and you came to me. – Matthew 25:34-36, WEBBE

Helping our brothers and sisters in need do not end by giving them some alms. It is truly fulfilled when we are really able to listen to their needs and when we attend to them with the resources, time and effort that it would take to alleviate their burden.

Quite often however, this is not an easy thing to do. We may be asked to help someone right when we're in the middle of a project. We may need to listen to the concerns of someone just when we're also having a bad day. How do we respond then?

We must always try to respond with love. We respond with the way we wish to be treated. We have often wanted to be invited at famous gatherings. We would certainly feel honored when we're invited by the head of the city or by a king or queen. Why then refuse Jesus when He comes to us as one who thirsts and needs our company?

November 7 :
When We Have Nothing

We can give so much more than what our money could buy. We can give someone our attention, our respect and our kindness.

Most certainly I tell you, because you did it to one of the least of these my brothers, you did it to me. – Matthew 25:40, WEBBE

There are times when we cannot provide what is being asked of us. We may not have enough money. We may not know what to do or what to advice to someone. We may even think ourselves to be less fortunate than they are – more burdened, more in need of money or other things.

But must this be the reason to raise our voice or embarrass those who ask for our help? If we could not even be of help, must we worsen their problems by bringing more darkness and ill will?

We always have something we can give. We can give our understanding and respect. We can give our smile and our sincere prayer that they find the help they're looking for.

November 8 :
 In The Image of God

For even the worst sinner was born in the image of God.

"But if the wicked turns from all his sins that he has committed, and keeps all my statutes, and does that which is lawful and right, he shall surely live. He shall not die. None of his transgressions that he has committed will be remembered against him. In his righteousness that he has done, he shall live. Have I any pleasure in the death of the wicked?" says the Lord GOD; "and not rather that he should return from his way, and live?" – Ezekiel 18:21-23, WEBBE

We must be able to see God in everyone. In the old and in the young. In the rich and in the poor ones. In the healthy and in the sick. In the good and even in those who seem evil.

We are all created in the image of God – capable of loving, capable of doing good. It may be difficult to see this image where people have so chosen to live otherwise, but we must ask for the grace to see it.

311

For as long as a person lives, he is capable of repenting from his ways and changing his heart. He still has a chance to be truly human, truly a vessel of God's love.

Let us leave the judging to God who alone knows the human heart. Our merciful God takes no pleasure in the death of wicked men and we should do the same.

November 9 :
   The Humble Soul

The more a soul humbles herself, the more she is loved by God.

Let your beauty be not just the outward adorning of braiding the hair, and of wearing jewels of gold, or of putting on fine clothing; but in the hidden person of the heart, in the incorruptible adornment of a gentle and quiet spirit, which is in the sight of God very precious. – 1 Peter 3, WEBBE

The humble soul benefits much from the grace of God. She does not lose hope nor does she despair from her imperfections. She knows her littleness, and because she is little she longs to be carried in the arms of her loving Father.

All things belong to the humble soul – truth, wisdom, mercy, love. She is able to receive all good things because she is not afraid to admit that she needs them.

She is content to disappear into obscurity because even in there, she knows she is not alone. She has the love of God, and that is enough, that is all that matters.

She does not need to speak out aloud for her life is already a testimony of God's grace. God Himself will uplift her. God Himself will defend her.

She knows she has nothing by herself, but with God, she possesses everything.

312

November 10 :
Something Good Can Happen

The bad things that happened yesterday could never block the good things God will accomplish for you today.

"Don't remember the former things,
 and don't consider the things of old.
Behold, I will do a new thing.
 It springs out now.
 Don't you know it?
I will even make a way in the wilderness,
 and rivers in the desert…
because I give water in the wilderness and rivers in the desert,
 to give drink to my people, my chosen,
the people which I formed for myself,
 that they might declare my praise."
-Isaiah 43:18-19, WEB

Something good can happen today! Let not your hopes vanish, but let it be strengthened. For we know not what will happen next.

Yesterday was full of troubles, and we cannot see how such can cease. But let not what happened before fill you with thoughts of gloom. Let it not rob you of the good things that can still take place.

For God's mercy is new every morning. Every day He makes the sun to rise. He upholds our every breath! Will He not save those whom He loves? Will He withhold any good thing from those who look forward to His compassion?

Something good can happen today. Begin your day in prayer. The answer you've been waiting for may come tomorrow, or it may come this very day!

November 11 :
Someday Soon

We must believe that no matter how troubled we are today, we have in God a future filled with hope.

313

He will wipe away every tear from their eyes. Death will be no more; neither will there be mourning, nor crying, nor pain, any more. The first things have passed away. – Revelations 21:4, WEBBE

Maybe not today, but one day, someday soon, your troubles will disappear and your tears wiped away. In that day, you will no longer need to ask because you will finally understand. You will discover how your every wound has made you stronger, how your sufferings have purified your love.

You will look back and you will be glad. You will see how you have been led all along to your dreams, to the deepest yearnings of your heart. Every delay had been there for a reason, every detour an answer to take you towards the safest path.

In that day, no sad memory can hurt you anymore because the happiness that shall be yours will be far sweeter, and far deeper than you could have ever dreamt about. You will be in that place where no one could ever take away your joy. You will finally be home and you will never ever be alone.

November 12 :
When God Forgives

When God forgives, He loves.

I, even I, am he who blots out your transgressions for my own sake; and I will not remember your sins. - Isaiah 43:25, WEBBE

"Come now, and let's reason together," says the LORD:
"Though your sins be as scarlet, they shall be as white as snow. Though they be red like crimson, they shall be as wool."
-Isaiah 1:18, WEBBE

When God forgives, He forgives us completely, He forgives us with love.

He does not hold any resentment towards us. He doesn't keep on reminding us of our faults.

He purifies us completely and looks at us seeing only His beloved child, not our past sins, not our previous shame.

The world may judge us. And even if someone forgives us, we may feel always guilty before his eyes.

But with God, all that remains is His love for us. A love so great it washes away every trace of darkness from our hearts, replacing it with the purity of His light.

November 13 :
Let God Heal You

Weary and bruised, God takes you by the hand, wipes away your tears and heals both your wounded body and your broken heart.

Then they cry to the LORD in their trouble,
he saves them out of their distresses.
He sends his word, and heals them...
- Psalm 107:19-20, WEBBE

Let God heal you. Hide not your wounds and your hurts. Present your every tear to God who can wipe them all away.

He knows your pain for He has suffered with you. Never think you are alone, for He Himself has gone through death itself even before you knew what darkness is.

Let God heal you. Let Him mend your heart. Rest in Him and let your soul find comfort in His gentle arms. You need not fear of anything for He will watch over you and keep you safe.

Rest for a while and let God do His work. It is not always for you to do everything. Surrender to your Father's embrace for He has waited so long to catch you and comfort you.

Let your tears fall one by one. Let all bitterness be revealed, let all worries leave your heart. You have a God who cares, who loves you so deeply He will never let you go.

315

November 14 :
Only Love

Only love can redeem us. We only rise up from death if we can live in love.

Love is patient and is kind…- 1 Corinthians 13,WEB

We can reprimand others in anger or force them one way or the other by use of fear, but unless one is changed by love, one is never truly changed. Only love penetrates the heart, and in penetrating its depths, it changes it in a miraculous way.

Let us not be surprised therefore if no matter how loudly we speak, we are not listened to. Let us not be surprised if no matter how we speak eloquently and win intellectually, we draw no one towards our beliefs.

People do not need so much knowledge as they need love. People do not need so much judgment as they need mercy.

November 15 :
One Mind and One Heart

We cannot love with our hearts only. When we love, we love with our hearts, our minds and our souls.

…you shall love the Lord your God with all your heart, and with all your soul, and with all your mind, and with all your strength. – Mark 12:30, WEB

One's mind and one's heart should not work against each other. Rather, both should work for the benefit of the other. We are not asked to leave our feelings in favor of our mind nor should we leave all our reason in favor of our feelings. They should both help us live our lives to the full.

We are human beings with a mind that can think and with a heart that can feel. If we keep on putting off reason because we are overwhelmed by our feelings, there will come a time when even our feelings will suffer much because we have failed to make the right decision.

We are not supposed to live in fragments. We are supposed to be fully human, we are supposed to be whole.

November 16 :
God Weeps With You

He who is infinitely merciful understands your loss, your fears and your hurts. He not only listens to you, He weeps with you and shares your every tear.

When Jesus therefore saw her weeping, and the Jews weeping who came with her, he groaned in the spirit, and was troubled, and said, "Where have you laid him?" They told him, "Lord, come and see." Jesus wept. – John 11:33-35, WEBBE

God understands what you're going through. He wants you to hope in Him and to trust Him, but that doesn't mean He cannot allow you to cry.

He knows what grief is. He went through pain Himself. He knows the very depths of our wounds.

Must we hide our tears from the One who loves us most? Must we think He could never understand us?

November 17 :
Love Forgets One's Wrongs

God knows that we often choose the wrong things, but that doesn't mean we are not capable of choosing the right things. He looks past all our falls and helps us each and every time to rise again.

Love... takes no account of evil... - 1 Corinthians 13, WEBBE

There are times when because of one sin, a person is condemned forever as though he could never do anything good anymore. Instead of seeing a person in the image of God, fully capable of

317

repenting his wrongs and correcting his ways, we see his sins always before us, focusing on them as though they would always define who he is.

Where is love then when we choose to see what is evil instead of looking for what is good? Where is love when we brand a person forever for one fault, for one moment of weakness, which we all must have?

Let love find its way to see beyond what's wrong, to look beyond what's already in the past. Love looks forward, it hopes for the very best, it sees the beloved in his best light.

Love forgets what was wrong. It buries such things and covers them with kisses and understanding, allowing a new seed to sprout and grow. With constant care and compassion, it will grow ever more beautifully than ever before.

November 18 :
Wounds That Do Not Heal

And let each wound be a window by which God's Light can enter in.

By reason of the exceeding greatness of the revelations, that I should not be exalted excessively, there was given to me a thorn in the flesh... to torment me, that I should not be exalted excessively. – 2 Cor. 12:7, WEB

GOD is the Lord who heals us. There will come a time when He shall completely heal our wounds and wipe away all of our tears. On that day, our joy will be far greater than our past suffering. On that day, we shall be truly whole.

Even today, God already heals us. There are those He restores to complete health and those whose emotional wounds are being healed.

There are some wounds however that may not heal completely in this life. For reasons known to Him alone, He allows certain

318

sufferings to afflict us. He leaves certain crosses we must carry from day to day.

Let this not take away our hope however. For as great as one's sufferings are, great also are the graces God confers upon us to help us bear them.

These sufferings become blessings also as they purify us and heal the deeper wounds of our souls. Bearing them allows us to gain courage. Seeing them reminds us of our frailty and sends us towards true humility.

Let us remember the wounds of Christ. Such are the wounds that gave out true compassion to those who also hurt and undergo great difficulties. Such are the wounds of love by which we are all healed in God's perfect time.

November 19 :
Giving and Receiving Forgiveness

When God forgave us, He also gave us the capacity to forgive.

Blessed be the God and Father of our Lord Jesus Christ, the Father of mercies and God of all comfort; who comforts us in all our affliction, that we may be able to comfort those who are in any affliction, through the comfort with which we ourselves are comforted by God. – 2 Corinthians 1:3-4, WEB

What's difficult with forgiving someone is the seemingly immediate pressure to focus on the offender: one is urged to have mercy on the offender, to understand the offender, to give the offender another chance, to love the offender.

But what about the one who was hurt? How about the one who was aggrieved? How about justice for the damage done? Is there no mercy for the one who was hurt?

Forgiveness is indeed a beautiful thing. It sets us free from an endless cycle of pain. It gives light in that part of the world filled with so much darkness. It gives peace and reconciliation a chance. It allows us to be more angelic and divine.

But let us not forget that in order to forgive, one must first have an abundance of mercy and love. One must be free to weep and to express how deeply one has been hurt and damaged. One must know that he or she will not be deprived of justice.

It is but human to feel hurt. To be able to rise above one's pain, one must receive healing. To be able to forgive, one must know that one is also loved and forgiven. Only by receiving God's mercy and understanding can we possibly be capable of giving it away.

November 20 :
   God's Mercy Is For You

Should you ever think that Jesus only died for the world and not for you? That His love is reserved for all mankind and not for you?

You are my servant, I have chosen you and have not cast you away.
Don't you be afraid, for I am with you.
Don't be dismayed, for I am your God.
I will strengthen you.
Yes, I will help you.
Yes, I will uphold you with the right hand of my righteousness.
-Isaiah 41:9-10, WEBBE

Unless you understand that God's mercy is not only for other people but for you, you'd never really know what God's mercy is. This is humility, knowing that you are also a recipient of the mercy of God.

It is true that you are called to be an instrument of His mercy and love, to show kindness to others, to help those in need. But you forget that you too, need to be shown kindness. You, too, need help and understanding and love.

God has not forgotten you. God gave His only begotten Son for you. God has redeemed you with His love.

For you, He makes the sun to rise each day; He makes the rain to fall. He orders the earth to give its fruits. He sets the limits of the seas.

He forgives you. He knows your limits and He understands when you fall.

He is patient with you. He pursues you even when you turn away.

He knows your hurts and He is the One who will heal you. He will defend you as He defends the widows and the orphans. He is the One who will avenge for you!

Mercy is not only reserved for others. It is yours as well. Why would He leave the ninety nine sheep behind if not for you?

God awaits you, always. He is the merciful Father who, instead of speaking words of scorn and blame, waits ever so patiently to embrace you and shower you with kisses!

Put away any thought of His condemnation. He has come to save you with His love. Put away guilt that thinks more about your misery than about the infinite goodness of God. Though your sins are as scarlet, they shall be as white as snow.

November 21 :
   People Are Gifts

Each person in our lives is a gift. In same way, our presence is a gift to another which no other person could replace.

But to each one is given the manifestation of the Spirit for the profit of all. For to one is given through the Spirit the word of wisdom, and to another the word of knowledge, according to the same Spirit; to another faith, by the same Spirit; and to another gifts of healings, by the same Spirit; and to another workings of miracles; and to another prophecy; and to another discerning of spirits; to another different kinds of languages; and to another the interpretation of languages. But the one and the same Spirit produces all of these, distributing to each one separately as he desires. - 1 Corinthians 12:7-11, WEB

Nobody is perfect. Even the best people can fail to meet our every expectation of them. But this should not deter us from appreciating what they can and do provide in our lives.

321

Each person that God allows to touch our lives brings with him a gift that only they could possibly give. One person may be there to give a word of encouragement when you feel down. Another may have a bubbling kind of personality that eases your troubles. Still another reminds you of the innocence of childhood and all its wonders.

Who are the people God has put into your life right now? Some were there to teach you, some to help you grow, others to try your patience, and still others to make you strong.

We need only to see what each person has to give so we can receive it and benefit from their presence. We have been blessed with their lives. May they also be blessed with ours.

November 22 :
Think of the Good Things

God never fails to give us little reminders, things of beauty and of wonder that helps us remember we are loved.

Finally, brothers, whatever things are true, whatever things are honorable, whatever things are just, whatever things are pure, whatever things are lovely, whatever things are of good report; if there is any virtue, and if there is any praise, think about these things. – Philippians 4:8, WEB

There are times when we may get so overwhelmed with the problems of everyday: a job undone, a client who declined, a terrible traffic jam, a bad whether. During such times, we may fail to see the good things that are still going our way. We may forget to see how we still have people who care about us, or how we can still get to enjoy little pleasures in life like a fine dinner or a walk along the beach.

Whenever you feel overwhelmed, try to take a break. Breathe. Listen to some music. Go to a chapel and pray. Light a little candle.

This may not be heaven yet, but there is value in the life we still possess. We are still given time. And with time comes much opportunity to love, to be loved, and to be happy.

322

A Walk In The Rain

A walk in the rain
my feet in the mud
a patter of raindrops
as I look up above
Streets are flooded
I wade my way through
like a child lost in wonder
like a child lost in awe
And if I can dance without tripping
if I can just sing once more
I'll thank the rain now washing my face
and I shall walk on and on and on…

November 23 :
You Are Loved

When you are burdened and falling, God reaches out and gives you wings. But you must choose to use them so you can fly!

Show your marvellous loving kindness, you who save those who take refuge by your right hand from their enemies. Keep me as the apple of your eye. Hide me under the shadow of your wings...
-Psalm 17, WEBBE

You have to let it sink in. You are loved. You are treasured. You are kept.

How beloved you are in the eyes of God. How valuable!

Let this truth heal you and be always with you. Let it guide you with light and with the innocence of childhood. Let it bless you with freshness like the morning dew.

Someone watches over you as you sleep. Someone is ready to take your hand as you rise.

323

You are more important than the stars, more beautiful than the moon. All that is made is made for you. For you are made in love and for love alone.

Arise from your sorrows and see. There is joy prepared without end for you!

November 24 :
   True Repentance

When someone repents with all his heart out of an abounding gratitude and praise for God's infinite mercy, is justice not met and satisfied also in all its depths, essence and fullness?

"Therefore I tell you, her sins, which are many, are forgiven, for she loved much. But to whom little is forgiven, the same loves little."– Luke 7:47, WEB

There is a kind of repentance that satisfies justice. It is that repentance that is not caused only by fear of punishment. It is not the kind that makes apologies only through words.

The kind of repentance that fulfills justice is that which is able to recognize and receive mercy. It is the kind that is moved by love and not by fear. It is one that comes sincerely from the heart and is able to manifest through both word and action, willing to do all because it has received everything out of love.

November 25 :
Love is the Foundation of True Justice

How could someone be just if one isn't even kind?

But he was pierced for our transgressions.
He was crushed for our iniquities.
The punishment that brought our peace was on him;
and by his wounds we are healed.
-Isaiah 53:5, WEB

God is just. He will never deprive us of justice. He will never remain deaf to the cries of the poor, the hurt and the oppressed.

His mercy moves Him to be just. His justice moves Him to be merciful.

He would rather pay the price Himself than deprive us of justice. He would rather suffer pain and humiliation than turn His ears away from our cries. He would rather die than deny us healing and new life.

It is unfathomable how He could place Himself in the place of a sinner and be punished as a criminal would. It is beyond our grasp how He Himself could bear the wounds that our offenders deserve, that we deserve also as we sin.

Jesus paid for our every debt. When the Father looks down from Heaven and sees the cross, He can't help but see both infinite mercy and perfect justice because Jesus Himself has paid in full for your sins and mine.

November 26 :
    When God is Silent

Love does not always need to be heard when it can be felt.

When he opened the seventh seal, there was silence in heaven for about half an hour. – Revelations 8:1, WEB

God loves us. This is true in moments when you feel His Presence and in moments when you do not. It is like the sun that remains shining even when it hides behind a cloud.

Hold on. Continue to believe in His love for you. Even when you can't hear Him. Even when He is so silent you don't know whether He's still there listening to you.

When the right time comes, you will know why He hid His face from you. And you will also know how He has never stopped watching over you even when you don't know it, even in times you fail to believe He's there.

November 27 :
A Space For God

You can never be so far away that God can't reach you. You can never fall so low that God cannot lift you where you are.

Behold, I stand at the door and knock. If anyone hears my voice and opens the door, then I will come in to him, and will dine with him, and he with me. – Revelation 3:20, WEB

There is no person in the world, no matter how lost he may seem to be, that God couldn't reach. God reaches out always to everyone. He has created our immortal soul, and there will always be that spark of the Divine in everything that He has made.

Let there be space for God. Make way even in the wilderness so He may come at last to those who need His consolation.

It is never too late. One is never too old. One is never so sinful as to not have hope for His mercy. For as long as one lives, there is room for hope and for healing. There can always be a new beginning for those who can believe and trust in God.

November 28 :
   Anger is Temporary

Anger is a temporary tool, not a permanent solution.

Don't let the sun go down on your wrath, and don't give place to the devil. – Ephesians 4:26-27, WEB

Anger is a tool to alert us of a dangerous condition. It gives us the power to fight or to flee from something that can harm us. It's an emotion so powerful as to evoke in us a horror for sin and evil.

What we must remember however is that anger shouldn't be a permanent solution. After the danger has passed, after we have recognized the horror of sin, and after we have taken the steps needed to protect ourselves and other people, we need to let it go. Otherwise, this heavy burden can trap us in the past, poison our hearts, destroy our peace and prevent our healing and happiness.

Surrender your anger to God. Surrender it and exchange it for hope in His justice, for faith in His mercy and for love that shines its healing light, making us whole again and giving us peace.

November 29 :
Forgive Yourself

God has forgiven you. Must you deny yourself what God has already given you?

However, for this cause I obtained mercy, that in me first, Jesus Christ might display all his patience, for an example of those who were going to believe in him for eternal life. – 1 Timothy 1:16, WEB

You've got to be more patient of yourself. If you have worked so hard trying to forgive others, shouldn't you also extend this forgiveness to yourself? If God can forgive you, can you not forgive yourself also?

Forgive yourself. Release yourself from the illusion that you can be perfect all the time. It is too heavy a burden to bear. Let grace do this for you, in God's perfect time. Meanwhile, as you journey towards the road of love, learn to love yourself also. Remember always that God loves you, is patient with you, and forgives you out of the depths of His mercy and love.

November 30 :

Let go and let God.

You shall not hate your brother in your heart. You shall surely rebuke your neighbour, and not bear sin because of him. You shall not take vengeance, nor bear any grudge against the children of your people; but you shall love your neighbour as yourself. I am the LORD. – Leviticus 19:17-18, WEBBE

While anger alerts us of immediate danger or evil, and is a temporary tool to help us fight or flee from harm, resentment poisons our soul slowly and becomes a burden too heavy to bear over time.

Have you a resentment? A need to forgive someone?

Sometimes, we don't even know we have resentments that have been buried for so long. We thought we have forgotten these, but quite often, they come out one way or the other. They can manifest through physical ailments, or they can suddenly erupt in explosions of anger when triggered by a stressful event.

We have to discover if we have hurts hidden deeply in our heart. How can we even begin to forgive if we can't even acknowledge we have been hurt?

Let us try to face these memories one by one so we can start the process of true healing. Only when we have truly been able to forgive can we be released from the pain. Only after finding this freedom can we find true happiness.

DECEMBER

December 1 :

Double Your Joy

If you become happy with the happiness of others, you have just doubled your joy!

Love is patient and is kind; love doesn't envy. – 1 Corinthians 13:4, WEB

We can be happy in two ways. First, we can be happy with our own lives. We can be happy for the things that we possess, for the things that are going well in our jobs and careers, for the relationships that we are blessed with, for our own spiritual growth and for all the happiness that God has showered upon us.

The second kind of happiness is being happy for the happiness of other people. It is being able to share in the success of a friend, in the good family life of a brother, in sainthood of a fellow man, in the unique blessings that people close and not so close to us possess.

Let us not remain closed to our own happiness. For this is what envy does. It blocks us from being happy with what others have and eventually, it makes us forget the blessings that have been given us.

Instead, let us have an open heart that is truly filled with happiness, and be happy for what we have as well as for what others have been given.

December 2 :

    The Tide Will Turn

I pray you do not give up. Your worst day may just be the day when your greatest desires can at last come true.

Therefore don't throw away your boldness, which has a great reward. For you need endurance so that, having done the will of God, you may receive the promise. – Hebrews 10:35-36, WEB

Never give up! Even when it's so dark you could hardly remember the last time you saw the light. Even when it's so painful you could hardly remember memories of joy and consolation.

It is not yet the end. The tide can still turn. Everything can change in a moment, and in that moment, you can receive all that you have ever prayed for.

But you must wait. Wait patiently for it then so you may receive the blessings coming your way!

Night is never the end, for morning shall definitely come. Rain may fall, but it can't keep on falling forever, the sun will shine again.

Gather your strength and keep your hopes up. Wait for your moment and trust the hand of God. No one who hopes in Him will ever be put to shame.

December 3 :
Make This Day Count

You can be in touch with eternity today. Enjoy the journey so at the end of it, you can say that it was definitely worth it, every wonderful day of it!

This is the day that the LORD has made.
We will rejoice and be glad in it!
-Psalm 118:24, WEBBE

There are many things we do every day because we need to. There are deadlines we have to meet, tasks that must be accomplished, house chores that needs to be done.

But can we pause once in a while and think how important today may be? What's today really worth? Is it even something we can look forward to each morning?

We can start to see things in a new perspective and thereby change the way we live and feel. We can start to see how important today is, how much we can really do, how we can make a real difference.

It is not only in the big things that we can accomplish something great. Many times, it's in the small and simple things that we can do so much difference, both in our own lives and in the lives of others.

Make this day count. Give a smile or a warm embrace that someone else can remember. Pause and see how beautiful is the sunrise and be in awe at all the beautiful things God has made.

December 4 :

The Angel In You

God believes in you more than you could ever believe in yourself.

For as many as are led by the Spirit of God, these are children of God. For you didn't receive the spirit of bondage again to fear, but you received the Spirit of adoption, by whom we cry, "Abba! Father!" – Romans 8:14-14, WEB

There are some of us who are so familiar with our imperfections that we sometimes forget the beauty that God sees in us as His children. We may have our weaknesses, but our origin is still of a divine nature. God has created us after His own image, and all that God has made is good.

We need to be reminded every now and then that there is still that spark of goodness that is within each and every one of us. We need to remember that we are more than our imperfection and our mistakes. We are more than our problems and our troubles.

There is also light and there is also beauty. There is still hope for us, and we have no idea what we can be if we allow God to purify us and make us as He is.

December 5 :
Your Secret Trial

We sometimes carry the heaviest of crosses in the dark, where no one sees and no one hears our cries, no one except for God.

But there is nothing covered up, that will not be revealed, nor hidden, that will not be known. Therefore whatever you have said in the darkness will be heard in the light. What you have spoken in the ear in the inner rooms will be proclaimed on the housetops. – Luke 12:2-3, WEBBE

There is a trial that is witnessed by God alone. In that secret trial, only God knows your anguish, only God could ever fathom the depths of your pain.

To the world outside, it's as though nothing peculiar is happening. But within your heart, your own martyrdom is already taking place.

Take heart however for you are not alone! Jesus goes with you to the very end and He will see you through until with Him you rise again.

335

December 6 :
Words That Give Life

By your words you can make or break a soul, you can build or you can destroy.

Death and life are in the power of the tongue;
   those who love it will eat its fruit.
-Proverbs 18:21, WEB

Our words have the power to hurt or to heal, to break or to raise up, to cause death or to give life. May we always choose what's good. May we always be watchful of what we say.

If there is nothing good that can be said, may we observe silence. For the effect of the words we utter remain long after they have been said. They are repeated over and over in one's mind, causing pain and inner wounds that take a long time to heal.

On the other hand, let us be more generous with praise and words of encouragement. Sometimes, all it takes are a few words of affirmation to build up another person's confidence. A few words are also often sufficient to inspire others towards their dreams.

December 7 :
    My Burden Is Light

There is no lighter burden than the cross God gives you and me.

Take my yoke upon you, and learn from me, for I am gentle and humble in heart; and you will find rest for your souls. For my yoke is easy, and my burden is light. – Matthew 11:29-30, WEB

We often feel so weary in life because we carry burdens God never meant for us to bear. We can't let go of our worries for we feel anxious of things we could never control. We can't let go of anger and resentment, and we fill our hearts with hatred and desire for vengeance. We take on more work than we could perform in order to chase dreams that could never really satisfy the soul. We strive and we labor, but our efforts seem often in vain.

Why not let go of these heavy burdens and take on instead the light burden that Jesus gives? It is light because it is free from anxiety and hatred, it is free from the love of the world and from fear. It is light because it is filled with peace and with love. It is light because we do not carry it alone. Jesus carries it with us, and this is the source of our strength and our joy.

December 8 :
God's Timing

The fact that God isn't in a hurry doesn't mean He isn't accomplishing much.

For the vision is yet for the appointed time, and it hurries toward the end, and won't prove false. Though it takes time, wait for it; because it will surely come. It won't delay. – Habakkuk 2:3, WEB

God is accomplishing so many things for us, but we often fail to recognize it because such things take time to fully manifest its wonders. It is like the slow evaporation of a cloud that sooner or later turns into rain. It is like a flower that slowly blooms or a tree that grows. Hardly do we take notice of any change, but one day, we suddenly see how things have already become as they are – the caterpillar has turned into a beautiful butterfly, the tree has produced its fruits, the young cub has become a mighty lion!

God does not work in a hurry, but He works precisely, and He works beautifully. Let us trust in God's timing for all the good things that are bound to happen in our lives.

December 9 :
The Opinion of Men

It is vain to try to gain the opinion of men. Why not try to seek the opinion of God?

Nevertheless even of the rulers many believed in him, but because of the Pharisees they didn't confess it, so that they wouldn't be put out of the synagogue, for they loved men's praise more than God's praise. – John 12:42-43, WEB

Our emotional stability must not be based on the opinion of men. Such opinions often change and are as fleeting as the wind. Also, they can't always be counted upon to be right. For it is not the quantity of opinion that counts. What shall always matter is the truth.

If we need to hear the truth, let us seek the opinion of God. He is Truth itself, and will never lie. His opinion is not based on any selfish agenda nor is it influenced by fame or wealth.

We can always find peace once we put God's opinion as the foundation of our decisions in life. His voice is true and pleasant and perfect. It is filled with wisdom and with love.

For am I now seeking the favor of men, or of God? Or am I striving to please men? For if I were still pleasing men, I wouldn't be a servant of Christ. – Galatians 1:10, WEB

December 10 :
   To Grow Old Beautifully

It is not age we must fear if we can grow old beautifully.

Gray hair is a crown of glory.
   It is attained by a life of righteousness.
-Proverbs 16:31, WEB

It is not only youth that has its gifts. Even old age has its blessings.

While youth is a time of physical vigor, old age can be a time of spiritual maturity.

While youth is a time of great hopes, old age can be a time of hopes fulfilled.

Old age can be a time of wisdom and of passing on that wisdom to those who are still searching for their way. It is a time of memories, beautiful ones that make the soul full and pure.

One that has aged is one that has been tested and made gold. One has become as a ripe fruit that is sweet to taste, a sturdy tree which no storm can break.

December 11 :
Being Fully Present Today

Why be in such a rush when you can be happy right where you are?

Therefore don't be anxious for tomorrow, for tomorrow will be anxious for itself. – Matthew 6:34, WEB

You can start to make the most of your life today. Here is the present moment. Here is the opportunity you've always been looking for.

You have the strength to face your challenges today. Cast away the shadows cast by the future and the past. You don't have to face them at the moment. All that is needed is to endure the present hour.

You can breathe today. You can feel the wind touching your face.

Life has been given you, and you can give so much back.

Savor each sweet moment you have with those you love. Make them feel you're really there!

In the stillness of the present moment, you can be truly alive. Take it all in and let the richness of the present empower you. Fill your soul with all the love you could possibly receive and in this prayer, find peace and healing and life.

December 12 :
The Love of Jesus

Nothing is more beautiful than the love of Jesus.

But God commends his own love toward us, in that while we were yet sinners, Christ died for us. - Romans 5:8, WEB

Jesus loves you. He loves you in your confusion, in your worries, in your moments of doubt. He loves you in your fear, in your anger, in your weakest, in your most vulnerable. He loves you when you feel most repulsive, when you are condemned and judged as unworthy of respect or care. He loves you in your sorrow, in your most desperate moments, He longs to bless you with His light. He saves you, He has saved you even before you ever tried to ask, and He will keep on saving you up to your very last beating of your heart.

December 13 :
To Be Truly Loved

We can never underestimate the value of loving another person. It is this experience alone, this encounter, this event, that changes us and makes us whole.

"Therefore behold, I will allure her,
and bring her into the wilderness,
and speak tenderly to her.
I will give her vineyards from there,
and the valley of Achor for a door of hope;
and she will respond there,
as in the days of her youth,
and as in the day when she came up out of the land of Egypt.
It will be in that day," says the LORD,
"that you will call me 'my husband,'"...
-Hosea 2:14-16, WEBBE

There is no experience like that of being loved. Nothing can ever compare to it. No wealth could ever be sufficient to replace it.

To be loved is to be noticed by another soul. It is to be truly seen for who we really are, to be accepted, to be cherished and remembered.

When we are loved, we feel valued, and we finally believe that we are precious.

The rest of the world can walk away, but as long as we know that somebody out there loves us, we are consoled. There is nothing that can take away our happiness.

When we are loved, we feel that we have finally found our true home. We are no longer lost because we have been found. We are no longer blind because we now see, and we are indeed seen for the core of who we are.

All The World Is Meaningless Without Love

The radiant sun is nothing
but a big ball of fire
that hovers above us.
If not for love,
what could the sunrise mean?
What could everything mean at all?

Even the brightest of stars grow pale,
Even the moon loses its mystery,
Nothing hides beneath the seas,
and no mountain is ever worth climbing for.

And yet with love,
even a candy wrapper
can be put in a special golden box,
even a torn ticket
can be held with the highest regard.

It is because you walked these streets,
that I come back here again and again;
It is because you sat in this chair,
that I sit as though
this is the most beautiful chair in all the world.

I touch this pen,
and I feel your fingers,
I hear a song,
and tears flow down my eyes.

Everything comes to life
because you have touched them,
but all the world is meaningless
without love.

December 14 :
   A Deeper Meaning

Much of our sufferings become bearable once we discover a deeper meaning beyond the pain.

Not only this, but we also rejoice in our sufferings, knowing that suffering works perseverance; and perseverance, proven character; and proven character, hope: and hope doesn't disappoint us, because God's love has been poured out into our hearts through the Holy Spirit who was given to us. - Romans 5:3-5, WEB

A mother about to give birth experiences much suffering, yet she is able to hold on and bears it because she knows she is going to give birth to her beloved child.

A soldier experiences hunger, loneliness and much discomfort. He may even be captured and beaten by enemies, but he endures all because he knows that he is defending innocent lives and upholding the freedom of his countrymen.

A saint experiences a painful sickness yet offers everything for the repentance of sinners and for the salvation of souls. She suffers bodily aches, sleepless nights and even emotional distress, but she knows that God accepts the value of it all for a far greater good.

Many times, it is not in our hands to avoid suffering. We get sick, we get hurt by others, we suffer emotional and mental pain. Much of these suffering could be so extreme as to be almost unbearable. But once we discover the value behind it, how it could save another life or inspire another soul, or how it could be united with the

344

suffering of Jesus to alleviate the distress of many, we begin to gain the strength to endure it. We start to have hope. Hope doen't lessen the pain. But it gives us the grace to carry on.

December 15 :
Our Full Attention

How we lessen our joy when we do not love in full!

He has also set eternity in their hearts… - Ecclesiastes 3:11, WEB

When was the last time you gave your full attention to those you love? Have you really looked at them? Have you really listened to what they are trying to say?

We have but a limited time. Must we not use it for the most important things? Must we be forever so distracted by unnecessary clutter that demand our precious time and attention?

Your child may be trying to show you something, give him your attention. It may not be long before he pays his attention to other things. Your mother or your father may be telling you a story, listen to their story. Even when you've already heard it, listen again. You have not yet listened to their story the way they're telling it to you today.

We say love is the most valuable thing, but where is love if our hearts and minds are filled with something else?

Give love your full attention today and you will rediscover what love is like. You will no longer need to rush, because when you get in touch with love, you will rediscover eternity.

345

December 16 :
Jesus in Disguise

Lord, open our eyes so we may see Jesus in disguise.

...for I was hungry, and you gave me food to eat. I was thirsty, and you gave me drink. I was a stranger, and you took me in. I was naked, and you clothed me. I was sick, and you visited me. I was in prison, and you came to me.' - Matthew 25:35-36, WEB

When Mother Teresa helps the poor, she doesn't look down on them. Instead, she sees in them the image of Jesus, the very image of God. Helping others then does not become a way to be proud of ourselves by being greater than those we help. It becomes a blessed opportunity to serve Him who loves us most.

For though God did not need to ask anything from us, He lowered Himself so we can reach Him, so we can have a chance to love Him back. How great is the love that not only gives but also receives humbly from His beloved!

May we all learn to see Jesus also in one another. May we be able to take every opportunity to find Him so we can serve Him and love Him back.

December 17 :
The Best and Worst of Times

The worst days can also be the best days with God's grace.

Even though I walk through the valley of the shadow of death,
  I will fear no evil, for you are with me.
Your rod and your staff,
  they comfort me.
-Psalm 23:4, WEB

As I look back at my life today, I begin to see how many of the worst of times had also been the best of times, not because of the darkness but because of the light that had shined through, because of the love that had been there. And I thank God for His merciful heart, because He has allowed such things to happen. For I wouldn't have chosen to undergo all those things myself. I would have been afraid! But God knew the good that would come out of it, and God's hand was strong enough indeed to guide me so I may not completely fall.

In times when all that you can see is darkness, cling to the belief that God is there, watching over you, guiding you, and will not let you suffer beyond what you can bear. He allows such things to happen not because He wants to hurt you, but because He loves you so much. He wants you to gather the sweetest fruits, the most fragrant perfume, and the greatest rewards which you can take with you through all eternity!

December 18 :
The Grace in Suffering

Suffering helps us to detach ourselves from worldly things and to fix our gaze upon heaven.

Not only this, but we also rejoice in our sufferings, knowing that suffering produces perseverance; and perseverance, proven character; and proven character, hope: and hope doesn't disappoint us, because God's love has been poured out into our hearts through the Holy Spirit who was given to us. – Romans 5:3-5, WEBBE

It is not God's will that we should suffer. But God is able to use all things, even suffering, so as to bring us a far greater good. He allows pain, which is temporary, to bring us to eternal rewards and lasting happiness, happiness which no one could ever take away from us.

When we suffer temporarily on earth, we are able to realize how fleeting all earthly things are. We see things for what they really are and we are taken away from things that could take our eyes away from God. We are thus protected from sin because we are taken away from being ensnared into a sinful way of living.

Every good thing comes from the Lord, even earthly blessings. But all such things will pass away, and it is best to make use of them only and not to have our joys attached forever on things that cannot last.

December 19 :
To Find The Beautiful

May we have eyes keen enough to see beauty even in the ordinary things.

"...The LORD, speaks, and calls the earth from sunrise to sunset. Out of Zion, the perfection of beauty, God shines out." – Psalm 50, WEB

There are times when our days seem filled with gloom and all we could ever think of are sad and dreary thoughts. It is during such days when we grow old within, and our soul hungers for its true food.

Hope however finds its way when we are able to catch a glimpse of the beautiful once again. It's as though all of a sudden, our spiritual eyes are opened and we could finally see something else in a colorful petal, in the flight of a bird or in the dancing of the pouring rain.

When we see beauty again, we are able to catch a bit of joy once more. We are able to live, to truly live, even in that short moment that takes our breath away.

December 20 :

To Gain What Matters Most

We can never gain all in God unless we risk everything.

For whoever desires to save his life will lose it, and whoever will lose his life for my sake will find it. – Matthew 16:25, WEB

Many times, it is when we have already detached ourselves from wanting to gain something that we start to receive what we have always prayed for. It is when we let go of everything to God that He blesses us with all things we really need.

When we arrive at that point in our lives when we are ready to lose everything else other than that which truly matters most, we arrive at that point when everything else that we receive from then on is gain.

December 21 :

Don't Miss Your Blessings

Let no difficulty turn us away from the blessings God has in store for us in the midst of all our troubles.

When you pass through the waters, I will be with you;
and through the rivers, they will not overflow you.
When you walk through the fire, you will not be burnt,
and flame will not scorch you.
For I am the LORD your God,
the Holy One of Israel,
your Saviour.
-Isaiah 43:2-3, WEBBE

There are blessings in store for us, but we must be willing to claim them. There are jewels of happiness along the way, but we must have the courage to walk the path that will lead us towards them.

Life will not always be easy. We are bound to encounter difficulties now and then. But we should never allow these difficulties to keep us away from living fully and joyfully.

Despite all the pain, we can still claim moments of happiness. Despite all the darkness, we can still see the brightness and beauty of the stars.

Don't miss your blessings. You will pass through this life only once. Yes, you will get hurt, you will fall down sometimes. But yes, you can also find light, you can find eternal treasures to keep if you do not give up and if you continue to hope and to rise again.

December 22 :
To Give More Happiness

We can never give more happiness than God is willing to have us receive from Him.

"If you want to be perfect, go, sell what you have, and give to the poor, and you will have treasure in heaven; and come, follow me." – Matthew 19:21, WEBBE

Let it be our resolution to give more and more happiness away. Let us be generous with our joy, for in being able to make others happy, we multiply our own happiness.

This world has so much need for the generosity of those who are overflowing with love and joy. Be that spring of life that touches other people's hearts, consoling those who bleed, and refreshing those who fall down.

It is by making others happy that you will chase away your own sorrow. It is by giving away love that you will receive it a hundredfold.

December 23 :
Never Too Old For Christmas

I pray that we can all be as happy as children are on Christmas Day.

When they saw the star, they rejoiced with exceedingly great joy. They came into the house and saw the young child with Mary, his mother, and they fell down and worshipped him. Opening their treasures, they offered to him gifts: gold, frankincense, and myrrh. – Matthew 2:10-11, WEBBE

I'm going to tell you a secret: we don't really grow old, we just pretend we're no longer like little children!

I'm not certain what has happened through the years that made us choose to grow old. Old and tired and afraid. In fact, we grew so old we could no longer remember how we were as children.

As little children we were so full of life and joy. Our eyes were filled with wonder! Our hearts beat with hope.

Who could have stopped us from peeking to find out whether Santa Claus was real? Who could have dared to tell us Christmas won't be there anymore?

We used to look forward to Christmas. We used to believe in Christmas.

And it's not just the gifts we wanted. Not just the good food or the new clothes to wear. Somewhere deep within our hearts, we felt that kind of joy which Christmas has brought us. We felt its warmth. We felt its wonder.

And if we could only cast away our fears, we can feel that wonder again. We can be like little children again who's not afraid to play or to open presents. We can be as children who can truly celebrate Christmas in our hearts!

December 24 :
God is With Us

Salvation has come when we find that we are no more alone, that God is with us.

"Behold, the virgin shall be with child,
and shall give birth to a son.
They shall call his name Immanuel;"
which is, being interpreted, "God with us."
-Matthew 1:23, WEBBE

I think that there is no other faith that is as unthinkable as the one that could believe in God coming down from heaven to become man. A faith that insists we need not remain in darkness because Light Himself has pierced through our shadows to illumine our path.

But as Christians, that is just what we believe, and Christmas reminds us of all that.

Christmas reminds us that it isn't our failures that matter, because there is One who can save us and make us whole again.

Christmas reminds us that it isn't our wounds that should overwhelm us, because there is One who can heal us and give us life.

Christmas reminds us that no matter how empty and alone we may feel, no matter how deserted by the world we think we are, we need not be alone.

God Himself has reached out to us from heaven. God Himself has walked the night to accompany us towards a new day. We are not on our own anymore because God has come, God is with us!

353

December 25 :
That First Christmas

When the best of things and the best of people fail us, let us try to look in the eyes of that little child in whose shoulders rest the salvation of the world.

For a child is born to us. A son is given to us; and the government will be on his shoulders. His name will be called Wonderful Counsellor, Mighty God, Everlasting Father, Prince of Peace. - Isaiah 9, WEBBE

This Is Christmas

God could have come in all His glory,
with trumpets and angels and all,
blazing like fire,
dazzling like lightning
as terrible as the raging of the seas!

But on that Christmas Eve,
He came as a newborn child,
small and gentle,
humble and innocent
as harmless as a dove.

Why He came like this
I didn't know,
until I looked at my own fears
and wounds.

How could I have come to Him
had I been so afraid?
How could I have even
looked at His face?

But as that babe,
I could cradle Him in my arms,
I could whisper to Him my heart's desires
I could look upon His eyes
without being judged

without being cast away.

And I love Him more
because He chose to come that way.
Because though He came for the whole world,
He also came for me,
and He knew me,
He knew how I longed to be loved.

But more than loving me,
He allowed me to love Him
and to care for Him,
to carry Him
even though He is actually the One
who carries me.

This is Christmas
This is Holy Night.
In that simple stable
silent and small,
I was saved,
I was healed,
I have been found.

December 26 :
    He Lived Among Us

Out of the darkness He called us and blessed us with His Presence that we may know, that we may never forget. God lives, and for as long as we live in love, He lives today in you and in me.

The Word became flesh, and lived amongst us. We saw his glory, such glory as of the one and only Son of the Father, full of grace and truth. - John 1:14, WEBBE

It is often hard to believe how God can be with us if we cannot even see Him. How many times have we sighed, "If we could only see Him, everything will be alright."

But could God really be so far away?

We may not always realize it, but God is near, within your heart, and with every heart that knows how to love.

He is in friends that talk to you when you are sad, in families that make sure home is always there for you at the end of the day.

He is in every hand that lifts you up, in every smile that cheers you, in every word that tells you how special you really are.

We may not always remember, for the distractions of this world often make us forget.

But in Christmas, we are given a chance again to realize the things that are truly important in our lives.

We remember once more the many people that gave us a glimpse of God's face. That gaze of love that made us whole again and strong again. That helped us carry on no matter how great our burdens were. That helped us dream again no matter how many times we fell.

Behold! God Himself came down from heaven to be with us. He revealed His face in the innocent face of a little child.

356

December 27 :
The Essence of Prayer

The essence of prayer is to know that God is there for you and that He loves you very much.

Seek the LORD and his strength. Seek his face forever more. – 1 Chronicles 16:11, WEB

The essence of prayer is not merely to lift up our petitions to God. It is not merely to ask for forgiveness or guidance or strength. It is not merely an obligation to praise Him who is indeed to be praised.

The essence of prayer is in being in the very presence of God. It is in basking in His love and tenderness, and in knowing you are dearly loved. It is in knowing you are understood, that you are not alone even in your deepest pain.

Prayer is communing with the God who has always watched over you and has long been waiting to embrace you and to reveal to you His love.

December 28 :
Blessings in a Storm

Our Lord is a Mighty God. He is Lord of Peace, and He is Lord of the Storm!

He said to them, "Why are you fearful, O you of little faith?" Then he got up, rebuked the wind and the sea, and there was a great calm. – Matthew 8:24, WEB

When a storm comes, the first thing we often feel is a great fear for all the devastation the storm could cause. We are gripped with both fear and sorrow, fear of losing what we have, and sorrow for not being able to do anything to stop the storm.

Yet if we could try to see things with different eyes, we can see that even in the midst of a storm, there are blessings we could claim.

It is often in the midst of a great trial that our faith is strengthened and our courage is forged. It is there when we discover our hidden strengths. It is there when we come to realize who our true friends are, friends who are not with us only when the weather is fair and good, but who are willing to go with us even in the fiercest of storms.

It is in the greatest storms of our lives that we learn the power of God. We discover that even if we have lost everything, God is still in control and with Him, we are never alone. We can overcome all things as long as God is there for He is after all, the Lord of the storm.

December 29 :
A Second Chance

Take this chance. Take this day and make it yours. Fill your empty heart with everything that can make it full. Let it overflow with gratitude and love.

Then Peter came and said to him, "Lord, how often shall my brother sin against me, and I forgive him? Until seven times?" Jesus said to him, "I don't tell you until seven times, but, until seventy times seven. – Matthew 18:21-22, WEB

The time that we have at present is a golden opportunity given us to try again, to strive again, to begin again. Think not of the things you have lost, think instead of what you can gain. Think not of what you have failed to achieve, think instead of the victories you can still win.

God is good. He makes the sun to rise each day to help us start anew. He gives us breath so we can go on living, becoming better persons, blessing each other's lives with our gifts.

What has been broken can be mended. What has been lost can be found.

There is nothing impossible by God's grace. He gives us as many chances as we need to change and to find our joy.

READY TO START AGAIN

There comes a time when you feel
that you're ready to start again.

You've spent enough time
looking at the past,
cherishing memories
learning your lessons,
healing the wounds that have caused you pain.

You may still feel some hurt
in some of the wounded parts of you,
you may have your regrets
and you may not have found
all the precious things you wish to carry with you.

But you move on.

One step at a time, you let go
and you release yourself from the past
that has held you captive all these years.

You may feel your heart skip a beat,
for there is still much uncertainty,
but you hold your ground
and with a firm resolve
you look ahead
instead of looking back.

And you begin to surrender,
as you begin to receive.
You welcome all the new things
life can offer you,
and all the new people
who'd welcome you in their hearts.

You become less afraid
and your courage increases
as you begin to follow your heart.

Everything has suddenly become new
and interesting
and blessed.
You see the world again
through the eyes of a child,
colourful,
magical,
and full of wondrous possibilities!

You are no longer too old for anything,
and it is no longer too late to try something else.

You hold nothing,
but you're ready for everything,
you are just beginning
but you're not afraid to pursue
what it is you really desire!

You are no longer the same
and you're not afraid to change some more.
You're no longer afraid to lose yourself
for you know who you are
and all that you have yet to gain

For the first time in a long time,
you feel free,
you feel so alive!

You've been prepared for this very hour,
for this very beginning,
You know there is yet much to do
but you won't be turning back.
You only move forward,
you only hope
and trust
and believe
that you're ready
never more ready than now
to START AGAIN!

December 30 :
Find God's Grace Today

No matter how difficult your present problems are, remember that God has already reserved sufficient grace for you to overcome them. God's grace is enough for you today.

Remember your word to your servant, because you gave me hope. - Psalms 119:49, WEB

Some people are held back by the past. But there are some that are held back by the future. Instead of seeing hope, the future is seen as a threat. Instead of being a door towards one's dreams, it is seen as an unyielding wall, blocking off whatever light there may be on the other side.

How can the future be so dark its shadow is cast even in the present? How can it be such a heavy burden we carry upon our shoulders? Is there even a way by which we can unchain its weight from our very souls?

The Lord Himself taught us not to be anxious of tomorrow. He taught us not to be afraid. Why else would He tell us so if He would not give us the grace also to accomplish what He desires?

It is grace that He gives us each morning. Every day, we can still find the key.

Fear not therefore. Be free! Everything is still possible for him who believes. Good things can still happen as we begin again today.

December 31 :
To Begin Again

Forget your past troubles. God calls you to begin again today.

"Don't remember the former things,
and don't consider the things of old.
Behold, I will do a new thing.
It springs out now.
Don't you know it?
I will even make a way in the wilderness,
and rivers in the desert.
-Isaiah 43:18-19, WEBBE

Do not be weighed down by the past. Let the past teach you. Let it inspire you. Let it make you a wiser and stronger person. But never let the past define who you are and what you can still do.

Unlock the chains that bind you. Set yourself free from all the burdens that keep you from being the person you were meant to be.

Storms come, but so does a season for rebuilding. Problems happen, but so does a chance to let them go. Wounds touch our hearts, but so does a time for healing and moving on.

Arise then and claim the life now given you! You can still dream. You can still love. And you have a God who can help you through and through.

BEGIN AGAIN

There'd be times when you'd mess up big
times you'd fail
times you'd trip so hard
you'd get knocked down bad
Times like that you'd want to quit
but BEGIN AGAIN.

There'd be times when you'd say
"Enough is enough,
I've really had it now,
why bother trying?"
Yeah, there'd be times you'd get so tired
but still, BEGIN AGAIN.

There'd be times you'd think
you've just lost everything
times you've risked it all
and got back nothin'
Times like that you'd feel
everything you've worked so hard for
were in vain, but BEGIN AGAIN.

Begin again,
try again,
believe again,
love again.

There'd be a second wind,
there'd be another star,
there'd be another hand,
to help you rise again.

Don't start quitting,
never stop dreaming.
A new tomorrow waits
for those who dare –
to BEGIN AGAIN.

OTHER BOOKS
BY Jocelyn A. Soriano

Mend My Broken Heart
Wisdom For The Journey
In Your Hour of Grief
Beloved
My Journal on God's Love
The Inspirer's Wisdom

Thank you for taking the time to read this book.
GOD BLESS YOU and keep you always in His care!

For Other Books and Inspiring Articles, PLEASE VISIT:
www.itakeoffthemask.com

For Free Android Apps, e.g. God's Promises, Hope in Difficult Times, My Daily Inpiration, Inspiring Bible Psalms, Help For The Grieving:
https://play.google.com/store/apps/developer?
id=Jocelyn+Soriano

You can also contact me at:
facebook.com/itakeoffthemask
instagram.com/itakeoffthemask
twitter.com/jocelynsoriano

Or write to me at itakeoffthemask@yahoo.com

About The Author

Jocelyn A. Soriano is an author, poet and blogger at **www.itakeoffthemask.com.**

She graduated Summa Cum Laude with a degree of Bachelor of Science in Accountancy and worked as a CPA and Internal Auditor before going freelance as a writer.

Am I Qualified to Write This Book?

I have lived a very simple life. There are no tragic events nor spectacular adventures I can boast of. My day to day activities are quite normal and may even seem boring to most. I am not rich but neither am I of utmost poverty. I am not a nun or a consecrated religious. As of the time of this writing, I am not even married, and I have no child of my own.

Yet through all these things, God has blessed me, too, with His love. He has revealed Himself to me in the ordinary course of life. He has directed my path and has helped me grow in wisdom. Truly, there is no person whom God couldn't reach. There is no life that couldn't become meaningful and beautiful by His grace.

He knows who I am - my gifts, my weaknesses, my natural temperament. He is the One who uses these among other things and circumstances to purify my soul and to fill me with wisdom and love.

I find it difficult to write each and every thing He did, how He did it through what seems to be an ordinary life. Many times, words are indeed not enough to describe it. At other times, I somehow feel it isn't appropriate to reveal everything, at least not yet.

But I do my best to write what I could, to somehow make a path for others to see, not me, but the many learnings I have received, and the many good things God has done and is still able to do.

Many people can say I'm not qualified to do what I do, that I haven't experienced this much pain or darkness, but then again, it's not about me. It's about God who can work through the most simple people, through even the life of the smallest child.

Jocelyn A. Soriano

Printed in Great Britain
by Amazon